Perspectives on Southern Africa

The Fractured Community

The Fractured Community

Landscapes of Power and Gender in Rural Zambia

Kate Crehan

University of California Press

Berkeley / Los Angeles / London

University of California Press
Berkeley and Los Angeles, California

University of California Press, Ltd.
London, England

Library of Congress Cataloging-in-Publication Data

Crehan, Kate A. F.
   The fractured community : landscapes of power and gender in rural
Zambia / Kate Crehan.
      p.   cm.
   Includes bibliographical references and index.
   ISBN 0-520-20659-2 (alk. paper).—ISBN 0-520-20660-6 (pbk. : alk paper)
   1. Zambia—Rural conditions.   2. Kaonde (African people)—Social
conditions.   3. Kaonde (African people)—Economic conditions.
4. Differentiation (Sociology).   I. Title.   II. Series
HN803.A8C74   1997
307.72′096894—dc21   96-51849

Manufactured in the United States of America
9   8   7   6   5   4   3   2   1

Contents

Preface and Acknowledgments

This book has taken me a long time to write. Its various parts have gone through many drafts, and been combined, torn apart, and recombined in many versions. Throughout this long gestation, however, my basic aim has remained constant: to tell something of the story of those living in two small rural communities in northwestern Zambia in the late 1980s, on the eve of the collapse of the one-party state. One reason why I found this so difficult was that I wanted to tell this story in a way that, on the one hand, reflected the realities of this rural world as these were lived by the people themselves, but on the other, also revealed how these local realities fitted into the larger landscapes beyond northwestern Zambia. Let me make it clear from the outset, however, that in no way am I claiming to speak *for* the people whose story I have tried to tell; this book is ultimately my mapping of their world. In drawing my map I tried very hard to listen to what those among whom I lived and worked in Zambia were trying to tell me. I wanted to understand how they themselves saw the world around them, but inevitably what I heard was filtered through my preexisting conceptual maps. However much I may have tried to lay aside these maps and attempted to see things through local eyes, and however much what I saw may have modified my maps, those maps remained a part of the intellectual baggage I carried with me. There is also the very important point that simply because those living a particular reality see things in a certain way does not automatically mean that their understanding reflects some ultimate truth; we all of us see through a glass darkly.

The story I tell in this book is in large part the product of a dialogue between those living a particular reality and me, as I attempted to make sense of the fragmented shards of data I collected, peering into my glass and trying to discern the patterns that seemed to glide in and out of view. But this dialogue included many other participants. Like any such book, this one is also the product of a long-running conversation with my intellectual forebears and contemporaries. Contemplating my much worked-over final manuscript, however, I find it impossible to enumerate my intellectual debts in any precise way. I can no longer retrace all the steps of the complicated paths my thinking has traversed, nor record the many and diverse points at which it has brushed up against the thoughts of others and how these encounters have shaped my thinking. All I want to do here is to thank in a rather general way various people and institutions who have been part of this intellectual journey. The book itself remains, of course, my responsibility.

My main debt of gratitude must be to the people of the two Zambian communities I am calling Kibala and Bukama, who allowed me to share something of their lives. I would also like to thank all those who have read and commented on various parts of the manuscript, as well as those who participated in the numerous seminars and conferences at which I have presented parts of this book. I do not now always remember just who it was who turned my thinking in a particular direction, or at precisely which seminar they did this; and some, no doubt, would be horrified at what I have made of their ideas. Let me just reiterate that this book has grown out of a long dialogue with many participants. Particular individuals I would like to thank by name are: Talal Asad, Tanya Baker, George Bond, Joseph Buttigieg, Ludgard DeDecker, Benedetto Fontana, Peter Geschiere, Karen Tranberg Hansen, Record Jioma, Norma Kriger, Louise Lennihan, Achille Mbembe, Ilse Mwanza, Achim von Oppen, Benjamin Orlove, Terence Ranger, Theo Rauch, William Roseberry, John Sender, David Turton, and Ken Vickery.

There were also a number of institutions whose support was crucial and whom I would like to thank. The primary research on which this book is based was carried out while I was the Smuts Research Fellow in African Studies at the African Studies Centre at Cambridge University, with the support of grants from the Smuts Travel Fund and the Nuffield Foundation. I also received important support from the New School for Social Research. I am especially grateful for a year's sabbatical leave that allowed me finally to complete the manuscript. In Zambia I received valuable support from the Institute for African Studies at the University of Zambia.

A Note on Orthography
and Usage

I have followed the orthography as used by J. L. Wright in his *English-Kaonde Vocabulary* (1985). Wright's main deviations from the revised orthography adopted after independence are the virtual omission of tone markers and the use of a single vowel to indicate both long and short vowels rather than a doubling of the vowel to mark a long vowel.

In line with what seems to be the current convention, I have in general omitted prefixes when writing Kaonde terms, except in the case of quotations. That is, I refer to the language as Kaonde, not KiKaonde, people as Kaonde not BaKaonde, and so on. I have also made extensive, to some readers perhaps excessive, use of quotation marks when using various English terms, such as *tribe* and *development*. This could be read as trying to have my cake and eat it: using these terms while simultaneously distancing myself from them. My intention, however, is rather to focus the reader's attention on them and by so doing to call them into question. The point is that we cannot simply escape preexisting names; we are parties to a dialogue in which they already exist as powerful ways of naming certain realities. My quotation marks are a way of taking issue with them.

Abbreviations

BSAC   British South Africa Company
ECZ   Evangelical Church of Zambia
IRDP   Integrated Rural Development Project
MCC   Member of the Central Committee
MMD   Movement for Multiparty Democracy
NWCU   North-Western Co-operative Union
RLI   Rhodes-Livingstone Institute
UNIP   United National Independence Party
VSR   Village Self Reliance
ZNA   Zambia National Archives

Citations to My Own Data Collected in North-Western Province

NE   From notes taken of an event in which English was being used, or of an interview conducted in English.
NK   From notes taken of an event in which Kaonde was being used, or of an interview conducted in Kaonde.
TE   Transcript of a tape-recorded interview conducted in English.
TK   Translated transcript of a tape-recorded interview conducted in Kaonde.

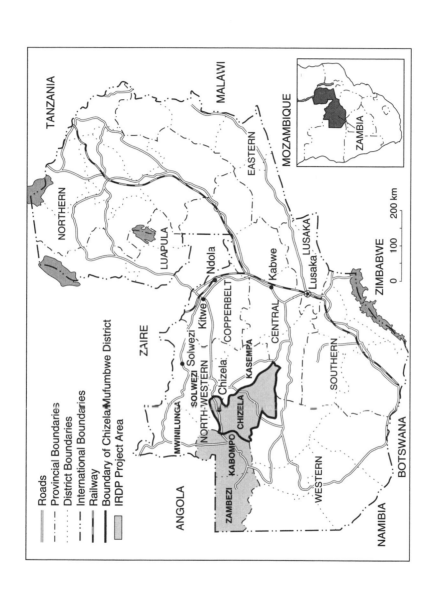

CHAPTER I

Introduction:
Theoretical Locations

*Human history is like palaeontology. Owing to a certain judicial
blindness even the best intelligences absolutely fail to see things
which lie in front of their noses. Later, when the moment has
arrived, we are surprised to find traces everywhere of what we failed
to see.*

Karl Marx, letter to Friedrich Engels, 1868

*The problem arises of whether a theoretical truth, whose
discovery corresponded to a specific practice, can be generalised and
considered as universal for a historical epoch. The proof of its
universality consists precisely 1. in its becoming a stimulus to know
better the concrete reality of a situation that is different from that
in which it was discovered . . . 2. when it has stimulated and helped
this better understanding of concrete reality as if it were originally
an expression of it. It is in this incorporation that its real
universality lies.*

Antonio Gramsci,
Selections from the Prison Notebooks

*Individual consciousness is not the architect of the ideological
superstructure, but only a tenant lodging in the social edifice of
ideological signs.*

Mikhail Bakhtin [V. N. Volosinov, pseud.],
Marxism and the Philosophy of Language

For six months in 1988 I lived and carried out research in
two small rural communities in the North-Western Province of Zambia,
one of the country's poorest and most remote provinces. This was a

return to the same province, and the same linguistic area, where I had done the fieldwork for my Ph.D. dissertation ten years earlier (Crehan 1987). I had stayed then for two years in Kasempa District. In 1988 I decided to base myself in one of North-Western's smallest and most impoverished districts, Chizela (see fig.1), in two communities I have called Kibala and Bukama.[1] This is a book about the lives of the men and women of Kibala and Bukama; and about the ways in which those lives were located within the larger economic and political order of post-colonial Zambia in the late 1980s. The book tries both to map out some of the basic contours of the landscapes of power within which lives were lived in rural Chizela, and also to trace out something of the complicated ways in which those contours shaped, and were in turn themselves shaped by, those lives.

This then is a book by an anthropologist based on two small and very specific case studies. The value of this classically anthropological, close examination of particular lives at a particular historical moment is that it enables us to glimpse something of what such large abstractions as "kinship," "capitalism," "monetization," "commoditization," and "the state" actually mean in the daily reality of people's lives. Michael Watts began a recent book by posing the question, "From what vantage point are we to understand the various guises, metamorphoses and reconfigurations of historical and contemporary capitalisms?" (Pred and Watts 1992:1). What I have tried to show in this book is that, however unlikely it might seem, the vantage point of this neglected corner of North-Western Province can throw an unexpected light on some of the concrete realities of "capitalism" in contemporary sub-Saharan Africa. Before, however, saying any more about the broader themes of the study, and why I used the particular approach I did, let me briefly introduce Kibala and Bukama and their inhabitants so that the reader will begin to get some sense of where and whom I am talking about.

1. I have used pseudonyms for the names of all individuals and places with the exception of the district itself, Chizela, and Chief Chizela, from whom the district's name derived. The incumbent of the chieftainship at the time of my fieldwork has since died. In fact, the official name of the district was not "Chizela," a name to which other local chiefs objected as slighting their authority, but the more neutral "Mufumbwe" (a local river). However, in practice everyone, including government officials, still used the name "Chizela," even in official documents, although in the latter "Mufumbwe" might be appended in brackets. Strictly speaking, "Chizela" should be spelled "Kizela" but again I have followed local usage.

Kibala and Bukama

Both Kibala and Bukama were located in the heart of the region associated with the Kaonde people which stretches over much of Zambia's North-Western Province, and both were seen locally as clearly *Kaonde* communities in which a Kaonde way of life was followed. The large majority of their inhabitants defined themselves to me as Kaonde, Kaonde was the language normally spoken, even by the non-Kaondes, and it was Kaonde chiefs who were described as "owners" of the area. The all-important kinship links, which, in local eyes, were what provided a community with its basic armature, were dominated by the Kaonde matrilineal pattern of descent. According to Kaonde kinship rules, a child belongs to its mother's clan, and marriage is forbidden within the matrilineal clan. The fluid and multidimensional nature of "being Kaonde," and how this was lived in day-to-day life, will, I hope, become clearer in subsequent chapters. But let me stress at the outset that, while this study focuses on two places in which there was a clear Kaonde predominance, it is not a study of *the* Kaonde.

The histories of the two communities were very different. Kibala was a long-established cluster of approximately thirty small settlements, crosscut by a dense network of kinship ties, with a population of close to 800[2] in 1988 and its own chief, Chief Kibala. Indeed, the people of Kibala maintained that in the late nineteenth century, at the time the region first came under the control of the British South Africa Company (BSAC), the Kibala chiefdom had been one of the most important Kaonde chiefdoms and that it was at that time senior to that of Chizela. Its importance, however, declined during the colonial period, and in 1944 the colonial government ceased to recognize it as a separate chiefdom, amalgamating it into that of Chizela. To the people of Kibala, however, and to many other local Kaonde, Chief Kibala was still a chief.

The people of Kibala produced relatively little in the way of crops for sale. Chizela District, like much of the region associated with the Kaonde, was a tsetse-infested area, and in 1988 cultivation was still for the most part based on a hoe-based, slash-and-burn cultivation system. This pattern of shifting cultivation (often referred to throughout Zam-

---

2. *Statistical Handbook no. II: North-Western Province* (GRZ 1988:28). Given the considerable mobility of rural Zambians generally, any population figures are bound to be approximate.

bia by the term for the Bemba variant, *citimene*) has a long history of being condemned by both colonial and postcolonial governments; only the degree of condemnation, and the reasons given for why *citimene* was wrong seem to have varied over the years.[3] At the heart of the Kaonde cultivation system, at least according to local ideology, was the cultivation of sorghum. Central to the idea of Kaonde identity, both when Kaonde people were describing themselves and when they were described by their neighbors, was that they were "sorghum eaters." "Being Kaonde" meant eating *nshima* (the solid porridge that constitutes the staple food throughout Zambia) made from sorghum rather than maize, millet, or cassava. In fact in the 1980s what people actually ate in Chizela was often maize, not sorghum, but in terms of ideology sorghum was still considered to be the "real" Kaonde staple. Chapter 5 looks at the local pattern of cultivation in some detail. The practice of shifting cultivation meant that the villages of Kibala had occupied many different sites over the years. The core meaning of the Kaonde term for village, *muzhi* (pl. *mizhi*), was not, however, a particular place but a particular kinship group, and as kinship groups many of the *mizhi* that made up Kibala were perceived as entities with histories stretching back into the precolonial period.

Bukama's origins were far more recent than Kibala's. It was established as a farm settlement scheme in 1977 as part of a Dutch-funded development project. The idea was to encourage "progressive" farming by providing properly "motivated" individuals with ten-hectare (approx. twenty-five-acre) plots in an area of relatively good soil on which they were supposed to grow some crops for their own subsistence but also maize and other crops for sale to the national marketing board. In the years since the scheme's founding the numbers of registered plot holders had fluctuated, reaching 40 at its peak, but never achieving the numbers planned by the scheme's architects and declining to 34 (of whom 12 were women) by 1988. In addition to these 34 there were 6 other households living just outside the scheme, but who were normally treated as part of the community. Also adjacent to the scheme was a farm belonging to the current chief, Chief Chizela, which he had established in 1964 just after independence, and where by the 1980s he was spending most of his time. The total population of the Bukama community (including Chief Chizela and the nonscheme farmers) was approximately 376 in

---

3. See Moore and Vaughan (1994) for an interesting history of the shifts in the colonial and postcolonial governments' attitudes to Northern Province's *citimene* system.

1988. The Farm Settlement Scheme Committee, which was elected by all the adults (*bakulumpe*) living there, was supposed to run things on a day-to-day basis but in fact seldom met, and any disputes within the community were taken to Chief Chizela for arbitration.

The original plan was that settlement farmers would be able to hire the services of government tractors, and on all the plots an area of 1.5 hectares had been stumped. The architects of the Bukama scheme, like those of many other similar schemes, believed that concentrating "progressive" farmers in this way would have the twin advantages of freeing them from what were seen as the constraints of "traditional" communities and of making it easier and cheaper to provide them with the various services they would need for "modern farming," such as the provision of inputs, extension services, and marketing facilities. By the late 1980s, however, the promised tractor services had ceased to materialize and few people were cultivating a significantly larger area than those in neighboring areas outside the scheme. All those who had settled on the scheme came from relatively close by, and even though there was not the same density of crosscutting kin ties, virtually all those living there had some kinship links with others in Bukama.

The composition of the Bukama settlement did differ significantly from that of Kibala, however, in that there was a far higher percentage of female-headed households, 35 percent as against 12 percent. In reality, whatever the intentions of those who had devised Bukama, many of those who had moved there had done so at the suggestion of Chief Chizela; and why he had suggested it was usually because there had been some dispute (often involving an accusation of witchcraft) that he had sought to resolve by encouraging one of the parties to move to Bukama. As a result Bukama had something of a reputation as a place full of troublemakers and witches. The significance of this, however, should not be overestimated given that, as we shall see in chapter 6, accusations of witchcraft were omnipresent in both Kibala and Bukama. Also, the fact that someone had a reputation as a witch did not prevent his or her neighbors from living peaceably with them. What is true is that Bukama had attracted a number of people, including a disproportionate number of widows and divorced women, who had found their previous villages less than hospitable.

Although virtually all the Bukama residents lived permanently on the scheme, people also continued to think of themselves as members of their former villages (*mizhi*). Many in fact described their "farms" in Bukama in the same terms as those in Kibala described their often distant fields (*majimi*), where they would live during the months of cultivation. Ironically, this yearly move to fields in the bush (*ku majimi*) was central to precisely that shifting system of cultivation so frowned on by both colonial and postcolonial governments. Whatever may have been the original motives of those who had moved to Bukama, the pattern of life there had increasingly come to resemble that of any other local community. Living first in Kibala, then in Bukama, what struck me was how similar the two places were. Over the ten years of Bukama's existence its settlers had essentially re-created the kind of community they were used to.

Both Kibala and Bukama were within striking distance of the small administrative center of Chizela District, Chizela town. Kibala was thirty-five kilometers from the town and Bukama twenty, although these distances were nonetheless significant given that there was no public transport and most people had to travel on foot. Only a small minority of men (and no women) owned bicycles. Both places also fell within the area of a large, mainly German funded, Integrated Rural Development Project (IRDP) initiated in 1979. This German IRDP had no links with the earlier Dutch project that had established the Bukama scheme.[4] Originally the IRDP covered only the Kabompo District of North-Western Province but it was later extended to Zambezi and Chizela Districts. Central to this project was the LIMA[5] program designed to encourage small-scale producers to produce more for the market by providing them with the necessary inputs (on credit), marketing facilities, extension services, and so on.[6] Although the scheme was originally intended to cover a range of crops, in practice what was usually grown was maize. The IRDP was funded jointly by Zambia and West Germany, and German "experts" of various kinds were closely involved in its implementation, which had led to local people referring to the project itself and everyone it employed simply as "the Germans," or *magermani*. The extent to which the whole enterprise was identified with "the Germans"

---

4. Smith and Wood (1994) provides a good account of the way international donors in Zambia, as in many places, tended to carve the country up into their own separate little national fiefdoms.

5. "LIMA," "LIMA farmers," "LIMA scheme," and so on refer to the program itself, while *lima* is the area measurement (0.25 hectares) on which the LIMA package, with its various inputs and extension messages, was based.

6. See Crehan and von Oppen (1988) for a detailed account of the history of the LIMA program in North-Western Province. Crehan and von Oppen (1994) deals with the LIMA program and the maize boom of the late 1980s in different peripheral areas of Zambia.

is illustrated by the puzzlement expressed by some farmers as to why Germany was so desperate for maize that they needed the people of North-Western Province to produce it for them.[7] During the time of my fieldwork "the Germans" were a significant local presence.

But what can the lives lived in this quiet corner of rural Chizela, or a view of the landscape of power of postcolonial Zambia from their vantage point, tell us that makes it worthwhile to focus so closely on them? How might such a vantage point, for instance, help us "to understand the various guises, metamorphoses and reconfigurations of historical and contemporary capitalisms?" (Pred and Watts 1992).

Mapping Capitalism

In recent years a number of theorists have become increasingly concerned with the complex interactions between the global and the local in the contemporary world. The world, it seems, is growing smaller and ever more homogenized at the same time that it is becoming increasingly fragmented. On the one hand, there is the undeniable, and growing, globalization of economies and cultures, which means, for instance, that there is almost nowhere on the planet where the ripples from the manipulations of the men in suits on the New York or Tokyo money markets sitting at their computer screens are not felt, just as an ever larger percentage of the world's population is apparently watching the same soap operas and the same CNN news on their television screens. On the other hand, the world also seems to be fracturing; nation-states are torn apart and all over the globe the cement that bonded together different regions, linguistic groups, ethnicities into unitary imagined communities seems to be crumbling. Some of the most interesting work on this complex contradictory phenomenon in the last few years has been done by geographers, particularly those working within a broadly Marxist framework, who have drawn attention to the importance of what we might call the politics of space. A seminal figure here is David Harvey (see, for instance, Harvey 1982, 1985, 1989, 1990),[8] whose *The Condition of Postmodernity* has been enormously influential.

---

7. Personal communication with Theo Rauch (IRPD North-Western Province planner).

8. See also Soja (1989); Bird et al. (1993); Massey (1984, 1991a, 1991b, 1994).

The geographer Michael Watts, whom I have already quoted, has done particularly interesting work from this perspective on Africa (see, for instance, Watts 1989, 1990; Pred and Watts 1992).

For Harvey a key phenomenon in the globalization of the contemporary world is that of "time-space compression" (Harvey 1989). In other words, the world we live in is one marked by ever-"diminishing spatial barriers to exchange, movement and communication" (Harvey 1993:4). If we want to understand the nature of particular localities, Harvey argues, we have to understand the ways in which this ever faster spinning world *itself* brings into being certain kinds of local diversity and particularity so that in an apparently paradoxical way "the elaboration of place-bound identities has become more rather than less important" (1993:4). For Harvey it is above all the logic of capitalist accumulation that provides the dynamic of space-time compression. Insightful as Harvey's work is in mapping out the broad contours of contemporary capitalism, it does, however, have certain lacunae, as another geographer, Doreen Massey, has pointed out. Harvey has little to say, for instance, about the significance of gender and ethnicity (Massey 1991b, 1993). Massey argues that if the notion of time-space compression is to be genuinely useful then it needs, as she puts it, "differentiating socially." There may indeed be ever-increasing interconnections between different points on the globe, and an ever increasing density of flows of people, goods, and information, but this is far from being a uniform process. It is in fundamental and structural ways profoundly uneven.

Different social groups and different individuals are placed in very distinct ways in relation to these flows and interconnections. This point concerns not merely the issue of who moves and who doesn't, although that is an important element of it; it is also about power in relation *to* the flows and the movement. Different social groups have distinct relationships to this anyway differentiated mobility: some are more in charge of it than others; some initiate flows and movement, others don't; some are more on the receiving end of it than others; some are effectively imprisoned by it. (Massey 1993:61)

Clearly, if we want to get to the rich specificity pointed to by Massey, we need to do some pretty detailed mapping. We need to be prepared to undertake the laborious work of unraveling the complicated interconnections of class, gender, and ethnicity in particular places at particular times. We need a mapping that pays attention both to the minutiae of daily life and to the larger structures of relations underpinning the surface diversity of individual and unique lives. This mapping needs also to move continually back and forth between them. Without this kind of nuanced mapping our analyses are unlikely to tell us much about just *how* the great surging narrative of contemporary capitalism translates into real power relations among real people in real places: too one-sided a concentration on the larger structures and their lived reality tends to disappear; too exclusive a focus on particular lives and we lose the connections with the larger realities in which those lives are embedded. Anthropology in general has excelled at teasing out local knowledges and meanings but, as Watts has justifiably complained it has often been weak as regards "situating local knowledge and meanings on the grand map of capitalism" (Pred and Watts 1992:15). My story of Kibala and Bukama is very much a story of the complicated relationship between the local and the global, and how large abstractions such as "the state," "the market," and "democracy" are translated into the lives of actual men and women in particular places at particular times. The way I have tried to tell this story is by tracing out some of the complex, and socially differentiated, political and economic locations inhabited by the women and men of Kibala and Bukama. In doing this I have tried to explore both the material realities of those locations and how they were imagined and understood.

I am, of course, using the term *location* here not simply in a literal, spatial sense, but also in a broader metaphorical one. Essentially what I am concerned with is the way these metaphorical locations, political, economic, imagined, and so on, come together in a particular geographical location, rural Chizela, at a particular moment (or location) in time. Particular places can in fact, as Massey suggests, be usefully "imagined as articulated moments in networks of social relations and understandings" (Massey 1993:66). I have chosen to describe these different moments in terms of different *locations*, and use the master metaphor of the map: firstly, as a way of drawing attention to their interconnectedness—they are all locations on a single map; secondly, because the boundaries of a map are always in some sense arbitrary—the landscape with its roads and rivers continues beyond the printed limits just as the relationships I am trying to trace often continue beyond the limits I have drawn; and thirdly, because a map is always so clearly a partial way of describing a reality—a way chosen to show certain features and certain relationships but one that makes no claims to re-create that reality in its totality.

But if we think of the way networks of social relations and understandings come together in space and time as multistranded and socially differentiated locations, and "society" as being the sum of these locations, to what extent should this cluster of locations, this "society," be seen as *determining* how particular individuals and groups act? Clearly they do play *some* shaping role. This shaping power is often seen as a laying down of certain limits to what is possible, but, as Raymond Williams stressed, this is not all that is involved.

"Society" is . . . never only the "dead husk" which limits social and individual fulfilment. It is always also a constitutive process with very powerful pressures which are both expressed in political, economic, and cultural formations and . . . are internalized and become "individual wills." (Williams 1977:87)

The locations that make up "society," therefore, both lay down limits and exercise a positive shaping force on what social groups come into being, on whether or not they persist, and on the forms in which they persist. And, crucially, they are also the context in which individual subjectivities themselves come into being. It is through their awareness of *where* they are—an awareness that always involves where they are *told* they are, or how their location is named—that individuals learn *who* they are, and how to articulate the raw impulses of the id as more or less appropriate, more or less "realistic" desires. Let me stress here that I am not suggesting any kind of crude mechanical determinism, only that the bundles of desires, fears, and experiences of the world that constitute individuals are always produced in particular *social* contexts.

A key part of my story is the socially differentiated nature of people's locations even within the small communities of Kibala and Bukama. These were both very much *fractured* communities; fractured along lines of gender, age, and relative wealth, to mention only some of the most significant. Within the general rural poverty there were, in local terms, very significant differences between, and within, households; everyone may have been poor but some were decidedly poorer than others. Rather than seeing Kibala and Bukama as two distinct communities, it may be better to think of the people of Kibala and Bukama as caught up in a whole range of different but entangled collectivities or communities, all of which were themselves socially differentiated, and which impacted on one another in complicated ways. These superimposed communities could be seen as forming something like a complex paisley design within which spiraled a multitude of smaller patterns—each pattern weaving people together into a different community, all of which were overlain one on the other so as ultimately to make up a single design. The character of these different "communities" varied enormously, however. There were, for instance, the overlapping communities based on kinship that stretched out from the smallest homestead to the village (*muzhi*), the village cluster and beyond, and included the imagined community of "the Kaonde" (or some other ethnic entity). There were also communities of neighbors that included kin and non-kin among whom links developed because they lived in close proximity. Then there were the various formal administrative divisions created by the Zambian state, from the ward to the district and the province, and up to the nation, Zambia, itself. How individuals identified with these various entities was not fixed in some primordial hierarchy; it depended above all on the context, with each community having its own particular salience.

In addition to the acknowledged communities, such as Kibala or Chizela District, there were other less immediately obvious nets of social relations that also tied people together, even though those linked together might be quite unaware of each other's existence. For instance, there were a wide range of imported manufactured goods, such as hoe blades, metal pots and pans, and clothes, which, as in the rest of rural Zambia, had long since become basic necessities. Finding their way into the countryside in often circuitous ways, these could link rural Zambians with some far-flung places in very material ways. For instance, insofar as events in China (which was the source of many manufactured goods in the 1980s) effected the supply and price of such commodities, and in as much as people in Chizela were the customers of Chinese producers, they were both part of a *single*, and ultimately global, economy.[9]

I have deliberately called all these very different kinds of collectivities "communities," and used the term *community* in this very wide sense, as a way of calling into question the term itself. The word *community* is always, as Raymond Williams put it, a "warmly persuasive" one; "unlike all other terms of social organization (state, nation, society, etc.) it seems never to be used unfavourably, and never to be given any positive opposing or distinguishing term" (Williams 1983:76). This cozy term also tends to imply something that is bounded and homogeneous, which, as I have stressed, neither Kibala nor Bukama were. One way of dealing with this problem would have been simply to avoid the term altogether,

---

9. A particularly interesting example of such international economic linkages is the burgeoning trade in Zambia in secondhand clothes imported in bulk from the West, about which Karen Tranberg Hansen (1994) has written.

but this would have been too easy a way out. Both in the eyes of those who lived in them, and according to my analytical maps, in certain undeniable ways Kibala and Bukama clearly *were* "communities." What I have tried to do is to use the term community, but simultaneously to interrogate it—the point being that the substantive reality of any given "community" cannot be determined a priori. Before we can say what kind of "communities" Kibala and Bukama were we need to map out the multistranded and socially differentiated locations inhabited by those who lived in them in the late 1980s.

A key set of locations were those having to do with the state. Seen from the perspective of Europe or the United States or even Zambia's capital Lusaka, North-Western Province, and especially Chizela, could seem a remote and isolated backwater inhabited by people whose connections to the political or economic world outside their own little rural corner were tenuous. But those connections were very real. Although the flow of migrant labor from the rural areas may have slowed down in recent years, virtually all middle-aged and older men had spent some time, and sometimes many years, living and working in the urban areas. Even among younger people and among women there were many who had experience living in town. Also, very important, the people of Kibala and Bukama were Zambian citizens, and one of the "imagined communities"—to use Benedict Anderson's marvelous term (Anderson 1991)—to which they belonged was that of the Zambian state. Most people very much wanted, and saw themselves as rightfully entitled to, clinics and schools provided by the state, and many were interested in selling at least some crops to the national market. At the same time, since the links were so often indirect, the larger world outside North-Western Province could frequently seem, both to those living there and to outside observers, a remote presence having little to do with local daily life. One of the locations of the people of Kibala and Bukama then was that of Zambian citizens and participants in the national economy, but this could mean something rather different in rural Chizela from what it meant in Lusaka, or even in other less remote rural areas.

The widespread contemporary pessimism about "Africa" and its future, shared by journalists and academic observers alike, often singles out the state as one of the major culprits. There is, it seems, wide agreement that there is some kind of general crisis of the postcolonial state in Africa, even if there are divergent views on the reasons for this.[10] While this study has little to say about *the* African state, it does try to throw some light on the substantive realities of one particular state, that of Zambia, as these were lived in one small rural corner at a particular historical moment. As I have stressed, in attempting to map this out, my strategy has been to move continually back and forth between the minutiae of daily life and the larger structures in which these are embedded. To do this I have used a theoretical approach that draws heavily on the work of Antonio Gramsci. Indeed, this whole study can be seen as framed within a Gramscian problematic of "hegemony." Since Gramsci is, as Foucault so neatly put it, "an author more often cited than actually known,"[11] and since what Gramsci meant by "hegemony" has been so disputed,[12] I want to explain in some detail what *I* understand to be the concept of "hegemony" and why I think it, and Gramsci's whole approach, are potentially so useful for Africanists.

In addition to Gramsci himself this will also involve some discussion of Marx and his theorizing of the commodity. I have also drawn on the work of Mikhail Bakhtin, using his approach to the production of knowledge, to complement that of Gramsci. I have used both Bakhtin's and Gramsci's work to reflect on how it is that certain groups in society possess what we might call the power to *name* reality, to describe and categorize the world, and what kind of power this power to name is. All in all then, this involves a fairly lengthy excursion into theory, which will take up the rest of this chapter. I hope, however, the reader will bear with me, since it is this basic theory that provides the tools needed to map out the landscapes of power and gender inhabited by the people of Kibala and Bukama. Where I want to start this intellectual journey is with the question of Gramsci's relevance for Africanists. Why should anyone interested in contemporary Africa go to an Italian marxist writing over half a century ago?

---

10. Bayart (1992) and Davidson (1992) are both stimulating though very different accounts of that crisis. Mbembe (1993) provides a particularly vivid account of the nature of the Cameroonian postcolonial state. Leys (1994) gives an interesting review of the debates on the postcolonial state in Africa. See also Mamdani, *Citizen and Subject: Contemporary Africa and the Legacy of Late Colonialism* (1996).

11. Quoted by Joseph Buttigieg in his introduction to the *Prison Notebooks* (Gramsci 1992:xix).

12. Among the many discussions of hegemony by Gramsci scholars, some of the key ones in English are: Anderson (1976–77), Buci-Glucksmann (1980), Femia (1981), Fontana (1993), Hall (1987), Hobsbawm (1982), Mouffe (1979), Sassoon (1987a), and Williams (1977).

A Gramscian in Zambia

In a well-known passage in the *Prison Notebooks* Gramsci wrote:

The starting-point of critical elaboration is the consciousness of what one really is, and is "knowing thyself" as a product of the historical process to date which has deposited in you an infinity of traces, without leaving an inventory. Such an inventory must therefore be made at the outset. (Gramsci, quoted in Forgacs 1988:326)

We and our analyses are always, as Gramsci reminds us here, embedded in history. Bearing this in mind, let me begin my discussion of Gramsci with a brief look at my own intellectual history. I first began studying anthropology in Britain in the early 1970s at a time when the old structural functionalist paradigm had already crumbled, and its ritual slaughter had become an annual academic rite. As far as I was concerned some of the most exciting work then being done was that of the French Marxist anthropologists, such as Godelier, Terray, Meillassoux, Rey, Coquery-Vidrovitch,[13] all of whom were working within the general problematic of the articulation of modes of production. This approach was particularly influential among the anthropologists and historians of Africa.[14] The modes of production literature, like structural functionalism (and every intellectual movement that has its moment of fame), has been subject to a radical critique in part for, as Jean-Francois Bayart's summary put-down has it, "in the familiar Althusserian manner, confusing structures, processes and actors" (Bayart 1993:104).[15] But justified and important as the critique undoubtedly is, particularly as regards the for-

13. Some of the key texts are Coquery-Vidrovitch (1969); Godelier (1972); Meillassoux (1964a, 1964b, 1972, 1973, 1981); Rey (1969, 1971, 1973, 1975); and Terray (1972, 1974, 1977). Allen's "Radical Themes in African Social Studies: A Bibliographical Guide" (1977) provides an interesting overview from a mid-seventies perspective, while Kahn and Llobera (1981) sums up the debates and the central issues from a slightly later vantage point.

14. Colin Bundy's seminal *The Rise and Fall of the South African Peasantry* (1979:4–13) has a discussion on the category "peasant" in the African context that is very characteristic of the way the issues were seen in the 1970s. Henry Bernstein's work on Tanzania was also highly influential in shaping Africanist debates; see, for instance, Bernstein (1978, 1979).

15. See, for instance, Thompson (1978) and Cooper (1993:99–104). A number of feminists, such as Guyer (1981), O'Laughlin (1977), Edholm et al. (1977), and Mackintosh (1977) drew particular attention to the inadequacy of the way the modes of production literature dealt with the dynamics of gender.

malism of much of the modes of production literature, and its inadaquacies in terms of the analysis of gender, the basic *problem* at the heart of this literature remains, it seems to me, as central as ever. Indeed, it is essentially part of the same general problem of the relationship between the local and the global explored by Harvey and the other Marxist geographers. How, that is, should we understand the place of "peripheral" rural communities within the overall trajectory of a global capitalist development that would seem to be continually expanding and reaching ever deeper into ever more corners of the world, and yet at the same time has traced such a grossly skewed and uneven path? And for me, the most powerful theoretical tools with which to explore this paradox remain those of the Marxist tradition despite the fact that this is a tradition rooted in Western history, and in the particular trajectory of that history.

Marxism, especially since the collapse of the Soviet Union—which many seem to think demolished marxism as it fell—is certainly not currently fashionable. Some would argue that the very categories of political economy are too Western-centered and too much part of the colonial legacy to be appropriate tools for the study of Africa. To what extent, for instance, do "categories like class or processes like proletarianization impose an external and misleading framework on the divisions and dynamics of African society" (Cooper 1993:193)? It is undoubtedly true that the basic categories of Marxist theory, like most in the social sciences, are the product of a Western-centered history. The way class societies develop, the kind of transformations they go through, and the nature of the classes that come into being have all tended to be mapped onto a European master narrative. And then there is the criticism that the political economy approach does not pay sufficient attention to the noneconomic, treating phenomena such as ethnicity and religion as mere epiphenomena of underlying and determining economic realities— not to mention what we might call Marx's (and many of his followers') "gender blindness." But does this mean that Marxism is so irredeemably flawed that if our aim is an analysis of African realities that does not artificially force these realities into boxes molded by Western history, does not neglect ideas and beliefs, and is attentive to gender dynamics, then we are better off not bothering with Marxism at all? I, as the reader will probably not be surprised to learn after my discussion of the work of the marxist geographers, would argue no, and that the Marxist problematic still has much to offer the student of Africa, even, surprising as it may sound to some, those of a feminist bent. Frederick Cooper expresses it nicely:

The development of capitalism is a historical phenomenon that has to be confronted, and the consequences of the commoditization of land and labor need to be worked out theoretically and historically. This territory may need to be remapped, but the problem which Marx made his life's work is not about to go away. (Cooper 1993:193)

Gramsci, it seems to me, is a Marxist who provides us with a particularly rich set of insights with which to set about this remapping. In Gramsci's writings, particularly the *Prison Notebooks*, we can find a wonderfully open Marxism, one that, to paraphrase Marx, is never solely focused on the economic conditions of power but is always centrally concerned with the ideological forms in which people become conscious of these conditions, and within which they struggle. There can, however, be dangers in using Gramsci. It is important that we do not mechanically transpose categories derived from European realities to African ones. If we are to use Gramsci, we need to be clear about what we can and what we cannot take from his work.

The first point to note is that Gramsci's analyses were always carefully grounded. Indeed, one way of seeing Gramsci's theoretical project is as an attempt to think through the concrete specificities of Italian history (up to and including Gramsci's own historical moment) starting from a Marxist problematic. Marx himself, after all, did not write much about Italy. This rethinking of Marxism in the context of a different history provides Africanists with an interesting example. For instance, Gramsci wrote a good deal about rural Italy and the peasantry,[16] but his discussion of *Italian* peasants was always firmly anchored in *Italian* history and attentive to the specifics of that history. As he wrote in the essay on "the Southern question,"

But the peasant question is historically determined in Italy; it is not the "peasant and agrarian question in general". In Italy the peasant question, through the specific Italian tradition, and the specific developments of Italian history, has taken two typical and particular forms—the Southern question and that of the Vatican. (Gramsci 1978:443)

16. In addition to Gramsci's famous essay "Some Aspects of the Southern Question" (in Gramsci 1978:441–62), see, for instance, the following passages in the *Prison Notebooks* (1971:5–15, 55–102, 210–18, 272–75, 280–87).

For Gramsci, understanding the great canvas of the South meant approaching it *both* as a single entity shaped by certain shared, economic and political structures, with a distinct place in Italian history, *and* as a collection of separate regions each with their own specific history and politics.

"The Southern question" is especially interesting for Africanists since southern Italy's predicament has a certain similarity to sub-Saharan Africa's unequal relationship with the West. In essence, "the Southern question" concerns the long-term and structural, economic, and political inequality between northern and southern Italy that apparently locks the "south" into its multiple disadvantages. Gramsci goes on in "Aspects of the Southern Question" to describe southern Italy as follows:

The South can be defined as a great social disintegration. The peasants, who make up the great majority of its population, have no cohesion among themselves (of course, some exceptions must be made: Apulia, Sardinia, Sicily, where there exist special characteristics within the great canvas of the South's structure). Southern society is a great agrarian bloc, made up of three social layers: the great amorphous, disintegrated mass of the peasantry; the intellectuals of the petty and medium rural bourgeoisie; and the big landowners and great intellectuals. (Gramsci 1978:454)

What is instructive here is not the details of Gramsci's analysis but rather the way he approached "the Southern question." This approach has nothing in common with the arid formalism of some of the Althusserian "modes of production" literature.[17] Gramsci does not take some ready-made theoretical schema and impose it on rural realities; what he does is to begin with the details of an empirical diversity, trying then to trace the threads linking these complex and specific realities back to various underlying structural relations. See, for instance, his careful discussion of the complexity and varied nature of those without land in the rural areas (the *morti di fame*) in the *Prison Notebooks*, where he stresses how they "are not a homogeneous stratum, and serious mistakes can be made if they are identified abstractly" (Gramsci 1971:273–74).

Obviously the history of southern Italy is quite different from that of Zambia, but there are nonetheless some broad commonalities in the histories of their rural areas. Both involve regional entities with their

17. Hindess's and Hirst's Althusserian *Pre-Capitalist Modes of Production* (1975), which was very influential for a time, is a good example of this kind of formalism. E. P. Thompson's *Poverty of Theory* (1978) is a savage critique of Althusser and his school.

own internal politics and economies, and linkage (and often subordination) to larger and more powerful economic and political entities that are not necessarily tidily confined within the boundaries of the national state. What is useful for the Africanist in Gramsci is above all the *practical example* Gramsci's work offers us of how to approach such fragmented wholes and how to trace out the complex power relations structuring them. As the Gramscian scholar Joseph Buttigieg has persuasively argued, it was in his grappling with the messy complexity of the empirical reality of Italian history, not through the elaboration of some previously worked-out formal theory, that Gramsci developed what has become one of his most borrowed concepts, hegemony.[18]

While I believe that the notion of hegemony has much to offer Africanists, we should not be too quick to transpose the specifics of Gramsci's analysis of Italian history to other times and other places. Gramsci, for instance, wrote that "the mass of the peasantry . . . does not elaborate its own 'organic' intellectuals, nor does it 'assimilate' any stratum of 'traditional' intellectuals" (Gramsci 1971:6)—a comment for which he is taken to task by Steven Feierman in his Tanzanian study, *Peasant Intellectuals* (1990:18), the very title of which can be read as a riposte to Gramsci. But Gramsci's comment here should not be taken as some "truth" about a general category "peasantry" always and everywhere unable to come up with their own accounts of their world. Gramsci's argument in this particular passage is that the *Italian* peasantry (a stratum that has been at the bottom of the social pyramid for close to a millennium) is incapable of elaborating an *effective* counterhegemony to an existing feudal or bourgeois hegemony. In other words, this statement of Gramsci's needs to be located within his argument as a whole.

To sum up, what we can take from Gramsci's writings on the Italian peasantry is not a ready-made set of analytical boxes into which we simply sort the particular bit of rural reality with which we are concerned. Rather it is an enormously suggestive example of how to approach the particular and complex histories of specific places in a way that never forgets either their specificity or their linkages to larger structures of power. And at the heart of this approach is hegemony.

Before elaborating further on Gramsci and hegemony, however, it is necessary to take a brief detour back to Marx himself to consider the fundamental concepts of value and the commodity, and what *commodi-*

18. Oral presentation, New School for Social Research, 1994.

tization means. If what we are interested in is "the remapping," as Cooper put it, "of the consequences of commoditization," then it is important to be clear at the outset as to just what we are talking about. A clarification of the notion of the commodity may not seem the most obvious place to begin a discussion of hegemony, but Gramsci's whole theorization of hegemony is in fact rooted in the basic marxist assumption that underlying and shaping political relations are key sets of economic relations.[19] Not that Gramsci (or Marx) saw this shaping as taking any easily predictable form; we are not talking here about any kind of mechanical determinism. To use a geological metaphor, the seismic forces underlying a landscape certainly play a powerful role in shaping its contours, but while it may be possible to identify the underlying geological fault lines, just how and when those stresses will break out remains essentially unpredictable.

Commodities and Commoditization

The thread of commoditization runs through the story of Kibala and Bukama. This thread began before the imposition of colonial rule, in the turbulent days of ivory and the slave trade; continued during colonial times with a sea of labor migrants flowing out of the rural areas and a tide of new consumer goods flowing in; and continues still through the economic crises of the postcolonial period. This is a process that has not charted a steady course, but, proceeding in fits and starts, sometimes surging forward, sometimes remaining stagnant, even at times moving backwards, it has nonetheless traced out an overall trajectory of increasing commoditization. More and more has wealth (or prosperity) come to consist of "commodities."

Commoditization, as Marx stressed in the opening words of volume 1 of *Capital*, is at the heart of the development of capitalist social relations.

The wealth of societies in which the capitalist mode of production prevails appears as an "immense accumulation of commodities"; the individual commodity appears as its elementary form. (Marx 1976:125)

---

19. Gramsci's groundedness in basic Marxist economic assumptions is often not sufficiently recognized. The new volume of selections from the *Prison Notebooks*, edited by Derek Boothman (1995), helps to redress this balance.

Commoditization is the process whereby an economic system comes to be one in which "exchange value dominates production to its whole depth and extent" (Marx 1973b:882). In other words, goods and services arc produced not to satisfy some need or want of the producer directly; they are produced in order to be *exchanged*, to be sold or bartered. It is the fact that they are produced *expressly* to be exchanged that defines them as commodities. However, even in the most advanced capitalist systems, this process is never complete; exchange-value may dominate, but it is not omnipresent. There are always significant parts of a society's production that remain uncommoditized. For instance, there are all those activities crucial for the day-to-day reproduction of individuals that even in the most developed of capitalist economies are often un-commoditized: the care of children, the old, and of those generally deemed unfit to participate in formal employment. Indeed, an important contribution of recent feminist scholarship has been to draw attention to the way in which capitalist economic relations *depend* on various social needs being met outside the sphere of the market.[20] What we are talking about, therefore, is a *dynamic* within the capitalist world, driven by capital's need to accumulate, whereby out of struggles between labor and capital, and between capitals, are generated contradictory pressures. On the one hand, there is pressure to commoditize productive activities not yet commoditized, while on the other, there is also pressure that certain areas of production should remain uncommoditized and be accepted as the responsibility of "the family" or private individuals. Indeed, there may also be struggles aimed at banishing parts of production already commoditized back to this private sphere. Two basic concepts that can help us to trace out the effects of this double-sided dynamic, whether in the advanced industrialized heartland or a rural periphery like North-Western Province, are those of use-value and exchange-value. Marx explains these concepts, which are central to my account of Kibala and Bukama, in the first chapter of *Capital*.

The products of any production process always have both a qualitative and quantitative dimension; the categories of use-value and exchange-value separate out these dimensions. Use-value is solely concerned with *quality* and derives entirely from the actual physical properties of objects or, in the case of services, their specific nature. A good or service from the point of use-value is

---

20. Anne Showstack Sassoon has edited an interesting collection of articles addressing this issue in the context of Europe and the United States (Sassoon 1987b).

a thing which through its *qualities* satisfies human needs of whatever kind. The nature of these needs, whether they arise, for example, from the stomach, or the imagination, makes no difference. Nor does it matter here how the thing satisfies man's need, whether directly as a means of subsistence, ie. an object of consumption, or indirectly as a means of production. (Marx 1976:125, my emphasis)

When we come to the dimension of exchange-value, however, we leave the whole sensuous world of quality behind and enter the purely linear world of quantity. "Exchange-value appears first of all as the quantitative relation, the proportion, in which use-values of one kind exchange for use-values of another kind. . . . As use-values, commodities differ above all in quality, while as exchange-values they can only differ in quantity, and therefore do not contain an atom of use-value" (1976:126–27). In other words, as goods begin to be exchanged for one another in any kind of regular, systematic way, the different goods involved come, through the social process of the market, to be invested by those doing the exchanging with certain *relative* values; so much of good A is worth so much of good B. Central to this process is usually the emergence of some form of money. Nonetheless, it needs to be stressed that while commoditization is closely associated with monetization, the two terms are not synonymous. *Commoditization* refers to production geared around exchange; goods and services are produced *in order* to be exchanged. *Monetization* refers to the process whereby exchanges come to use a universal equivalent (some form of money) in which the relative values of different goods can be expressed.[21]

According to Marx, what in fact is being equated when good A comes to be worth so much of good B is human labor. For example, good A will be worth twice as much as good B if, within given conditions of production, Good A takes on average twice as much labor to produce as good B. This average amount of labor time within given conditions of production Marx terms *socially necessary labor time*. It is important to stress that Marx is not saying that all the day-to-day fluctuations of price are the result of differential amounts of socially necessary labor time; this is a theory about the underlying relation through which goods and services acquire basic values around which their market prices fluctuate.

An implication of this that has profound repercussions for rural Af-

21. The complicated history of different monies in West Africa, and of the effects on local currencies of incorporation into wider economic circuits, is explored in a stimulating collection of articles edited by Jane Guyer (1994).

rican producers, such as those of Kibala and Bukama, is that the "value" of the crops they produce for sale, or the tools they make, is determined not by the amount of labor actually invested by them (included in this labor is the labor that has gone into producing the fertilizer and other inputs they must buy), but the *socially necessary* labor time. In an age of global markets this tends to be set by the far smaller quantity of labor needed by more "advanced" and highly capitalized farming systems, such as those of North America, and modern factory production. This is why, for instance, local iron smelting in southern Africa disappeared virtually as soon as mass-produced iron became available. However skillful the local smiths may have been, their labor-intensive processes resulted in iron that was simply too expensive. Although a number of men in 1980s Bukama and Kibala knew how to work metal and there were still skin bellows hanging up in many of the shelters, these were only used to rework scrap metal. In the colonial archives, however, there is an interesting reference from 1934 to local men beginning again to make hoes and axes, which is seen "as a measure of the poverty not the prosperity of the local natives."[22] In other words, it was only when people were not able to buy the factory-produced iron, either because they did not have the necessary cash or for some other reason, that a temporary revival of local production was possible.[23]

A very important thread in the story of how exchange-value comes to "dominate production to its whole depth and extent" is the thread of gender. Marx himself, who tended to treat the division of labor within the family as essentially "natural,"[24] did not, it is true, have much to say on the subject of gender—a good example of how "even the best intelligences absolutely fail to see things which lie in front of their noses." Nonetheless, I would argue, exploring the nature of the particular relationship, in different times and places, between those human wants that are met through the production of commodities and those met

22. ZNA, ZA/7/1/17/2, *Provincial Annual Report, Central Province, 1934.*

23. The labor theory of value has been much debated over the years, and even among economists sympathetic to Marxism has often been discarded. However, leaving aside the more specialized debate within economics, at the very general level at which I am applying it, it still seems useful. Also, even if we reject the argument that it is labor time that lies at the heart of exchange-value, the relationship between use-values and exchange-value still holds.

24. When describing the origin of the division of labor in *Capital* Marx writes, for instance, "Within a family . . . there springs up *naturally* a division of labour caused by differences of sex and age, and therefore based on a purely physiological foundation" (1976:471, my emphasis). See also 1976:171.

through the direct consumption of use-values produced outside the market can help us understand the specific ways women and men are located in particular societies. Everywhere, as the process of commoditization advances, there tends to be, it would seem, a broad division of labor that disproportionately allots the primary responsibility for the uncommoditized part of production—particularly that whole loose bundle of so-called domestic labor—to women rather than men. The *content* of domestic labor can vary enormously between different societies and different historical periods, but the existence of a bundle of tasks centered on the day-to-day reproduction of individuals and involving uncommoditized labor seems to be more or less universal, and seems, again almost universally, to be primarily associated with women rather than men.

Similarly, the commoditized sector itself tends to be significantly gendered. The ways in which women and men are incorporated and the kinds of access they have to commodity production tend to be different, often precisely because of their differential responsibilities within the noncommoditized sector.[25] Not, of course, that gender is the only factor structuring access; race is also highly significant here. Understanding the place of gender in the history of commoditization, and the complicated way in which gender intertwines with the threads of class and race, necessarily involves the careful mapping out of the basic contours of that commoditization. And here, it seems to me, Marx's theorization of use-value and exchange-value is an immensely useful starting-point that enables us to engage in a genuinely *gendered* Marxism.

Mapping of the consequences of commoditization, however, involves tracing out not only the underlying contours, but also how men and women *live* them in their daily lives. And this means exploring the complicated relationships between the underlying economic contours and particular historical landscapes of power, which brings us back to Gramsci and hegemony.

The Problematic of Hegemony in the *Prison Notebooks*

Let me begin by stressing that my reading of Gramsci here is very much guided by Gramsci's own advice on how to read Marx:

25. For an example from rural Senegal of just how quickly commodity production is gendered when it is newly introduced, see Mackintosh (1989).

"[The] search for the *Leitmotiv*, for the rhythm of the thought as it develops, should be more important than that for single casual affirmations and isolated aphorisms" (Gramsci 1971:383–84).

Hegemony is a much-used term nowadays among many social scientists.[26] Very often, however, it is taken, particularly by anthropologists, solely to concern the realm of ideas and consciousness. James Scott's gloss captures this reading: "*Hegemony* is simply the name Gramsci gave to this [i.e., the process of ideological domination as formulated by Marx and Engels in *The German Ideology*] process of ideological domination" (Scott 1985:315). As I read Gramsci, to reduce hegemony to the purely ideological is to turn a potentially illuminating, and multidimensional *approach* to the whole problem of power into no more than a label to be attached to certain phenomena.

Hegemony for Gramsci certainly is concerned with the ideological, as in the much-quoted passage about the way a group of people may have "for reasons of submission and intellectual subordination, adopted a conception which is not its own but is borrowed from another group; and it affirms this conception verbally and believes itself to be following it" (Gramsci 1971:327). But to take this as being *all* that hegemony is about is, in my view, to adopt a sadly impoverished version of Gramsci, and one that easily collapses into the much-criticized notion of false consciousness. Hegemony is also very much about real material forces, embodied in institutions like schools, churches, and the media, which both bring into being specific landscapes of power and mold the individual subjectivities that feel at home in those landscapes. Hegemony, as it were, focuses attention on the complex, and two-way, passage between the economic and the political. To put it another way, hegemony is a way of formulating the problem of the interrelations between the infrastructure and the superstructure. Indeed, it seems to me, through the notion of hegemony Gramsci manages to go beyond the not always helpful infrastructure/superstructure dichotomy[27] in a way that neither collapses into a vulgar mechanical Marxism nor slides back into a voluntaristic idealism in which ultimately the true dynamic of history is that of ideas.

26. Two recent and influential studies by Africanists that use the notion of hegemony and draw explicitly on the work of Gramsci are Feierman's *Peasant Intellectuals* (1990; see 26–27), and Jean and John Comaroff's *Of Revelation and Revolution* (1991; see 18–32).

27. Interestingly Marx himself only uses this dichotomy once in the whole of volume 1 of *Capital*, and that is when he is quoting himself in the famous preface to *A Contribution to the Critique of Political Economy* (Marx 1970:175).

Gramsci's *Prison Notebooks* are an extraordinarily open text that can be read in many different ways; nonetheless, there are certain readings that seem to me to go against the spirit, if not the letter, of his work. Crucially, I would argue, however many different facets there may be to Gramsci, the fundamental problematic within which he located himself was a solidly *Marxist* one, and to deny this is to misread him. Underlying all Gramsci's writings, from his earliest journalism to the major prison writings, is the assumption that fundamental economic relations provide societies with their ultimate dynamic, and it is from this substructure that—although always *ultimately*—ideas and consciousness flow, rather than the other way around. In the *Prison Notebooks* we find him writing,

Though hegemony is ethical-political, it must also be economic, must necessarily be based on the decisive function exercised by the leading group in the decisive nucleus of economic activity. (Gramsci 1971:161)[28]

What makes it possible to deny Gramsci's rootedness in the Marxist problematic is precisely its taken-for-granted nature in his thinking. The assumptions of historical materialism—or, as it is usually termed in the *Prison Notebooks*, the philosophy of praxis—were such basic assumptions for Gramsci that they were not something he was continually reiterating; they were simply his starting point. Gramsci's concern was always with the complex ways in which the passage from the underlying relations of production and exchange to history is brought about by the actions of individuals and groups of individuals.

For Gramsci the economic and the political are inextricably intertwined: "the State is the concrete form of a productive world" (Gramsci 1971:117). And the kind of problems he addresses are: What does the power of states consist of, how is it achieved and how is it linked to economic relations? It is in the course of working through such questions that Gramsci gradually develops the concept of hegemony in the *Prison Notebooks*. It is through what I would like to term a *problematic of hegemony* that Gramsci explores the nature of state power and the conditions of its existence—not, that is, the power of states in some formal

---

28. Similarly in an early journalistic piece, Gramsci wrote on the importance of Marx for the rethinking of the relationship between ideas and history. Prior to Marx,

History was a domain solely of ideas. Man was considered as spirit, as pure consciousness. . . . With Marx, history continues to be the domain of ideas, of spirit, of the conscious activity of single or associated individuals. But ideas, spirit, take on substance, lose their arbitrariness. . . . *Their substance is in the economy, in practical activity, in the systems and relations of production and exchange.* (Gramsci quoted in Forgacs 1988:37, my emphasis)

sense but the concrete and specific ways in which particular states at particular historical moments either do, or do not, maintain dominance.

Gramsci refers to hegemony and the state in many places in the *Prison Notebooks*, but, as has been frequently pointed out, the meanings he gives these terms are by no means consistent. Indeed, Gramsci has often been taken to task for failing to provide neat and bounded definitions of a number of his central concepts, such as the state, civil society, and hegemony.[29] I would argue, however, that the irritation that some people seem to feel because they cannot pin down *exactly* what Gramsci means by *hegemony, exactly* how he understands the relationship between the state and civil society, and so on, is misplaced, and that Gramsci's flexibility in the way he used basic theoretical concepts is in fact central to his analytical strategy—a strategy that insists that it is the relationship *between* things, not the things themselves on which we must focus. It is these *relationships*, which are always dynamic, never static, and always historically specific, that define entities such as "the state." There is a necessary fluidity—something that is signaled by Gramsci's liberal use of quotation marks. It was Gramsci's rigorous refusal to turn away from the ever shifting complexity and general messiness of history that is both his strength and the source of much of the "difficulty" of his writings.[30] It is precisely Gramsci's refusal to provide rigid theoretical boxes that makes his writings on the state so useful for tracing out the ways in which particular states, at particular historical moments, translate into the lived realities of individual lives.

If we look carefully at the different references to the state in the *Prison Notebooks*, what we begin to see is the broad outline of an underlying power relationship that is always in motion. Thus in one note we find Gramsci describing the state as

the entire complex of practical and theoretical activities with which the ruling class not only justifies and maintains its dominance, but manages to win the active consent of those over whom it rules. (Gramsci 1971:244)

29. The editors of the standard English language edition of the *Prison Notebooks* themselves reiterate this criticism. "What is, however, true is that Gramsci did not succeed in finding a single, wholly satisfactory conception of 'civil society' or the State" (Gramsci 1971:207).

30. See Joseph Buttigieg's introduction to the new complete English language edition of the *Prison Notebooks* (only volume 1 of the planned five volumes has so far been published) for an extremely thoughtful discussion of Gramsci's methodology. Sassoon (1990) provides an interesting way of approaching Gramsci's use of language in the *Prison Notebooks*.

While in another note the state is defined more succinctly as "political society + civil society, in other words hegemony protected by the armour of coercion" (1971:263). But in the context of a discussion of the role of intellectuals, the state is described rather differently.

What we can do, for the moment, is to fix two major superstructural "levels": the one that can be called "civil society", that is the ensemble of organisms commonly called "private", and that of "political society" or "the State". These two levels correspond on the one hand to the function of "hegemony" which the dominant group exercises throughout society and on the other hand to that of "direct domination" or command exercised through the State and "juridical" government. The functions in question are precisely organisational and connective. The intellectuals are the dominant group's "deputies" exercising the subaltern functions of social hegemony and political government. These comprise:

1. The "spontaneous" consent given by the great masses of the population to the general direction imposed on social life by the dominant fundamental group; this consent is "historically" caused by the prestige (and consequent confidence) which the dominant group enjoys because of its position and function in the world of production.

2. The apparatus of state coercive power which "legally" enforces discipline on those groups who do not "consent" either actively or passively. This apparatus is, however, constituted for the whole of society in anticipation of moments of crisis of command and direction when spontaneous consent has failed.

(1971:12)

Running through these different accounts is the identification of the state as a particular moment in a continuing struggle between different interests in which, as it were, a specific configuration of power carrying with it its particular historical legacies is, for however long or short a time, congealed. For Gramsci any such configuration of power always rests on some combination of force and consent in which the two elements, domination and hegemony, are linked together in a complex dialectic relationship that is itself continually shifting. Because the state is in this way the outcome of struggles fought not only on numerous different sites but on sites that are themselves subject to shifts and changes, it is impossible to define in any fixed and permanent way certain institutions as inherently part of civil society and the sphere of consent, and others as inherently belonging to the sphere of coercive state apparatuses. Indeed, even the line dividing force from consent can be difficult to draw. The analysis of specific states and their historical trajectories necessarily involves tracking the complex dialectic of force and consent as it moves through institutions and practices, often dragging these into new configurations.

Inasmuch as the state in any class society represents an ultimately coercive domination of subordinate groups by the dominant classes, the moment of force necessarily dominates, and in some sense incorporates that of consent and hegemony. Here the state corresponds to Gramsci's definition of "hegemony protected by the armour of coercion." In certain contexts, however, it is important to focus on the difference between force and consent, between the state and civil society. For instance, understanding why particular patterns of domination persist involves analyzing a whole range of institutions that appear not to be part of the formal state apparatus, and to be based not on force but consent. And yet civil society cannot be seen as totally independent of the state; indeed, a crucial part of its analysis involves tracing out the threads linking it with the state, and the degree to which the institutions and practices that constitute civil society *are* autonomous, and the degree to which they are not—and the nature of this autonomy.[31] Gramsci refers to Hegel's description of the parties and associations of civil society as "the 'private' woof of the State" (1971:259). To develop this metaphor: if we see consent and the institutions associated with it as the woof, or weft, of society, and force and its associated coercive institutions as the warp, then woof and warp together make up the fabric of the state as a coherent set of power relations that sustain a particular topography of power. Inasmuch as the warp cannot exist without the woof, civil society is an integral part of the state. But weft and warp are nonetheless different, and, if we want to understand the particular strength of a given fabric, it often helps to unpick it into its component strands and analyze these separately.

As should be evident from the passages cited, the notion of hegemony is part and parcel of Gramsci's theorization of the state. But, as the quotations also make abundantly clear, hegemony is a highly complex and shifting notion. That is why I prefer to think of hegemony as a *problematic*, rather than some distinct, and clearly bounded, analytical category; that is, as a way of approaching the problem of power, and especially state power, that focuses attention on "the entire complex of practical and theoretical activities with which the ruling class not only

31. See Buttigieg (1995) for a helpful account of Gramsci's notion of civil society.

justifies its dominance, but manages to win the active consent of those over whom it rules." Hegemony as a *problematic* continually brings us back to the fundamental questions. How does power work? How is it that even the disadvantaged in a society seem so often to accept their disadvantage as legitimate—or at least inescapable? What is the nature of this subordinated consciousness and why is it unable to articulate a coherent alternative view of the reality in which it lives? How does such a consciousness come into being and how might it be transformed? These are questions that for Gramsci are always about *process*: the processes by which ruling groups exercise relationships of domination, leadership, and organization; the processes through which consent is created and maintained, or challenged. At one point, for instance, Gramsci, writing about France, describes hegemony as follows:

The "normal" exercise of hegemony on the now classical terrain of the parliamentary regime is characterised by the combination of force and consent, which balance each other reciprocally, without force predominating excessively over consent. Indeed, the attempt is always made to ensure that force will appear to be based on the consent of the majority, expressed by the organs of so-called public opinion—newspapers and associations. (Gramsci 1971:80)

Note that hegemony here is not *opposed* in any simple way to force; rather the concept of hegemony serves to highlight the problematic relation between force and consent, and to draw attention to the way in which they are entwined, and how force may be concealed behind a facade of consent. Secondly, however apparently monolithic and unchallenged it may appear, hegemony is, as it were, a smooth veneer applied to a disorder of contending forces that are always threatening to crack it apart. Hegemony is never secure because it always describes a relationship between groups or classes in struggle (even if this struggle may be latent and unacknowledged for long periods).[32] It must be continually produced and reproduced.

While it is important to stress that hegemony is not just about ideas and beliefs, struggles over how reality is described are certainly an important dimension of a society's power relations. And as we shall see in the case of the term *tribe* in colonial Zambia, struggles over the nature

32. James Scott's work on Indonesian peasants who engage in what he terms "everyday forms of resistance" to the hegemony the state attempts to exercise has been very influential in directing attention to this level of struggle, and also in shaping the debate on hegemony in anthropology. See, for instance, Scott (1976, 1985, 1990).

of reality, over "how things are," and how this reality is to be named can have very material effects. The power to *name* is a crucial one. And here I want to introduce the third major theorist on whose work I have drawn to tell the story of Kibala and Bukama: Mikhail Bakhtin.

A problem to which Bakhtin, like Gramsci, continually returns is that of the *social* production of knowledge. How is it that certain shared accounts of the world come to be so firmly embedded within individuals' consciousnesses as to seem to those individuals part of the very texture of their own subjective being? Bakhtin, again like Gramsci, is a theorist who is read in very different ways by different readers. This is perhaps appropriate given that one of the central themes of his work is the active role of the reader in determining meaning. One area of disagreement concerns the attribution of certain texts to him. A more general area of dispute is the nature of Bakhtin's relationship to the Marxist tradition.[33] Part of the problem is that, even in those texts that are unquestionably by him, Bakhtin adopted many different voices. The particular voice that I have drawn on is one that seems to me to speak from within the Marxist tradition, but that continually questions that tradition in a productive way. So let me now in the final section of this chapter elaborate a little on how Bakhtin's insights can be brought together with Gramsci's notion of hegemony in a productive way.

The Power of Naming

At one level all social life can be seen as an ever-continuing dialogue in which everything that is said is said in a *context*, and always derives a certain amount of its meaning from that context. All of us, whatever society we live in, are continually interpreting what the people around us do and say, and shaping what we ourselves say and do according to our interpretations of what others "mean" by their speech and behavior. In other words, the process by which specific words and

33. Clark and Holquist's biography of Bakhtin (1984:1–15, 146–70) provides a helpful summary of the disputes over the various texts produced by the Bakhtin circle and of the problems involved in pinning down Bakhtin's work in any theoretically tidy way. The main texts I have drawn on are Bakhtin (1981, 1984, 1986a, [Vološinov, pseud.] 1986b, and 1988). For my purposes the question of precise attribution is not a crucial one and for the sake of simplicity I cite Bakhtin throughout with the understanding that strictly speaking this "Bakhtin" sometimes refers to the Bakhtin circle.

actions come to have particular meanings in a particular social universe is always profoundly *social*: meaning is produced through social interaction. Speakers, whether explicitly or implicitly, are continually imagining how what they are saying will be heard by their listeners, how it will be interpreted, and are trying in the light of this to express their meaning in such a way that it will be "understood" by the hearer. A speaker's meaning, however, is never simply duplicated in the mind of the hearer. A speaker is always engaged in a *dialogue*, and always expects some kind of response, whether agreement, disagreement, sympathy, or perhaps the carrying out of some action if what was said involved a command or request. This response may well not be openly expressed, but inasmuch as the hearer is another human being it is always there, and it is out of this spoken or unspoken dialogue that meaning emerges.

Sometimes when we are given an account of how things are in the world that seems to conflict with what we know, or believe, we may be prepared to accept this, whether because we are genuinely convinced that we were wrong or because in this particular context we feel intimidated and unable to defend our beliefs. If, however, we do challenge what we are being told then we are engaged in a struggle over meaning. This is so whether our dissent was open or remained unspoken, and whether it was radical or nothing more than a minor modification. Such struggle involves both the question of what it was we actually heard and the fit between that and *our* understanding of "how things are."

Over time, within a given society with its particular configurations of power, certain meanings, and certain ways of understanding the world, acquire a greater or lesser degree of authority and hegemony. For while social life may involve a continual struggle over meaning, our freedom to interpret the world around us is limited. As Bakhtin put it: "Consciousness takes shape and being in the material of signs created by an organised group in the process of its social intercourse" (Bakhtin 1986b:13). No child, wherever and however it is brought up, ever simply discovers either its own individuality or the world around it; it is continually being told, both explicitly and implicitly, who it is and what the world around it is. Raw experience is continually being named, categorised, interpreted, evaluated, and explained. Even as individuals learn to name and categorize for themselves, they do this within preexisting languages and preexisting principles of categorization, which confront them as external realities, explained to them by others. Much of what individuals "know" they have absorbed almost unconsciously simply in the course of growing up in a particular place at a given moment of history. Much of this knowledge is in fact embodied in the very institutions and practices of their society, often in the form of implicit assumptions buried in explicit statements about the nature of reality. Because this knowledge is so hegemonic and taken for granted by everyone around them, and because, whether explicitly or implicitly, they are so often told it by powerful authority figures, it can be difficult for members of that society even to find the words in which to express doubt. One such deeply embedded idea within modern industrial society is that the basic unit of society is the independent and autonomous individual. It is indeed our assimilation of a certain substratum of beliefs and ideas that binds us into our particular historical time and place. It is almost as if we do not so much think such ideas as they think us; they are the stuff out of which the basic elements of our consciousness are formed. In the course of their development individuals may fashion very different garments out of this stuff, but they have to use the basic fabric given to them. Bakhtin provides a wonderfully vivid and precise description of the place of such structuring ideas in individual consciousness, and of the nature of their relationship to the social life of collectivities. In the chapters that follow I will come back again and again to this passage.

The point is that all the fundamental social evaluations which develop directly from the specific conditions of the economic life of a given group are not usually uttered. They have become flesh and blood of all members of that group, they organize actions and behaviour, they have as it were, fused with the objects and phenomena to which they correspond, and for this reason they do not need special verbal formulations. It seems that we perceive the value of an object together with its being, as one of its qualities; in the same way, for example, we sense the value of the sun together with its warmth and light. And thus all phenomena of being which surround us are fused together with our evaluations of them. If an evaluation, is in reality conditioned by the very being of a given collective, then it is accepted dogmatically as something understood and not subject to discussion. (Bakhtin 1988:13)

Individuals, however, have considerable latitude in terms of the ways in which basic hegemonic assumptions about reality are interpreted in any given situation. That witches exist, for instance, may be a basic assumption, but whether or not a specific death is due to witchcraft can be argued about. Also, very important, ideas about the nature of reality are over time measured against experience of that reality, and if the two cannot be brought into some kind of meaningful fit, then *ultimately* the ideas are likely to be discarded. This assumption makes this a materialist account of meaning, while the stress on *ultimately* saves it from being vulgarly materialist.

It should also be stressed, however, that the dichotomy between an external reality and subjective consciousness is an analytical separation rather than an empirical description. Or, to put it another way, while it can be assumed that there is such a separation it does not manifest itself at the level of the empirically observable in any clear way. A key point, it seems to me, is that while it is true that the idea of such a separation needs to be problematized, unless we assume there *is* some kind of separation we cannot even ask questions about it. The question of how individuals perceive the reality in which they live is always complicated; and one of the questions addressed by this book (particularly in chapter 6) is how and why ideas are "plausible" in a particular context. But nonetheless, I would argue, ultimately there *is* some kind of irreducible hard reality "out there," and if our beliefs about this reality are to retain their plausibility, those beliefs have to take this into account; but this is something that is always mediated in complicated ways and only happens over time. Let me again emphasize the *ultimately*.

There is in fact a continual tension between *knowledge* of the world and *experience* of it—knowledge always being subject to challenge and experience always mediated by our preconceptions. And it is out of this process that new names and new understandings come into being, albeit always dragging fragments of the old with them. This process is always, even when carried out by the most solitary of individuals, a *social* process since it cannot but use language, that most social of creations. New names and understandings emerge as a result of an ever-continuing struggle over meaning in which individuals and groups try to establish *their* account of the world as the correct one; as, for instance, "morally right," or "logically correct," or "the only one possible in the circumstances," and so on. While some of the namings involved may be idiosyncratic there are also those that derive from specific experiences that are shared by certain groups, such as a particular location within a society's economic relations, which describe that experience in a satisfying and plausible way. Such a shared account of "how things are" (which may well contain its own contradictions) can be seen as constituting that group's worldview, even though all its members may not share this worldview in its entirety. At the level of the social formation these different accounts vie with one another. Certain of them, essentially those that represent the position of the dominant groups, achieve—for however long or short a time—a degree of hegemony while others, those of the subordinated groups, are denied or suppressed. The degree of hegemony achieved is reflected in the degree to which dominated or subaltern groups find it impossible to name their own experience and are thrown back onto the names given to them by the dominant group.

At the level of the individual, a certain degree of bricolage is possible, whereby individuals are able to construct their own identities out of found fragments; but they also, again to a certain degree, emerge into consciousness of themselves as individuals already named. From their first conscious moment they are continually being told who they are, and they learn to recognize themselves in existing names, such as: mother, daughter, brother, Kaonde, Zambian. These names are, as it were, held up in front of them like mirrors: you are a mother, *this* is what mothers look like. All the various shards of identity out of which individual lives are pieced, however, are always the product of particular histories and are always embedded in power relations. The ways in which individuals come to inhabit particular identities necessarily involve power struggles and contestation, even if these struggles are implicit and unacknowledged. Individuals neither stand outside history nor are they determined in their entirety by it. Similarly, while they live within hegemonic power relations, hegemony is never complete.

Complete hegemony, although it might be a logical possibility, is never an empirical reality. Hegemony is always in some degree partial and limited; it is a power relation that must be continually produced and reproduced. For instance, insofar as a prevailing hegemonic account does not adequately articulate the experience of subordinated groups, there is always the potential threat that this experience will find an articulated form that can effectively challenge the particular web of meaning the dominant group has cast over certain realities. The production of such articulated expressions is one of the functions of intellectuals as a distinct group. Very importantly, the hegemonic accounts that dominant groups succeed in imposing on subordinate groups represent the outcome of a struggle in which the former may have been forced to give way at certain points and incorporate elements of subordinate accounts.

Hegemonic accounts are also relative depending on from where we are viewing them. Within the communities of Kibala and Bukama, for instance, there was a set of shared assumptions about the way the world is, and a set of moral expectations, to which people certainly did not always adhere but which were generally agreed (at least in any public setting) to represent the way people *ought* to behave. One needs to be bear in mind, however, firstly, that these expectations and assumptions operated at a very general level so that there was always plenty of room for competing interpretations of their precise meaning in any actual context. Secondly, this version of "how things are" represented a hegemony in which the interests and experience of senior men, and above all married men, were represented at the expense of that of women and younger unmarried men. And these cleavages along lines of age and gender were not the only ones of rural life. Concealed beneath the hegemonic front that the community tended to present to the outside world there were a number of different voices, some of which will, I hope, emerge in subsequent chapters.

Let me bring this rather long introduction to a close with a brief explanation of how the chapters in this book are organized. As I have stressed, the red thread that runs through all the chapters is the act of *naming* and *locating* (a term I am using in a broad metaphorical sense). To set the scene for my mapping of Kibala and Bukama, I began by laying out in this introduction the basic theoretical tools I am using and explaining my own theoretical location. In the next chapter I turn more specifically to the theoretical and practical location of both myself and the anthropological enterprise in Zambia. The first part of the chapter explores my particular location as a white woman anthropologist from Britain within rural Zambia in 1988. The second part looks at a particular historical example of anthropological naming: the story of how "the Kaonde" became a "tribe" in colonial Zambia. It is a case study demonstrating in a concrete way the complicated and always historically located nature of the production of knowledge. This case study also serves as a good introduction to my account of Kibala and Bukama, not only as a warning against hubris, but also because, again in a concrete fashion, it forces us to ask the question, Just who are the people of Kibala and Bukama, analytically speaking? This is a question I will come back to in the conclusion.

Chapters 3 to 6 are all concerned with mapping out the various locations inhabited by the people of Kibala and Bukama, but each focuses on a different dimension of their location. Chapter 3 is concerned with political locations within what I am calling "the imagined community of kin," and with how this community of kin was incorporated into the colonial and postcolonial state. Chapter 4 concentrates on the local political topography of the postcolonial state of the Second Republic and the intertwining of the community of kin with that of citizens of the national state. In chapter 5 the focus shifts to economic locations and what the processes of monetization and commoditization have meant for the lives of individual women and men. Throughout the book as a whole I have attempted to include local voices and pay attention to how they saw themselves as located and how they named their world; in chapter 6, however, this becomes the main focus. As a way into these local understandings and namings I have taken the phenomenon of *bulozhi* (witchcraft), to which the people of Kibala and Bukama attributed almost all deaths, sickness, and other misfortunes. In essence I argue that the local discourse on *bulozhi* can be seen as providing a mirror in which local notions of the good society can be glimpsed in a perverted, negative form. When people spoke about *bulozhi* they were in fact drawing on a set of taken-for-granted assumptions about moral behavior and human relationships, which those who practice *bulozhi* were seen as transgressing. Finally, in a brief conclusion I come back to the question of how the mapping of this little corner of Zambia can help us understand the broader picture of contemporary capitalism.

CHAPTER 2

Observing Power

Ever tried. Ever failed. No matter. Try again. Fail again.
Fail better.

Samuel Beckett, *Worstward Ho*

Part One: Failing Better

To insist on field research as the fundamental source of
anthropological knowledge has served as a powerful practical
corrective, in fact a contradiction, which, philosophically
speaking, makes anthropology on the whole an aporetic
enterprise.

Johannes Fabian, *Time and the Other*

Local Colour. Work it in all you know. Make them accomplices.

James Joyce, *Ulysses*

This book is about the political, economic, and imagined
landscapes inhabited by the people of Kibala and Bukama. These were
landscapes that were certainly not contained within the boundaries of
those communities themselves; nonetheless, to gather data for their
mapping I relied primarily on what might be seen as the rather traditional anthropological approach of the "community" case study. In the
first part of the chapter I explain why I chose an approach based on
participant observation and the small-scale case study. I also try to locate

myself and my attempts at naming what I saw. Having done this I then go on in the second half of the chapter to tell the story of a particular example of colonial hegemony and naming: how it was that the Kaonde came to be a "tribe." I look at what the name "tribe" signified from three vantage points: the anthropologists of the Rhodes-Livingstone Institute, colonial officials stationed in North-Western Province, and, finally, those called by this name of "Kaonde."

One reason for introducing *my* mapping and *my* naming of Kibala and Bukama with this historical case study of anthropological and colonial naming is that it demonstrates in a very concrete way the inevitable limits to the aporia of fieldwork. However open to doubt the anthropologist may try to be, ultimately he or she is always imprisoned within a given historical moment; we always join a dialogue already in progress in which certain ways of naming reality have become hegemonic. The two halves of the chapter can be seen then as in dialogue with each other. The story of how the Kaonde became a "tribe" will also, I hope, be present as a questioning voice in the chapters that follow, where I refer frequently to such entities as the *Kaonde* discourse on authority, *Kaonde* kinship terminology and *Kaonde* cultivation patterns. My hope is that the example of the colonial use of "tribe"—since these things are always so much easier to see in hindsight—will remind the reader (and me) to keep questioning just what *Kaonde* means in any given context.

Participant Observation and Context

The primary value of a fieldwork strategy based on participant observation, it seems to me, is that it provides a certain kind of insight that is difficult to obtain in any other way. It is not that living in a place and watching its daily life ebb and flow around you somehow enables you to capture its totality or its essence; it is rather that the small bits of its life that you do see, you see in some kind of *context*. The great advantage of data collected through participant observation, rather than through direct questioning in a formal interview, is that they are produced not as a response to some hypothetical question but, as it were, occur spontaneously. The quarrel that erupts outside your front door between the secretary of the local co-operative and the farmer who claims he is owed money is a quarrel between two individuals you know, just as you know something about the local co-operative society. The "thick description" this allows—to use Clifford Geertz's phrase—is of a different order to that you are likely to get when your information comes from a formal interview with the co-operative secretary conducted during an afternoon's visit when the secretary and you are meeting for the first time.

This is not to say that the anthropologist is ever a neutral, fly-on-the-wall presence, and a fortiori not when she is a westerner living in a small African village. Anthropologists cannot but be to some extent alien and in various ways politically charged presences, who by their very presence necessarily alter the reality in which they are trying to participate. The encounter between a foreign fieldworker and rural Africans is never neutral or disinterested; each side has their own interests, brings their own assumptions and beliefs as members of a particular society, and has their own preconceptions as to what is involved in the encounter, what the encounter "means." And this remains true even when anthropologists do fieldwork in their own society. But the fact that the anthropologist can never be a purely disinterested spectator does not mean that she cannot, within certain limits, be a *relatively* disinterested one. We may be condemned to engage in a dialogue of the partially deaf, but not the stone deaf. Despite all the different agendas and the inevitable misunderstandings, *some* form of dialogue is possible. The limits to this dialogue, however, are not something that can be fixed in any kind of rigorous theoretical way, since they depend so much on the idiosyncratic and particular circumstances of each field study—circumstances that include the nature of the personal relationships that develop between the anthropologist and local people. "Doing fieldwork" is always as much an art as it is any kind of science.

My accounts of Kibala and Bukama are necessarily fragmentary and incomplete, but this would be true of any accounts, even ones given by members of those communities. Women and men, the young and the old, the less and the more prosperous do not always see things the same way. Also, any account is given in a context and it is the specifics of that context that determine which elements are selected and assembled as the relevant and significant ones and which are denied or repressed. Crucially, when anybody gives any kind of account it is always in some sense answering a question. As Bakhtin put it, "Anything that does not answer a question is devoid of sense for us" (Bakhtin 1986a:145). What fieldwork is often about, it seems to me, is the struggle to discover the questions we have not asked but which our informants hear and are struggling to answer in their attempts to make sense of the questions we do ask. It is these unasked questions, if only we can make our way back to them, that often reveal how reality appears from those informants' vantage point.

For instance, in some of my more formal interviews in Bukama I asked people how much maize and other crops they had produced for sale. Toward the end of my time there my research assistant explained to me that most people exaggerated these figures because they assumed that, whatever I might say to the contrary, I would tell the powers that be how much everyone was producing, and those deemed not to be producing enough would be "chased" from the settlement scheme. The threat that unproductive farmers would be expelled from the scheme was a staple of the exhortations delivered by various visiting bureaucrats and politicians at public meetings in Bukama. Although such threats were, as far as I could tell, purely rhetorical and no one had ever actually been expelled, however meager their production, nobody was about to take any chances. What the answers to my questions about yields were actually telling me about, therefore, had less to do with productivity and more to do with the relationship between local farmers and officialdom. In other words, what those I questioned heard was a question about whether they were "progressive" and properly productive farmers.

Much of this study is based on participant observation that involved the reconstruction of the various contexts—including the context of power—out of which my fragments of data were torn. The task was all the more difficult because so much of this context involved unspoken, taken-for-granted assumptions that were so much a part of the fabric of people's lives that, as Bakhtin wrote, "they do not need special verbal formulations." In the next section I attempt to describe my position in Chizela as a female, white anthropologist from Britain and how I fitted into the local power landscape.

A Powerful Visitor

I arrived in Chizela laden down with more possessions for my six-month stay than all but the very richest inhabitants of Kibala and Bukama owned in total. By the standards of those amongst whom I was to live I was fabulously wealthy. With my impressive letters of introduction from Lusaka and the provincial capital and my apparent access to that scarce and vital resource, transport, I clearly belonged to the world of government, missionaries, and foreign aid workers—a world of whose power rural Zambians were fully aware. Given the lack of public transport in Chizela District, for most people journeys longer than could be managed on foot usually meant long waits by the side of the road on the chance of a lift from one of the vehicles that would occasionally roar by in a cloud of dust. Sometimes such a lift could be begged in advance, but this was far easier for a visiting anthropologist. Although I did not have my own transport, I could usually count on lifts from any passing government or aid project vehicle when I needed them. And whereas local people were often asked to pay for these lifts, I, who unlike them could so easily have afforded to pay, was almost never asked. The world to which I so obviously belonged was the world that controlled crucial resources, such as clinics, schools, and marketing services, and which determined the prices of so many of the goods people needed to buy. As an emissary of this powerful but remote world, so hard of access for rural people, it was inevitable that I would appear as a potential channel through which local interests might be able to make themselves heard in influential circles. At the very least I was recording what went on locally, and would later tell people outside Chizela (whether in Lusaka or Britain) what I had learned. This meant it was important that I was given "correct" accounts. In short, it was quite impossible that I would be perceived as a neutral observer.

Very few westerners ever *live* in Zambian villages. At the time of my fieldwork the only people belonging to the wider world of government, foreign aid, or the missionaries who did were a few lower-ranking government employees, such as primary school teachers or agricultural assistants. The rest, whether Zambian or expatriate, lived, if they were rurally based, in district centers, like Chizela town, or on mission stations. They did, it is true, visit rural communities to hold meetings or church services, or maybe to buy local delicacies such as game meat or fish. Arriving in their official vehicles, they would address the assembled "masses" (assuming that those responsible had managed to assemble them), and then get back in their vehicles and return to the comforts of urban life. Occasionally they might spend a night in a village but almost never longer. The only people from this world who have sometimes lived in rural communities for longer periods have been those carrying out research of some kind, most commonly anthropologists. But these have been few and far between, especially in the Kaonde-speaking region of North-Western Province. I first came to North-Western in 1979 and was the first anthropologist to stay for any length of time (I stayed for two years) in a Kaonde speaking area. William Watson had spent a few weeks in the area in the early 1950s (see Watson 1954), before moving on to Northern Province for his main study (Watson 1958), and Dirk Jaeger had carried out a geographical study (Jaeger 1981), but that was all.

When I returned ten years later I was still the only anthropologist to have carried out extended fieldwork in a Kaonde-speaking area. There were, therefore, at least some local people, particularly among the more educated, who were pleased that finally there was someone who was interested in their region, and interested enough actually to live with them. Some of these were Kaondes, anxious that their history, their "traditions," and their way of life should be recorded. Other local people who were often interested in my project were those government employees who do actually live in rural communities: the teachers, the agricultural assistants, the clinical officers. These were people who were likely to be from another language group and, partly for this reason but even more because of their education and government salary, were in the eyes of the local community, most definitely outsiders. They and I had in common membership in a world of education and the English language stretching out beyond the "village"—a world suffused with the bright glow of modernity and wealth.

Part of what I represented to the people of Kibala and Bukama, was a way of telling "the world out there" about their world. To avoid any possible misunderstanding here, let me stress, in no way am I claiming to speak *for* the people of Kibala and Bukama, let alone for "the Kaonde"; all I am saying is that at times I represented an ear into which people could speak. However much an anthropologist may wish to let anthropological subjects "speak for themselves," they do not and cannot unless the anthropologist has surrendered all editorial control and has merely facilitated their own publications. Of course anthropologists do sometimes do this, but the kind of folk histories that tend to result are seldom allowed entry into the hallowed halls of "serious scholarship."[1] While I believe that anthropological research and the production of academic texts should involve dialogue and debate with those whose lives provide the raw data, I also believe that anthropologists should not delude themselves that they can have it both ways—that they can "let the other speak" and yet at the same time retain a control that enables

1. Robert Papstein provides an interesting account of the kind of political problems such endeavors can run into in "From Ethnic Identity to Tribalism," in Vail (1989).

them to guide the voices of these "others" so that the tunes they sing obey the harmonics of the academy.

For those who feel themselves to be outside the circles of power—whether these are rural Zambians or others excluded in different ways in different societies—simply to be listened to and taken seriously by someone from those circles of power, may have a value. Anthropologists, because they are often interested in, and take so seriously, things in which no one else—possibly not even those within the society itself—shows much interest, can at times become a rather special kind of audience. Sometimes the mere fact of being asked by the anthropologist to "explain" some piece of behavior, that to any member of the society is obvious and taken for granted, may have the effect of forcing someone to think consciously about that little fragment of everyday life for the first time. For those from whom the anthropologist seeks information and explanations, the anthropologist can sometimes become something like a mirror in which people see their identity, their "culture," their "tradition," or whatever, reflected; and not only reflected, but in some way validated. Of course, what the anthropologist mirror "sees" is not necessarily the same as that which those looking *into* the mirror see reflected.

Anthropologists and those among whom they work are always and inescapably engaged in a dialogue embedded in power relations of various kinds, and it is always out of such dialogue that "facts" are produced. But this is not to say that those facts are therefore false, or that somewhere beyond the dialogue, if only we could get there, we could find a realm of pristine objectivity. Like it or not, we are condemned to scrabble about with our secondhand categories in a tension-laden field. The best we can do is to try conscientiously to follow the threads dangling from the "facts" we have excavated back to their origins. Why might X have told us this? What kind of associations might those terms have in this particular context?

An important set of limitations to what anthropologists can learn through fieldwork have to do with the names and the categories we inevitably use to process what we see. How much of the life going on around me in Kibala and Bukama was I *capable* of seeing? Part of the baggage I took with me was a whole intellectual legacy acquired in the course of fifteen years of anthropological studies, and inevitably this kept telling me what I was seeing: *this* is significant, *that* insignificant, *this* falls into that category, *that* into that one, and so on. In other words, what I was seeing had already been named in the literature with which

I was familiar, and it was impossible for me to think about it without using those names. Central to the experience of anthropological field-work is a continual struggle between the preexisting names anthropologists carry with them and the hard and untidy realities in which those anthropologists have chosen to submerge themselves. But while it is never possible to experience these realities in any direct, unnamed way, the world "out there," which is never purely a world of discourse, however much it always appears to us clothed in our names, can sometimes stretch and tear those names in such a way that we are forced to rethink them. While it is important not to underestimate the difficulties of seeing a different reality, especially one that does not conform to the received hegemonic perception, it is surely equally important not to retreat into an arid skepticism that argues that the difficulties are so great that it is simply not possible to gain *any* knowledge that refers to anything beyond discourse.

My strategy in Chizela for disturbing my preconceptions, a standard anthropological one, involved, firstly, attempting to undermine my own assumptions and preconceptions through, as far as possible, submerging myself in this alien reality and allowing it in all its empirical richness to flood over me and challenge my ready-made names—to embrace, as it were, aporia. I also conducted numerous interviews, fifteen of which I tape-recorded. However, although I took to these interviews a set of topics, I used these more as a way of starting conversations than as a way of getting the answers to specific questions. Rather than relying solely on direct questioning to elicit data, I also concentrated on information that, as it were, presented itself to me, trying to observe what people did rather than what they said they did, and listening to what people said spontaneously in a particular context, whether this was an aside to one of my questions or was said to someone else on an occasion when I happened to be present as an observer. I would also try and obtain information about a particular topic when it happened to come up in conversation. Nonetheless, it is important to remember that, however much I might try to stray beyond the public arena, the very fact that I was present had a tendency to transform any occasion into a public one. I always to some extent represented the eye of the outside world.

The alert reader is likely to notice that certain people in Kibala and Bukama are often cited, in particular two men I have called Sansoni and Mukwetu, both of whom at times acted as my research assistants. Sansoni was an educated man of thirty-nine who had completed his secondary school education. The son of a teacher, Sansoni had spent most of his adult life in town, where he had held various white-collar jobs. In 1985 he had moved to Kibala and was employed as a teacher at Kibala primary school. He was also the secretary of the Kibala ward. Mukwetu, who was twenty-seven, had also attended secondary school but only up to Form 3, not Form 5. At the end of Form 3, after three years of secondary school, students have to pass another exam to be accepted for the final two years and many, like Mukwetu, fail. In 1988 he had been living in Bukama for three years. Partly because of their education, both Sansoni and Mukwetu were highly articulate, and both were probably able to relate more easily to me and my project than were some others. I tried very hard to find local women to work with me as research assistants, but in general it was simply too difficult for women to find the necessary time to work with me on any kind of a regular basis.

Another source of data I have used are the Kaonde versions of the folktales told throughout Zambia. *Bishimi* (sing. *kishimi*), as they are termed in Kaonde, were often told in Kibala and Bukama at night around the fire, and were one of the ways in which ideas about the nature of the world and "how things are" were transmitted from one generation to the next. *Bishimi* tell of the doings of people—frequently identified not by name but by kinship status, *nkasanji* (young sibling), *mwisho* (mother's brother), and so on—and of supernatural beings and anthropomorphized animals. During my time in Chizela I tape-recorded a total of fifty-seven *bishimi* from eighteen (ten women and eight men) different storytellers, simply asking people to tell me *bishimi* and leaving the choice of stories up to them. After someone had told me a story I then asked them to tell me what they thought the story meant, and what lessons it could teach children. Of course the question of how such explanations should be interpreted raises thorny theoretical issues, but it seems legitimate to me to use such explanations to establish certain very general patterns of association. I also found asking for explanations an interesting way of eliciting statements about moral expectations— although, of course, this tells us nothing about the relationship between this moral discourse and how people in fact behaved.

I also worked in the national archives in Lusaka for a month after my six months in Chizela, which helped me locate my Kibala and Bukama data in their historical context. In addition I spent time in the district and regional centers collecting material on how rural Chizela looked from their vantage point.

Writing anthropological accounts, such as this one, necessarily involves a power relationship. Inevitably it involves claiming the right to name. My account is the product of a dialogue in which the participants were not only the people of Kibala and Bukama, but also a whole body of anthropological and scholarly theory that defined certain questions as important, others as irrelevant, provided analytical categories, and so on. Ultimately, however, although I hope it is a polyphonic rather than a monologic account, it is *my* account. I make no claims to be speaking *for* the people among whom I worked, rather, starting from various vantage points within Kibala and Bukama, I tried to understand as far as I could both *what* things looked like from down there and *why* they looked like that. It is not so much that the subjects of my story would necessarily disagree with what I have written (though some well might), but that much of it, even were it to be translated into a language they could understand, is likely to have little meaning for them, seeming to be about finding answers for questions they have no interest in asking. However, the profound gulf here is not primarily about Western versus non-Western, or "African" versus non-African, but about intellectuals versus non-intellectuals. To take an example from another part of north-western Zambia, Victor Turner's Ndembu informant and friend Muchona the Hornet was probably able to engage with Turner's scholarly exegesis of Ndembu symbolism in a way that most Ndembu not only could not, but would not have wanted to, as Turner himself recognized (see Turner 1967:131–50).

Given the partial and fragmentary nature of my information about Kibala and Bukama, in what sense can I claim that my mapping of the power landscape is "true"? And since I am not presenting it as a piece of fiction, or simply my "impressions," I am necessarily making some kind of claims to some kind of "truth." Before answering this question, I want to reflect a little on some aspects of the general problem of the "truth" of anthropological accounts.

Telling It How It Is

Providing "truthful" accounts of places and times, of which the reader is unlikely to have any firsthand knowledge, is always problematic. In the case of anthropological accounts dealing with non-Western societies the problems are particularly obvious, but in reality most of us know few worlds at first hand. How many professional New Yorkers, for instance, have any real knowledge of the world of the homeless, even though they may pick their way through them daily? So how can the accounts of anthropologists be evaluated by those ignorant of the realities these accounts claim to map?—particularly given that the same reality can appear very different when looked at by different observers. I want to illustrate this by providing two accounts of the same place.

Account I

Chief Chizela's personal farm borders the Bukama Farm Settlement Scheme, and this is where he spends most of his time nowadays, rather than at his official capital. Chief Chizela, now in his eighties, has had a farm here since the mid 1960s, and a small village has grown up around the Chief's enclosure. Let us imagine a visitor from a Western country, maybe one of the numerous tribe of development "experts," or a newly arrived anthropologist arriving at the Chief's. What would they see? First, a battered fence of broken poles half-heartedly marking out the Chief's space. In the rainy season maybe the visitor's eye would be caught by patches of bright green creeper trailing over the poles; the single sign of tropical abundance. In the enclosure itself is a huddle of dilapidated buildings apparently set down at random: houses, cooking shelters (separate ones for each of the Chief's three wives), and the special shelter built to house the Chief's aged, and usually broken down, tractor. There is also a collapsing pit latrine, the use of which demands a secure sense of balance. In a slightly better state of repair (although its skeleton of roof poles has been waiting for its new layer of thatch for some months now) is the Chief's official shelter, where court cases are heard and public meetings held. A couple of the houses are built from sun-dried brick, the others from plastered mud. Two have corrugated iron roofs held down by a collection of chunks of termite mound, lumps of scrap metal, and anything else heavy and to hand, but most have grass roofs that hang untidily over the walls except for here and there where someone once began trimming them only, it seems, to lose heart after a foot or two. Many of the grass roofs are thin and discolored with large bald patches, looking as if they too have become discouraged by prolonged contemplation of the cracked mud walls, crazily skewed door frames, and general lack of care.

As the visitor approaches, a horde of curious children assemble out of nowhere; many are obviously malnourished, bellies swollen with parasites; most are wearing no more than the last tattered remains of a pair of shorts or a ragged dress, any pattern they might once have had having long since given up the struggle against the relentless sun and harsh detergents. Many of their elders wear clothes that are scarcely in better shape, grime and wear having reduced all colors to a dull democracy of grayish brown. The few manufactured goods there are seem similarly to have had their spirit broken by their hard life, and loll listlessly about in odd corners: enamel plates no longer bothering to hide their chips and cracks; aluminium pots mended for the nth time, and still leaking; a three-legged iron cooking pot, its one remaining leg rearing defiantly in the air.

But what if we provide a little more context? Chief Chizela is a Kaonde chief, and the Kaonde have long been associated with a shifting cultivation system. Given a population density low enough to allow the necessary long fallows, such a system is an efficient adaption (especially in terms of returns to labor) to local ecological conditions.[2] This was a cultivation system, however, that involved both the relatively frequent relocation of settlements and, since fields were normally some distance from these settlements, an annual move for much of the cultivation season to temporary shelters erected close to the fields. Living close by one's fields was seen as necessary to protect the ripening crops from birds and other predators. Before the coming of the missionaries with their churches, schools, and hospitals and the provision of government services such as roads, this mobility was not a problem; it was simply how "the Kaonde" lived. However deep in the bush a settlement might have been, it was not "remote," simply because, in this highly decentralized society, there was nothing to be remote *from*.

Linked to this pattern of shifting cultivation with its high mobility was a material culture in which things needed either to be highly portable or to have a minimal amount of labor invested in their production since they would soon be abandoned. In addition, it was a society where it was only on the eve of colonization, during the time of slaves, ivory, and guns, that any form of centralized chieftainship had begun to emerge. The absence of a well-established system of chiefly power meant a corresponding lack of importance of material markers of majesty and of imposing physical spaces in which power and authority were given physical form. In general, as we shall see in chapter 6, this was a society characterized by strong sanctions against the accumulation of surplus by individuals. To parade material wealth was profoundly dangerous and risked provoking accusations of witchcraft, leading to social ostracism if not worse.

Lives in Bukama were not lived, as they are in industrial societies, amid a vast and ever-proliferating assemblage of commodities, where, as in the tale of the Sorcerer's Apprentice, the tide of commodities hurled forth at an ever-increasing rate at times threatens to engulf the mere

2. See Allan (1965) for a discussion of the benefits and problems of this kind of shifting cultivation.

mortals they were supposed to serve. People in Bukama met many of their basic subsistence needs through their own production. Most individuals owned no more in the way of consumer durables than could be packed in one of the cheap cardboard suitcases that were such a rare and prized possession. Recycling was such a fine art there that the rubbish pits, which since colonial times people have been continually urged to dig, would have remained empty—if, that is, people had actually heeded this advice and dug them. Clothes were not discarded because they had become a little worn or faded, and certainly not because they had fallen out of fashion. They were worn until they literally fell apart; two pairs of shorts, for instance, with holes in different places, would be worn one over the other. Even mending and patching clothes was a problem because of the scarcity of needles and thread. Less worn-out clothes tended to be carefully hoarded and worn only for church or on other special occasions. Sometimes itinerant peddlers on bicycles brought secondhand clothes to sell. When looking these over, local women would more often discuss their strength and durability than their aesthetic qualities.

Looking at Chief Chizela's Bukama homestead in the light of this history and present-day realities the visitor might see it rather differently. This would occur particularly if he or she were aware that this was not regarded as a true "village" (*muzhi*) but rather as an equivalent of the cluster of temporary shelters to which people moved during the cultivation season.

Account II

Marking out the Chief's enclosure is a simple fence designed not to keep anything out, but rather to draw a symbolic line demarcating a space infused with a particular chiefly authority, within which language and demeanor must be constrained. This space and its buildings are organized not according to the kind of rectangular geometric grid that industrial societies see as embodying order; but according to a different map of authority reflecting the complex overlapping hierarchies of kinship and gender and expressed in circular rather than linear forms. The houses themselves, which are used for little except sleeping and storage, are also simple, making use, for the most part, of local resources, such as poles, bark-rope, and grass, all cut from the nearby bush, and mud dug similarly close at hand. The two corrugated iron roofs are not only symbols of wealth and modernity, but are significantly more durable, and less hospitable to insect life than thatched ones, even if iron has none of the insulating power of grass. Grass must be frequently replaced; the collection of enough grass for a good roof and the correct combination of different kinds of grasses (good thatching grass is not always easy to find) require a considerable investment of labor. Once the shock of the overwhelming, crushing poverty—and the shocking lack of "commodities"—has begun to wear off, the visitor may slowly begin to glimpse a way of life with its own rules, its own structures, and its own rhythm, one not driven by the insistent beat of the commodity.

The two accounts I have given of Chief Chizela's homestead are very different, and yet neither is false in the sense of describing something that is not there. The difference has to do not only with the providing of some context, but with what has been picked out to be described and, very important, the *style* used. What makes the accounts different is how the reader is drawn in, the various associations that are not stated explicitly but which the author assumes the reader will make, and the overall moral tone that suggests a certain response. Neither account is neutral; each involves claims about the nature of the reality it describes. Each in its own way, like Joyce's Stephen Dedalus, seeks to work in local color and make the reader an accomplice. To the eyes of someone socialized in a modern industrial environment, whose world is constructed out of commodities, an absence of commodities often appears in one of two ways. It can be seen, as in the first account, simply as the most abject poverty, in which individuals can scarcely be recognized as having their own individuality, but appear as featureless and passive victims— their lack of personal possessions automatically signifying a lack of control over their lives in general. It can also, as in the second account perhaps, be romanticized as some kind of preindustrial idyll free from the crass materialism of modern consumer society.

Account I caricatures a writing style more common among journalists writing on the non-Western world (but borrowed from time to time by anthropologists), while the tone of Account II, with its appeal to context, is more recognizably "anthropological." My reason for juxtaposing them is to illustrate the point that *all* accounts, even those apparently solely concerned with describing material realities, are precisely that: "accounts"—particular representations embodying whole sets of assumptions, never raw unmediated "reality." And once we move from simple descriptions of place and attempt to portray how people *experience* their world, the layers of mediation thicken dramatically. But while anthropological accounts and mappings can never capture pure, objective, "out there" reality, they can, I would argue, be "truthful" to a greater or lesser degree. This truthfulness is always a matter of degree, concerned not with some absolute truth but with answers that are more truthful or less truthful, within the limits set by the assumptions inherent in the questions to which they are answers. The pursuit of "true" accounts of social realities is a pursuit that is necessarily doomed to failure, but, as Samuel Beckett put it, we have to try to "fail better." Part of what that pursuit involves is a continual self-consciousness as to the context and the specific power relations within which our "facts," and indeed our questions, are produced. A concrete example of this was provided by my attempts to interview Kibala's ward chairman, Kabaya.

Throughout my three-month stay in Kibala I made numerous efforts to set up an interview with Kabaya, only to discover when I arrived for the scheduled meeting that he had left that morning for a fishing trip in the bush, or just as I was starting out for his place a child would arrive with a message that he was sick and could we please postpone the interview to another day. Finally, just before I left Kibala, thanks to the help of Sansoni, the ward secretary who had promised Kabaya that he would help with any "difficult" questions, the interview took place. In view of Kabaya's obvious uneasiness about the interview I decided not to tape-record it but simply took notes. For Kabaya, the interview was clearly fraught with anxiety. Whereas in his own world of Kibala Kabaya felt at home and in control, in this other world, the world of government, education, and English (although the interview was in Kaonde, this was nonetheless what I represented to Kabaya), he was profoundly ill at ease. Since I so obviously belonged to that alien world, Kabaya was probably afraid not only of revealing his inadequacies to me, who he may have feared would then go and report on him to the higher-up party officials, but also of revealing locally his lack of skill in coping with the world of English and officialdom. When talking to me Kabaya's overwhelming concern was probably, even more than was normally the case in my interviews, to give me the "right" answers, or at any rate not to say anything "wrong." The point here is not whether Kabaya was "lying," but rather that while I learned little from this interview about Kabaya's agricultural and other economic enterprises, or his actual role as ward chairman in Kibala, I did learn a lot about *his* understanding of what the government expected of a ward chairman. What Kabaya was trying to do, it was clear, was to reflect back to me as accurately as he could what he imagined those expectations to be.

For instance, I had learned from other people in Kibala that Kabaya's most profitable economic activity was fishing. Fishing had in fact long been an important part of the Kibala economy; the fishing grounds of the Mufumbwe River have been famous since colonial times.[3] Private traders have been coming to the fishing camps to buy ever since the development of the dried-fish market during the colonial years. Given the urban areas' permanent high demand for dried fish, fishing was both a profitable and relatively low-risk source of income. The technology involved, fish dams, required little in the way of inputs that had to be bought, only a certain investment of labor, which could be timed so as not to clash with other labor demands. Also, whereas in the case of cultivation months of labor can be wiped out by unfavorable weather, crop disease, or some other natural hazard destroying the harvest, fishing is closer to a form of gathering, which involves very little investment of labor prior to the actual catching of the fish. In addition, and very importantly, marketing fish from the Mufumbwe did not rely on inherently unreliable government transport services; large quantities of dried fish could be transported relatively easily on a bicycle. Fishing would seem, therefore, to have been an eminently sensible and rational economic activity. Kabaya, however, when I asked him about his economic activities scarcely mentioned fishing; it was only others who told me that this was Kabaya's main source of income and that he spent much of his time away in the fish camps catching and drying fish.

Kabaya's silence here can be explained by the official government attitude to this kind of fishing. It was not that fishing was forbidden. If asked, government officials would acknowledge its importance both in terms of meeting local food needs and those of the urban areas, where dried fish is a crucial source of protein. Nonetheless, the emphasis, as when officials addressed local meetings, for instance, was always on the primacy of agriculture and the need to produce maize and other food crops for sale. Fishing was rather tolerated than encouraged, and even then only as long as it did not interfere with cultivation. Kabaya himself repeated this orthodoxy to me when I asked him what were the main problems in Kibala. One of the main problems hampering development (*bukomo*), he told me, was that local people spent too much of their time away at the fishing places killing fish.

Before beginning my own mapping of Kibala and Bukama, I want in the second part of this chapter to look at how the Kaonde were named during the colonial period. I want, that is, to tell the story of how the Kaonde became a *tribe*—a story that illustrates one dimension of the

3. See, for instance, ZNA, sec. 2/134, *Kasempa Annual Report on Native Affairs, 1935–1937*; and sec. 2/943, *Kasempa Tour Reports*, Tour Report no. 3, 1953.

practical reality of the hegemony of the colonial state and shows in a very concrete way what an important power the power to *name* can be. This story demonstrates how powerful a role the naming of reality plays in shaping the political and economic landscape within which the different actors struggle, and how the naming of this landscape locates particular actors in particular ways. The emergence of the Kaonde as a "tribe" is also an example of how certain ways of seeing the world, and certain names, are able to achieve such a degree of authority that even those who want to challenge them are likely to frame their challenge in terms that accept their basic assumptions.

Part Two: How the Kaonde Became a "Tribe"

The tribe is at once the only bulwark we have against anarchy and the only foundation on which to build progress in local government.

ZNA, *Annual Report on African Affairs,*
North-Western Area, 1951–1952

One's conception of the world is a response to certain specific problems posed by reality.

Antonio Gramsci, *Selections from the Prison Notebooks*

The name Chizela was taken from the local senior Kaonde chief and the district was in the heart of the region most closely associated with the Kaonde. But what kind of an entity *are*, or were, "the Kaonde"? In the 1980s, as I discussed in the introduction, "the Kaonde" certainly existed in the sense that people would identify themselves as Kaonde and point to a particular way of life as being "how we Kaondes live." It is doubtful, however, whether prior to the colonial period "the Kaonde" existed as any kind of distinct and self-conscious entity either politically or "culturally," even if by the end of the colonial period such an entity did indeed exist. This kind of "creation of tribalism" (to borrow the title of Leroy Vail's 1989 volume) has been common throughout Africa, and has been well documented in recent years.[4] There are many

4. Hobsbawm's and Ranger's *Invention of Tradition* (1983) was very influential in opening up this field. Vail (1989) collects together a number of examples from southern Africa. Mamdani, in his *Citizen and Subject: Contemporary Africa and the Legacy of Late Colonialism* (1996), claims the construction of colonial subjects around their membership of different "tribes" is one of the central characteristics of colonialism in Africa.

parallels to the story of the category "Kaonde."[5] Nonetheless, it is worth looking in some detail at the specifics of how the Kaonde, like other peoples in the region, became a *tribe*, with all the colonial baggage that implies.[6]

There was a hegemonic, taken-for-granted assumption within the British colonial world that the basic social unit within which rural Africans lived was the "tribe"; it was as "tribes" that African communities were named and theorized. For colonial officials, for example, the answer to the question, What kind of entity are the Kaonde? was simple: the Kaonde were a *tribe* with an origin lost in the mists of time. In fact, however, what this category "tribe" came to mean in British colonial Africa was the outcome of a long, drawn-out dialogue between colonizer and colonized. The particular meanings it acquired in the case of particular "tribes" in particular places depended both on the overarching colonial discourse on the African "tribe" and the specifics of particular localities and the nature of their economic and political realities. A crucial party to this dialogue were the anthropologists, who played a major role in the development of the notion of the "tribe" as a purportedly "scientific" category. In telling the story of the emergence of "the Kaonde" as a "tribe" I have focused on three groups: firstly, the colonial anthropologists of Northern Rhodesia's Rhodes-Livingstone Institute; secondly, the colonial officials stationed in North-Western Province; and thirdly, the Africans whom the name "Kaonde" attempted to locate. While these three groups can be seen as engaged in a complex three-way dialogue, it was a dialogue in which the different groups were far from equal in their power to "name" in an authoritative way the social realities of the colonial state. The data I am using to recover this dialogue are taken primarily from the archives or from secondary sources, in both of which the little corner of Chizela is a rather shadowy presence. Inevitably, therefore, there are few actual Chizela voices; this is a more general story of the mapping of the conceptual terrain that those living in places like Kibala and Bukama were told they inhabited, and also how in a particular colonial context the name "Kaonde" acquired a particular set of meanings.

I want to begin the story of how the Kaonde became a "tribe," and

5. Papstein's article in Vail (1989), for instance, tells the story of two other "ethnic" identities in North-Western Province, the Lunda and the Luvale.

6. A pioneering article on the ideological significance of the concept of "tribe" is Asad (1973).

what the implications of this "tribal" identity were, with the more general concept of the "tribe," and how it shaped, and was shaped by, the untidy and dynamic realities it was supposed to explain. To do this I have chosen to focus on the nature of the "tribe" as a theoretical concept in the work of one of the most prominent anthropologists to work in colonial Zambia (Northern Rhodesia), Max Gluckman. Gluckman was the director of the Rhodes-Livingstone Institute before leaving Northern Rhodesia to take up the newly created chair in social anthropology at Manchester University in Britain.

Max Gluckman and the Rhodes-Livingstone Institute

The Rhodes-Livingstone Institute (RLI) was founded in 1937 with a dual mission.[7] On the one hand, it was to be an independent institution, free from direct control by the colonial state, that would use the procedures of the relatively newly professionalized discipline of social anthropology to generate "scientific" knowledge about the subjects of British colonial rule in Central Africa. On the other hand, it would also provide the colonial authorities with useful information that could be used to facilitate the smooth and humane operation of colonial rule. Such information, it was argued, "is necessary if we are to base on any sure foundation the improvement we are seeking to make in African conditions" (quoted in Brown 1973:184). Colonial officials and Northern Rhodesia's white settlers may, as Brown shows, have been somewhat skeptical as to the validity of the latter argument, but it was an important strand in the RLI's own understanding of the role of anthropology. Godfrey Wilson, the institute's first director, was an especially strong believer in the important role that anthropology (and the social sciences generally) could, and should, play in solving social problems.[8] Like Wil-

7. The RLI has been extensively written about. See Werbner (1984) for a comprehensive overview. Vincent (1990:276–83) provides an interesting contextualization. Van Binsbergen (1985) examines the RLI anthropologists' use of the concept of the "tribe." Brown (1973) explores the complicated relationship between the RLI (particularly under its first director Godfrey Wilson) and the colonial state.

8. In a hearing in 1940 to decide whether he should be granted exemption from military service as a conscientious objector, Wilson argued for the vital role of his research at the RLI, the lack of such research being, as Wilson saw it, one of the reasons why Europe was now at war. His argument was met with some skepticism by at least one

son, whom he succeeded in the early 1940s, Gluckman was convinced of the importance of anthropology beyond the academy. The range of the RLI's aims under Gluckman, which he explained in his "Seven-Year Research Plan" (Gluckman 1945), was reflected in its different publications. There was the scholarly *Journal of the Rhodes-Livingstone Institute*, produced for an academic audience; but there was also "provision for presenting the results of scientific research to laymen" (1945:28) in the journal *Human Problems in British Central Africa*, while *Communications from the Rhodes-Livingstone Institute* provided the "detailed data beyond what the sociologist customarily publishes . . . [which] 'Government often requires' (1945:28)."

The colonial authorities themselves remained distinctly ambivalent about the value of anthropological research, and as the RLI developed the emphasis became increasingly scholarly and academic. The relationship between the RLI and the colonial state was always, however, a complicated one. It would certainly be a gross oversimplification to see anthropologists like Wilson, as certain critics of colonial anthropology have done, as "the handmaidens of colonialism." What I am interested in here, however, is the rather different question of the extent to which a theoretical concept such as that of the "tribe" and its associated problematic embody *in themselves*, quite independently of the explicit aims of those who use them, specific ways of naming the world that have implicit in them their own political claims.

A key feature of the colonial state in British Central Africa from the late 1920s was its commitment to the principle of Indirect Rule. This combined a cheap form of administration that used locals to police its lower tiers, with a comforting illusion of local autonomy. For Indirect Rule to work, both ideologically and practically, it was essential that everybody involved—or at least everybody whose voice was likely to be heard—believed that rural African society did indeed in some essential sense retain its old precolonial structures of authority and forms of social organization. In fact, however, the imposition of colonial rule represented a moment of fundamental rupture. Even if a genuine de facto colonial presence was slow to establish itself in many areas, *analytically*, I would argue, colonialism has to be seen as introducing a real discontinuity. One of the great silences underpinning the British colonial state's

---

member of the exemption board who remarked that he did not see how "a study of the native laws of Bantu society would solve many of Europe's social problems" (ZNA, sec. 1/1650, vol. 1).

enthusiasm for Indirect Rule in sub-Saharan Africa was the unspoken denial of the basic fact that the establishment of *pax Britannica*, and of the colonial power as the ultimate authority over land, law, and so on, necessarily eroded radically the power base on which precolonial political authority rested. It is against this silence that the project of understanding and controlling the colonized society takes shape; and it is within this project that the work of the RLI anthropologists was located.

Central to this work was the concept of the "tribe." When fledgling anthropologists (such as Victor Turner, Elizabeth Colson, Clyde Mitchell, A. L. Epstein, William Watson, and Norman Long, all of whom did fieldwork in Northern Rhodesia) arrived at the RLI to carry out their first fieldwork, they were sent off on a preliminary trip to a designated "tribe." Clutching a bundle of RLI index cards, they had the task of plotting out the basic structures of this "tribe." A characteristic piece that resulted from one of these first forays was an article by William Watson (who went on to write *Tribal Cohesion in a Money Economy: A Study of the Mambwe People of Zambia*) on "the Kaonde" entitled "The Kaonde Village" (Watson 1954). After this initiation the neophyte anthropologist would then return to the RLI and set out for his or her main fieldwork in some other area. Whatever the ultimate topic of their research, the starting point was always a particular "tribe"; for instance, for Victor Turner the Ndembu, for Watson the Mambwe, for Elizabeth Colson the Tonga.[9] An unquestioned assumption was that the basic community within which rural Africans lived was the "tribe." To trace out something of what lay behind this name of "tribe" for the RLI anthropologists, I have chosen to focus on a single text by Gluckman, *Politics, Law, and Ritual in Tribal Society* (hereafter *Politics, Law, and Ritual*).

There are several reasons why I chose this particular text. Firstly, there is Gluckman's dominating role within the RLI and in the anthropology of Central Africa. Secondly, while it may not represent Gluckman at his best, because it was a book written as a teaching text for undergraduate anthropology students in Britain, in it Gluckman is very much concerned with laying out what he saw as some of the fundamental concepts in the discipline. Finally, *Politics, Law, and Ritual* (published in 1965) was written in 1964 at the precise moment when Northern Rhodesia was gaining independence as Zambia, and it can be seen as representing

9. See Turner (1957), Watson (1958), and Colson (1960). Colson and Gluckman (1951) collects together essays on seven central African "tribes."

a summation of one variant of colonial anthropology. Indeed, by this point functionalist anthropology of this kind was already being attacked as ahistorical, as, for instance, in Leach's *The Political Systems of Highland Burma* (1954). Consequently *Politics, Law, and Ritual* is very much a defense by Gluckman of his approach, and he takes pains to explain very precisely just what that approach is.

Gluckman describes *Politics, Law, and Ritual* as "a statement of how one social anthropologist, working in the full tradition of the subject, sees *the general problem of rule and disorder in social life*" (Gluckman 1965:xxiv, my emphasis). This a formulation that surely echoes a central concern of the colonial state. The particular area *Politics, Law, and Ritual* deals with is that "of political struggle and order, of law and social control, and of stability and change in tribal societies" (1965:xxi). Gluckman explains his choice of the term *tribal* as follows:

By "tribal society" I mean the kind of community which was once described by the term "primitive society", a term now rightly rejected. Others call this type of community "pre-literate" or "pre-industrial". These are appropriate terms, but I prefer "tribal", since "tribe" was used to describe most of the communities of Europe, virtually up to feudal times. And forms of social organization akin to those communities, are what I am dealing with.

Gluckman goes on to define the characteristics of tribal society:

Basic to a tribal society is the egalitarian economy, with relatively simple tools to produce and primary goods to consume. The powerful and wealthy use their might and goods to support dependants; for they are unable to raise their own standard of living with the materials available. (1965:xv)

He explicitly distinguishes "tribal" societies from peasant societies.

On the whole I judged that the study of peasants was another field. The study of tribal society has stimulated, and been stimulated by, the study of peasants. It would have produced a far more superficial book had I tried to draw on the wealth in this somewhat distinctive field, even though many of the social processes with which I am concerned are represented there. (1965:xxv)

We are not told, however, *what* it is that constitutes this "distinctiveness"; significantly there is no entry in the index under "peasant."

For Gluckman the category "tribe" is essentially descriptive and unproblematic, referring to a straightforward "fact" of colonial life. Taking the passages I have quoted, we can summarize the basic characteristics of Gluckman's category "tribe" as follows. Firstly, "tribes" represent a distinct type of social organization, and one that was characteristic of an earlier, prefeudal stage of European history. Secondly, this social organization is based on an "egalitarian" economy. Since this egalitarian economy can also have hierarchies of wealth and power, its egalitarianism would seem to refer to the fact that the wealthy and powerful "are unable to raise their own standard of living with the materials available" and instead "use their might and goods to support dependants." Thirdly, its technology is that of "relatively simple tools" producing "primary goods." What I want to argue is that much of the meaning of this model of the tribe is to be found not so much in its explicit features, but in its silences—the questions with which it is not concerned. It is on some of these I want to focus, and on their significance within a colonial context.

Although "tribal" social organization is located as a particular stage within the development of Europe, the question of *how* "tribal" societies become transformed into nontribal societies is not addressed. The question of history, in the sense of nonreversible change, is for Gluckman, as for other functionalist anthropologists, not the business of anthropology. "Anthropologists analyze a society as if it were in a state of equilibrium"—equilibrium here being "the tendency of a system after disturbance to return to its previous state" (1965:279). In this context Gluckman goes on to explain, "While we are concerned with tribal societies it is easier to make this kind of analysis [i.e., assuming a tendency to return to equilibrium] because they were restricted in their external relations and their economies were stationary" (281). "Tribal" economies therefore are not only outside history, they are self-contained entities that can be analyzed in isolation from the wider colonial economy. By the time Gluckman was writing *Politics, Law, and Ritual* he was sensitive to the growing criticism of the functionalist paradigm, criticism which he saw as essentially misguided, insisting that "Every study of a particular tribe that I have cited in the course of this book, *after analysing the tribal equilibrium*, considers the tribe's position since it came under European domination" (285; my emphasis). This formulation merely emphasizes that the key entity to be analyzed is the "tribe" and that, although colonization may have brought changes, this basic entity, the "tribe," persists, a particularly problematic assumption given that Gluckman's definition of tribal social organization defines it in terms of particular *economic* structures. Even if we accept "simple" technology and the lack of the possibility of direct economic accumulation as features of precolonial African economies—and this is questionable in itself—

these are characteristics that are likely to be profoundly affected by incorporation into a wider colonial economy; we certainly cannot simply assume that they will persist.

Just as Gluckman's model of the "tribe" is silent as to how a "tribe" might cease to be a "tribe," so too is it silent as to the history of how this form of social organization developed. The very nature of the model represses questions about how the structures of the rural areas in British Central Africa have come to have the specific form they have at this particular historical moment. However much the turbulent history of nineteenth-century or even eighteenth-century Africa may be acknowledged, there is an implicit, unspoken assumption that all this history *happened to* some basic entity, the "tribe." Individual "tribes" may have disappeared and others come into being, and all may have been subject to that favorite process of functionalist anthropologists, "fusion and fission," but in some essentialist sense the "tribe" as a form of social organization persisted.

It was this implicit assumption that enabled the RLI anthropologists to assume so confidently that it was possible to uncover the "tribal equilibrium" of peoples whose structures of political life had undergone a radical transformation little more than a generation previously. A crucial dimension of the Yao people's economy, for instance, prior to the imposition of *pax Britannica*, was slave raiding; similarly the precolonial Lozi state depended to an important extent on tribute labor. Yet Clyde Mitchell, who wrote about the Yao (1956), and Gluckman himself, who wrote about the Lozi,[10] nonetheless treated these "tribes" as if such radical changes could be ignored and the continuing Yao and Lozi "tribal" structures, surviving since precolonial times, could be discovered through research on contemporary communities living under colonial rule. The point here is not that such a claim is ipso facto false, but that neither Mitchell nor Gluckman—nor the other RLI anthropologists— felt it necessary to demonstrate *why* this continuity could be assumed.

As I have stressed, Gluckman's brief definition of "tribal society" is not concerned with distinguishing this form of social organization from other forms, those characteristic of peasant society, for instance, or with explaining why "tribal society" can be treated as an autonomous entity despite its embeddedness within a colonial state. Essentially, the model is a descriptive rather than a theoretical one. I would argue that

10. Gluckman wrote a number of monographs and articles about the Lozi, one of the most influential being *The Judicial Process among the Barotse of Northern Rhodesia* (1955).

why Gluckman can, as it were, get away with presenting this vague and incoherent definition of the name "tribe" as a "scientific" and rigorous model is because standing behind it, and providing it with its real substance, is a powerful "commonsense" or popular notion of the "tribe." A commonsense "fact" within colonial discourse—a "fact" that survives remarkably unscathed in current popular discourse about Africa—is that the basic set of social relations within which Africans live is the "tribe"; it is the nature of "tribal customs" that explain Africans' identities and behavior. Ultimately, what the definition of "tribe" boils down to in practice is simply "the unit within which Africans live." What *Politics, Law, and Ritual* is concerned with is the exploration of aspects of this *empirically* given entity, the "tribe"; and the empirical reality within which the category "tribe" assumed its particular African meaning was that of colonialism and the problems of colonial "rule and disorder." The reality was that there were colonized peoples among whom order had to be maintained and disorder avoided. Part of what the name "tribe" does is to locate the colonized not in terms of a power relation between them and their colonial overlords, but in terms of a separate world that they, but not their colonizers, inhabit. This is a way of seeing colonial society that, regardless of the intentions of individual theorists, helps divert attention away from its real power relations.

But if "scientific" categories gain resonance and power through their unspoken links with lay or popular categories, so these in turn gain authority and credibility through their links with "scientific" discourse. Indeed, many popular notions represent odd fragments of earlier scientific or philosophical discourses that have over time gradually drifted down into the great sedimented stratum of "common sense." As Gramsci put it:

Philosophy and modern science are also constantly contributing new elements to "modern folklore" in that certain opinions and scientific notions, removed from their context and more or less distorted, constantly fall within the popular domain and are "inserted" into the mosaic of tradition. (Forgacs 1988:360–61)

The substantive meaning the term *tribe* acquired in British colonial Africa is a good example of the complex way in which "scientific" and commonsense categories reciprocally inform and shape one another.

In the next section of this chapter I want to shift the focus from the place of the name "tribe" within the work of Gluckman and the RLI anthropologists to the way "tribe" was used by locally based colonial officials. And this is where our story returns to North-Western Province and to the local dialogue between the colonial state and its inhabitants as to the identity of "the Kaonde." Given the hegemony of the name "tribe," for colonial officials this dialogue could not but center on the question, What are the characteristics of "the Kaonde tribe," and what are the differences and the similarities between "the Kaonde" and other "tribes"? That "the Kaonde" were a "tribe" was simply taken for granted. Part of what hegemony means is precisely this establishment of particular names as no more than a way of indicating obvious and banal "facts," the existence of which nobody but an overzealous pedant could question. Colonial officials seeking to understand the nature of their colonial subjects therefore could not but use the notion of the "tribe." Using the reports and other writings of colonial officials stationed in what is now North-Western Province, I look first at the place of the general notion of the "tribe" in the thinking of these officials whose concern was not academic research but the practical problems of administration. I then go on to look at how such officials used the notion of the "tribe" to explain to themselves the nature of "the Kaonde." Having described something of what could be termed the theoretical landscape in which the colonial state located "the Kaonde," we can finally return to the question of how those so named, "the Kaonde" themselves, understood "being Kaonde." Until that point, in order to keep, as it were, a question mark over the nature of this name I have usually used quotation marks when writing "Kaonde."

Administering "Tribes"

The situation of British colonial officials stationed in rural districts, and especially those in the more remote regions such as the northwest, had a very particular character. Such an official was one of a tiny band of Europeans made up of a handful of other officials—all male—together with some wives and families, set down in the midst of a sea of Africans, often with a couple of hundred miles or more of dirt road between them and the nearest other Europeans. The autobiography of one such official stationed in Kasempa in the 1950s, gives a sense of the intoxication of power this could lead to—and of the heavy baggage of British literary references that these men brought with them.

Kasempa was real, the outer world but a shadow, and letters from it, from
ghosts. It made many Europeans terribly assertive. One acted one's part
upon an enormous empty stage: the "compleat man" was untrammelled if
unseen. Grey of Falloden feeding pigeons, Gladstone hewing at trees, even
Dr. Watson with a brisk manner and a bottle of iodine. One could play out
such fantasies in real life with real people. (Short 1973:56)

The job of the colonial official involved being both a clear and un-
ambiguous symbol of the might and authority of an empire beyond
challenge; it also involved managing the practical day-to-day realities of
colonial law and order, collecting taxes, punishing criminals, and so on.
In addition there was always a concern on the part of the colonial administration as a whole that the costs of administration, especially in
areas like the northwest, seen primarily as labor reserves, should be kept
to a minimum. This concern made the idea of Indirect Rule a very
attractive one. Co-opting local authority figures as a cheap lower tier of
colonial administration was one way of reducing the number of vastly
more expensive British colonial officials.

The mental and physical boundaries between colonial officials and
the colonized world over which they were set were always fraught and
dangerous. On the one hand, the maintenance of their position as awe
inspiring symbols of the empire—and indeed their security as isolated
individuals usually far from much tangible imperial might—demanded
that they maintain a proper distance between themselves and the colonized. This was also important for their own psychological well-being,
particularly since the social conventions of colonial society were severe
on those who strayed across this all-important boundary, and in such
small isolated communities ostracism was a powerful sanction. The danger of "going native" was always one of the structuring fears of European colonialism. This is indeed one of the collective nightmares that
underpins Joseph Conrad's *Heart of Darkness*, and gives it much of its
power. On the other hand, the need to be effective administrators demanded that colonial officials *should* "penetrate" the mysteries of the
colonized society; their "effectiveness" depended on their understanding
of local realities. Then too there was the psychological need to impose
some kind of conceptual order, and to be able to explain at the very least
to oneself, *why* so much of what one was trying to do, such as implement
the various colonial schemes for "development," was not working. The
colonial official therefore, had simultaneously to "get to know," and
remain aloof from the colonized. One result of this was a knowledge

structured around essential, unalterable difference, a difference that explains why "we" (the colonizing power) have a "natural" right to rule "them" (the colonized).

For British colonial administrators throughout sub-Saharan Africa the central name in which this notion of difference was gathered together was that of the "tribe." Within colonial discourse on Africa it was hegemonic that the basic unit of rural society was the "tribe," and that "tribes" were the primary actors in rural life. The people colonial officials were charged with administering were seen as "tribal" peoples living according to "tribal" norms. The "tribe" was both a comfortingly familiar and yet "scientific" category. It should be remembered that almost all these colonial administrators were the product of an education system in which the classical authors of Greece and Rome loomed large; accounts of barbarians, Germanic tribes, and ancient Britons formed a basic part of their mental furniture. This was how Europeans themselves had lived in some distant past. The familiarity of the term meant that its meaning did not have to be spelled out; what *tribal* meant could be simply taken as self-evident, which removed any need to look too closely at just what it was that differentiated the colonized from the colonizer. It could function as a marker of difference, but a marker that also apparently explained that difference.

One colonial official was F. H. Melland, who spent eleven of his more than twenty years of colonial service in northwestern Zambia in a Kaonde-speaking area and wrote a book about "the Kaonde" entitled *In Witch-Bound Africa: An Account of the Primitive Kaonde Tribe and Their Beliefs*. A "historical digression" from this book illustrates how parallels from the Ancient World could be seen as offering lessons on the nature of local "tribal society."

One of the most close parallels to our rule in tropical Africa is furnished by the Romans in Britain. For some time the Romans thought of nothing but law, order and discipline. Boadicea's rebellion taught Rome a lesson, and under a more enlightened policy . . . the Britons were taught to build houses instead of huts, to cultivate, to start industries, develop mines, export their produce, and so on: result, progress and peace. . . . That Roman policy laid the foundations of a progress that made those despised savages advance further than any advance dreamt of by the Romans. (Melland 1923:304)

The concept of the "tribe" was used both to explain Africans in general—*all* Africans were "tribal" and shared certain characteristics that marked them out from Europeans—and to explain differences between

Africans. As Melland stated in the preface to his book, he hoped that although he had focused on the Kaonde, the book would be useful for

all who are going to live and work among similar Bantu peoples, even if far from the BaKaonde; for, while their customs, habits, and beliefs differ there is, still, a great similarity in these matters. . . . To acquire an insight into one tribe helps one to understand others. (1923:8)

And it was the "tribe" that was the basic unit in the system of Indirect Rule, even if the uncomfortable reality that some "tribes" did not seem to conform to the stereotype would insist on complicating things from time to time. The lack of fit between the "tribal" model colonial officials took for granted and what they saw happening around them could induce extreme irritation at the apparent failure of some rural Africans, such as "the Kaonde," to behave as a "tribe" ought. The following two extracts are from reports written by the same colonial administrator in 1930 and 1931, the period when Indirect Rule was being introduced.

The difficulty in the Kasempa district is that the Kaonde have little or no tribal organisation. . . . the idea of sitting together in a Court, is extremely repugnant to them. As one elderly petty chief. . . . put it to the writer, "I am a lone elephant bull, I wish to walk alone," and this is the attitude taken up by the majority of petty chiefs which is not conducive to the success of native courts as at present constituted.[11]

In the Kasempa Province we have the Bakaonde, the Alunda, the Andembo and other lesser tribes, all of a low standard of intelligence, who . . . now have very little tribal sense.
The Bakaonde tribe in particular, now have little, if any, tribal organisation or cohesion. . . . If the people were intelligent, and not so scattered, it would be easier to revive a tribal sense, and with it there could be a better application of indirect rule.[12]

The basic category "tribe" included a wide range of different "tribes" with different "tribal customs," and within colonial discourse there developed an extensive repertoire of "tribal" stereotypes. The annual reports and district notebooks that colonial officials were required to keep reveal the major role played by these stereotypes and the way the different characteristics of different "tribes" were evoked to explain what was happening in particular areas. Each official would tend to have his

11. ZNA, ZA/7/1/13/6, *Provincial Annual Report, Kasempa, 1930*.
12. ZNA, ZA/7/1/14/6, *Annual Provincial Report, Kasempa, 1931*.

own favored "tribe," or "tribes," and his own *bêtes noires*. In the north-western region two groups of people who were continually contrasted were "the Kaonde," and "Luvale" and "Chokwe" people. One basic difference between the two groups was their association with agricultural systems organized around different staples: sorghum in the case of "the Kaonde" and cassava in that of "the Luvale" and "the Chokwe." The tribal stereotypes used in the district notebooks and other official documents, however, go far beyond any simple difference in cultivation patterns, as the following quotations illustrate.

In 1940 we find one official writing,

The Kaonde are naturally of fine physique being often six feet or more in height and well proportioned. As these people have no cattle largely owing to tsetse fly their physical condition must it is presumed be largely due to the high dietic qualities of the kaffir corn.[13]

While in 1948, another writes,

The two elements in the population present a contrast in health and fitness which one cannot but ascribe to diet to some considerable extent. The immigrant element in the population [i.e., Luvale and Chokwe] are well fed, and cheerful, whilst the Kaonde are under nourished morose, and diseased. Not one was free from some deformity and I can only say that they represented about the lowest ebb of humanity that I have yet seen in Northern Rhodesia. They had no nuts, cassava, or goats at their villages, and were short of the kaffir corn which is their staple diet. "We are Kaonde: we don't grow groundnuts or cassava or keep goats, we leave that to the Chokwe and Lwena [Luvale]" which was the invariable reply heard over and over again on this tour, epitomises the inertia of the Kaonde who would prefer to remain under nourished and diseased rather than expend a little more energy in cultivation and adopt new practices.[14]

Ten years previously, another official, more enthusiastic about "Kaonde potential" had noted, "As a whole the Kaonde build good villages with well thatched huts and kitchens attached and should form a fairly fertile soil in which to start a movement for village improvement."[15] This view was echoed in 1948: "I was disappointed in the living

13. ZNA, sec. 2/936, *Kasempa Tour Reports, 1940–47*, Tour Report no. 2, 1940.
14. ZNA, sec. 2/936, *Kasempa Tour Reports, 1940–47*, Tour Report no. 2, 1947. Interestingly, the writer of this particular comment was C. M. N. White, who in addition to his administrative duties also wrote at least sixteen anthropological articles on the Luvale, most published under the auspices of the RLI; see, for instance, White (1948, 1953, 1960).
15. ZNA, sec. 2/934, *Tour Reports, Kasempa, 1933–1939*.

conditions amongst the immigrants [i.e., Chokwe, Luvale, Luchazi, Mumbunda]. Their villages were, on the whole, extremely dirty with poor houses. The Kaonde villages had large, well built houses and were usually much cleaner."[16] This view was not shared, however, by another official in 1957: "Village housing is, generally, good amongst the Chokwe, who take a pride in their houses . . . and poor among the Kaonde, who prefer to spend their money upon bicycles rather than sound houses."[17] About the same time, yet another official, who clearly did not have much faith in "Kaonde potential," wrote, "The Kaonde as a whole are not a tribe which believe in a vast amount of exertion and it is, therefore, here that one finds the element of self-help less well developed than in some other parts of the Province."[18]

These comments on physique and housing are particularly illuminating about the role of "tribal" stereotypes and their power to shape what colonial officials saw when they looked at the rural world around them, in that ostensibly what was at issue were straightforward, observable "facts." Those who saw either Kaonde of "fine physique," "often more than six feet tall," or "under nourished morose, and diseased" Kaonde, all of whom had "some deformity" and who "represented about the lowest ebb of humanity . . . in Northern Rhodesia," were observing the same population at more or less the same time. Just as those who saw "good" or "poor" Kaonde housing had traveled through the same rural areas.

There are also more obviously subjective comments.

We visited one Mbundu village and one Lovale village. Apart from the fact that they have grown groundnuts and the Kaonde do not, I could see nothing of worth in these two villages; they have few children, are very dirty, and their housing standards are poor. *They were obviously more primitive and less manly than the Kaonde who treat them with considerable contempt.*[19]

Quite often, as here, the concept of the "tribe" shades into that of the "race." The notion that humankind is divided into distinct "races," each with its own specific characteristics passing from generation to generation, had become increasingly hegemonic in nineteenth-century discourses not only around colonialism, but around history in general. As

16. ZNA, sec. 2/939, *Tour Reports, Kasempa District, 1949.*
17. ZNA, sec. 2/947, *Kasempa Tour Records, 1957,* Tour Report no. 2, 1957.
18. ZNA, sec. 2/137, *North-West Province Annual Reports, 1954–55.*
19. ZNA, sec. 2/940, *Kasempa Tour Reports, 1950–51,* Tour Report no. 7, 1950 (my emphasis).

with the "tribe," the notion of "race" was used both in academic and "scientific" discourse,[20] and in that of popular common sense. What "race" named in the interwar period is captured in the first edition of the enormously influential *Cambridge Ancient History*, published in 1924.

Ancient peoples come upon the stage of history . . . in a certain order . . . each with a make-up congruous with the part they will play . . . history presupposes the formation of that character . . . in the greenroom of the remoter past: and the sketch which follows . . . is intended . . . to describe how men came by these qualities of build and temperament. (Quoted in Bernal 1987:389)

As with "tribe," much of the explanatory power and persuasiveness of "race" as a category was, and indeed still is, its combination of being apparently "scientific," describing what seem to be undeniable "facts" (such as that there are inherited physical differences between people), and at the same time including a shifting range of highly subjective psychological traits and propensities. The "scientific" authority here provides credibility to the purported mental characteristics. The power of these porous grab bags of mental and physical qualities, which makes them so impervious to specific challenge, depends on them being both ordinary "commonsense" terms whose meaning is shared within a particular culture, and inherently vague. Take a quality like "manliness," used in the earlier quotation, for instance. We can assume that within the British public school culture of colonial officials, everybody "knew" what "manliness" meant but at the same time would probably have been hard put to explain in any precise way just how you could measure a "tribe" on the scale of manliness "scientifically." As with the predictions of astrologers, terms that seem to say something but which can be so stretched as to fit almost anything, can be profoundly reassuring. In the cloudy soup of tribe or race, as Raymond Williams puts it, "Physical, cultural and socio-economic differences are taken up, projected and generalized, and so confused that different kinds of variation are made to stand for or imply each other" (Williams 1983:250).[21]

20. Martin Bernal, in *Black Athena* (1987), explores in careful detail the development of the nineteenth-century concept of race and its structuring role in the various academic disciplines that grew up around the study of the Ancient World.

21. A comment by one district commissioner is particularly revealing of the way "tribe" and "race" could merge with one another:

Administratively, the only thing which these people [i.e., Luchazi, Chokwe, and Mbundu immigrants] understand is firm control without any compromise. . . . Discussion is fatal. . . . They have remarkable resemblance mentally to another immigrant race so well

But how did those the colonial officials so confidently named "Kaonde" identify *themselves?* And what part did they play in the dialogue about who and what "the Kaonde" were?

The Administered

Did the people living in the northwest during the colonial period describe themselves as belonging to "tribes"? Clearly at one level they did. As in the quotation on page 66, people would indeed refer to themselves as "Kaonde," "Luvale," or some other "tribal" label. Local interpreters used the term *tribe* when writing up court cases in English for the records. and there were ready answers when the district officer, or a visiting anthropologist, asked about "tribal" law, or "tribal" customs. But the meaning of this term *tribe*, and the resonances it had, were not necessarily the same for those who belonged to "tribes" as they were for the colonial officials or the RLI anthropologists.

There are four main linguistic groups associated with the northwestern region: the Kaonde, Lunda, Luvale, and Luchazi. Oral traditions suggest that the Kaonde-speakers came from Luba country to the north, partly in response to the emergence of the Luba and Lunda states, in a long series of migrations from the sixteenth to the nineteenth centuries. These migrations, as Roberts argues, "were probably a prolonged and mostly rather haphazard process of small kinship groups gradually moving to the south and east in search of new land" (Roberts 1966:106; see also Jaegar 1981:46–68). The Lunda, Luvale, and Luchazi came from the north and west, and were still pushing east in the nineteenth century (Roberts 1966). In the course of these migrations existing populations tended over time to be either displaced or incorporated. The Mbwela was one group of people to whom this happened in the area now associated with Kaonde.

---

known in the medieval and modern world. (ZNA, sec. 2/941, *Kasempa Tour Reports, 1951,* Tour Report no. 9, 1951)

This statement is also revealing of a pervasive undercurrent of anti-Semitism in the shared culture of British colonial officials, it being assumed here that the reference to Jews will not only be obvious but that it can be taken for granted that "we" (those reading this report) will share a basic stereotype of what Jews are like. Lacking such an assumption, it is difficult to see any particular resemblance between the Angolan immigrants and Jews beyond their shared position as objects of a particular kind of racist stereotyping.

It was during the long period of their migrations that the Kaonde language emerged as a distinct language, and it is the Zairian languages, Sanga, Luba, and Hemba, to which it is most closely related (Wright 1977:109). When I was collecting oral traditions in the late 1970s, people would often begin their account of Kaonde history with the formula, "Atweba twi baSanga" (We are Sanga people). Indeed, prior to the imposition of colonial rule, it is unclear to what extent the Kaonde constituted any kind of political entity. In the previous half century or so, certain Kaonde headmen[22] had managed, with the help of guns, ivory, and slaves, to raise themselves and their lineages above those of their fellows, and it seems as if some kind of a centralized power structure was beginning to emerge; but things were still very fluid when the imposition of colonial rule froze a particular moment in a continuing and turbulent power struggle. The largest political unit in the period prior to colonialism appears to have been a groups of clans. It was as leaders of senior lineages within particular clans that chiefs seem to have emerged and began to amass power, gradually gaining dominance over a whole clan. Over time certain clans might manage to establish themselves as royal or chiefly clans—the emergence of a royal clan meaning that other clans were now commoner clans.

The Kaonde term for clan is *mukoka*, and interestingly the only English-Kaonde dictionary in print (Wright 1985)[23] gives *mukoka* (pl. *mikoka*) as one of the translations of *tribe*. The other translation of *tribe* it gives is *mutundu* (pl. *mitundu*), a very general term that can be glossed as "kind" or "type," and can be applied to people, animals, and plants as well as inanimate objects. The point here is that there is no term in Kaonde which refers to a particular kind of political organization, the "tribe." There were, and are, only *mikoka* and actual empirical entities, the Kaonde people, the Lunda people, the Europeans, all of which may

22. I have used the English terms *headman* and *chief* despite their colonial overtones precisely because the meaning these statuses came to have in the colonial period, and how they are understood nowadays in northwestern Zambia, are so inextricably entangled with their existence as an element within the colonial state apparatus.

23. Unfortunately, little has been published on Kaonde, and there is no adequate Kaonde dictionary in print, only a short English-Kaonde word list produced by J. L. Wright (1985). The longest-established missionaries in the area (now the Evangelical Church of Zambia), responsible for the standard Kaonde Bible, while producing a considerable amount of material on the language for their own missionary language training, have published little. In addition to the 1985 word list there was the earlier *A Kaonde Notebook* (Wright and Kamukwamba 1958) and one main article (Wright 1977). I was kindly lent an unpublished Kaonde-English word list, also prepared by Wright (Wright n.d.).

constitute a distinct entity in many different ways. These apparently "ethnic" categories are in fact highly protean.

At the time of my fieldwork, people would use labels such as "Kaonde" or "Luvale" to refer to a whole variety of different things, not only particular settlements or whole regions, but also agricultural systems, ways of life, particular beliefs, and so on. Such "ethnic" terms were used in a taken-for-granted, unselfconscious way, and, because such categories were so unquestioned and undefined, people had no problem in using them in different contexts to refer to a bewildering variety of realities. Given the lack of precise linguistic terms in the language, it seems reasonable to assume that this fluidity was also characteristic of the colonial period. The comment quoted on page 66 illustrates one usage of the category "Kaonde": "We are Kaonde: we don't grow groundnuts or cassava or keep goats, we leave that to the Chokwe and Lwena [Luvale]." This statement was made to silence a colonial official bent on "developing" the Kaonde, not given as a definition of some primordial Kaonde identity. Indeed, there may have been individuals who would have described themselves as Kaonde, possibly living in the next village, growing groundnuts and cassava and keeping goats. Probably all that is common to these ethnic labels is that these were groups who perceived themselves—or were perceived by others— as groups sharing a language and into which people were in general born; and even then, an individual's ethnic identification might change over the course of her or his lifetime.

In the 1980s the Europeans connected with the local, and primarily German funded, Integrated Rural Development Project tended to be seen locally as part of a common entity, *magermani*. Not all the Europeans working for the project were German, and local people were sometimes puzzled to discover that not all *magermani* spoke the same language. *Magermani* could indeed be seen as sharing a common culture, the culture of the "development expert" and foreign aid worker. Although this is by no means a homogeneous and uniform culture, from the perspective of local people those who belonged to *magermani* constituted a distinct "tribe" just as much as did "the Kaonde" or "the Luvale." But this local understanding of the name "tribe" as signifying no more than some empirically existing group, whose shared characteristics could take many very different forms denied the basic premise of the colonial discourse on the "tribe" that "tribe" named a particular kind of social organization associated with a particular level of social development. However much it might have represented local perceptions, any definition of "tribe" that went against this colonial hegemony had little chance of becoming a part of the dialogue between the RLI anthropologists, the colonial state, and the people of the northwest.

Whether or not the Kaonde constituted a distinct political entity at the beginning of the colonial period, during the colonial period they certainly learned that in the world of colonial administration Africans were located within "tribes" and it was primarily in the name of a "tribe" that claims could be made on the colonial state. This was the only voice with which Africans were allowed to speak. And this is why by 1951 we find one Kaonde chief saying in a meeting of Kaonde chiefs organized by the colonial government,

We are not here to discuss matters of precedent or to discuss totems. We have heard about the Barotse and the Bemba tribes; we must throw away the totem barriers [i.e., think in terms of "tribes" rather than clans] and be one people. We must be proud to be called Kaonde.[24]

It had become clear that the only language in which the colonial state was prepared to listen to claims by Africans was a language of "tribal" law and "tribal" customs, a language that assumed that these laws and customs derived from an ancient and unchanging past—in other words, that they were "traditional." Since the model of the "African tribe" whether that of anthropologist or colonial official, presupposed homogeneity within the "tribe," the question of just which interests within the "tribe" were reflected in "tribal" law and custom did not arise within the colonial discourse.[25] But to what extent and in what ways did the name "tribe," as it was used in colonial Zambia, help more generally to shape the realities it was supposed to explain? Answering this question provides a good example of what hegemony looks like in practice.

Of "Tribes" and Hegemony

For the anthropologists associated with the RLI and the colonial officials, the concept of the tribe helped map the reality of the colonized world. It gave a particular shape to what they saw as

24. ZNA, NR 4/529, *Courts of Appeal and Meeting of Kaonde Chiefs, 1951.*
25. See Channock (1985) for an account of the development of "customary" law in Zambia and Malawi.

the problems of "law and disorder" in British Central Africa—as when struggles around working and living conditions on the mines were seen as a problem of rural "tribesmen" becoming "detribalized" rather than, say, struggles between labor and capital. This naming also had a number of powerful effects for those categorized as "tribal." The hegemonic naming of Africans as "tribal" within colonial discourse contained them in a particular way. It froze them into supposedly homogeneous communities, *gemeinschaften*, remote both from the workings of the world capitalist economy and from history, ruled by "tribal law and custom" handed down from an ancient past. In line with the principle of Indirect Rule, questions of the role and nature of the state and its relation to individual colonial subjects were deflected onto the role and nature of the "tribe," which for the African, as the colonial eye saw it, *was* the state. Similarly, inasmuch as major realities such as the development of a huge copper-mining industry in Northern Rhodesia were pushed to the sidelines of analysis while the searchlight shone on the "tribe," the notion of the "tribe" did alter the landscape that was seen by colonial officials, the RLI anthropologists, and indeed by the colonial state's African subjects—just as the colonial administrators' stereotypes of "manly" or "diseased" Kaonde affected how they saw those they met on their tours.

Africans were inescapably enmeshed in the reality of institutions based on the category of the "tribe," such as the Native Authorities of Indirect Rule. In addition, they were also enmeshed within an overarching colonial hegemony with at its heart a notion of irreducible difference—and not only difference but inequality. What this difference consisted of in Africa was above all a difference between the modern, the civilized, the developed, and the tradition-bound "tribe," which was condemned by its very "tribal" nature to slumber in a sleep of superstition and indolence until awakened by the kiss of the colonial prince. Those Africans who had the temerity to awaken on their own to any of the new opportunities offered by the new colonial world were likely to be dismissed as dangerously "detribalized."

The miscalled "mission boy", the worker on the mines and on farms, the house boy (all equally anathema to the chiefs and headmen), pick up bits of knowledge, lose their old tribal and religious checks and become a disintegrating, destructive element. (Melland 1923:305)

The name "tribe" helped provide those engaged in the colonial enterprise with a morally justifiable gloss explaining why colonial rule was necessary. Africans were "tribal" and therefore simply could not handle the economic or political institutions of "modern" society. At the same time, the name "tribe" helped those engaged in running the colonial state to feel that they understood the world of the colonized, that they knew where the roots of colonial "law and disorder" lay, and that their little world of busy administration had some purpose and function. The fear that the whole colonial enterprise might in the end be absurd and meaningless, and ultimately doomed, is another of the basic fears that underlies many novels of colonial life, from Conrad to Orwell and Forster.

What the "tribe" as a name came to mean in colonial Zambia is in part a story of what "hegemony," or one dimension of it, can mean as a lived reality. The relationship between names such as "tribe" and the realities they point to is like that between maps and the physical topography they represent. Just as particular maps take particular forms depending on what they are to be used for, and are judged ultimately on how useful they are, so too in the case of the names used to map social reality. There is always a dialogue between our representations and that which they represent, as we attempt, concepts and categories in hand, to chart our way through the ever-shifting sands of social life.

One measure of hegemony is the degree to which the conceptual maps of dominant groups, and *their* naming of reality, manage to maintain their unassailable authority for subordinated groups even in the face of a lack of fit between those subordinated groups' experience and how this experience is named to them. After all, the authority of a map depends to a large extent on its provenance and the professionalism with which it was produced; only some in society have the necessary resources to produce authoritative maps. The problem for the subordinated is, How do you move from a sense that you cannot trust the maps and, even though you may pack them in your rucksack, it is best not to use them, to a confidence that not only can you make your own maps, but that they are superior to the existing maps? And this shift is not only about confidence; hegemony is also about the power to demarcate arenas of struggle—in other words, the degree to which a ruling group is able, through its *practical* control of institutional structures, to confine the challenges of subordinated groups within a terrain mapped out by the dominant group. However creative Africans might have been in "imagining" their social relations, and however perceptive as to the real relations underpinning colonial society, they were confronted with a colonial order that in very concrete ways insisted that demands or claims put forward by Africans use the discourse of "tribes."

The story of the "tribe" in colonial Zambia provides a good introduction to my attempt to map out the various landscapes of power inhabited by the people of Kibala and Bukama. Firstly, because it illustrates something of what hegemony means in practice, and the important role played by the power to name. Secondly, it shows us the complex interaction there is between the supposedly scientific categories produced within the academy and those of nonscientific "common sense." Finally, the story of the "tribe" reveals with a particular clarity the embeddedness of the academic pursuit in existing hegemonic relations. Social theorists are necessarily embedded in their historical moment; all accounts of social reality, whatever their claims to scientific rigor, are always produced in a particular political context that necessarily shapes how that social reality is approached. This book too, of course, is imprisoned in its time just as much as were those of earlier anthropologists. My story of the "tribe" will, I hope, not be read as an exercise in the "condescension of posterity," but rather as a reminder of the complex threads that bind theorists to their times. And bearing that salutary lesson in mind, we are now ready to begin mapping out the political and economic landscapes of Kibala and Bukama.

CHAPTER 3

Political Locations I:
The Community of Kin

Mansunsu kechi akile mutwe ne.
The shoulders are not higher than the head [that is, young people should respect their elders].

Waendaenda, wamonapo bainobe, mwanamukazhi muntu ungi kesha ukusha mu mambo.
When you travel go and see your mothers; a woman [your wife] is a stranger and tomorrow she will desert you.

John Ganly, *Kaonde Proverbs*

In this and the next chapter I trace out some of the main contours of rural Chizela's political landscape and something of the character of its political spaces. In part what these chapters are about is the substantive realities into which a particular colonial and postcolonial state were translated in this particular place. Key questions I address are: In what specific ways were people in this rather remote corner bound into these larger political entities and how did they experience these relations of incorporation in their everyday lives? In order to answer these questions, however, it is necessary to look in some detail at certain local political relations and at how these were imagined. Much of this chapter, therefore, will be taken up with an exploration of the political institutions and practices of Kaonde kinship, and with the political discourse associated with what I am calling the community of kin.

In thinking about the state in these chapters, my starting point is Gramsci's broad definition that I have already quoted:

The State is the entire complex of practical and theoretical activities with which the ruling class not only justifies and maintains its dominance, but manages to win the active consent of those over whom it rules. (Gramsci 1971:244)

In other words, one way of understanding this large, abstract concept, "the state," is as *all* the multifarious power relations that help produce and reproduce a particular political and economic configuration. Some of these relations will be those formally labeled as belonging to the domain of "politics" narrowly understood, but also included will be some that may seem at first sight to have little to do with the specifically political domain. Then again, some of these relations concern the state as a repressive power able to compel compliance, while others are concerned with the state as a hegemonic power that constructs consent. To avoid possible misunderstandings, let me also say a word about how I understand Gramsci's use of the term *ruling class* in this definition of the state. What Gramsci is referring to here, I would argue, is not some precisely defined analytical category but rather a general power relation. This is the same kind of power relation Gramsci has in mind when he insists elsewhere that "It really must be stressed that it is precisely the first elements, the most elementary things which are the first to be forgotten. . . . The first element is that there really do exist rulers and ruled, leaders and led" (1971:144).

In these two chapters on political location I will be exploring something of what the state, in Gramsci's broad definition, translated into as a day-to-day lived reality in rural Chizela. This exploration will involve tracing out the general shape of the historical trajectory of this heterogeneous bundle of power relations during the colonial period and the postcolonial years up to the fall of Kaunda. Although my focus here, and in subsequent chapters, is on rural Chizela, it important not to forget that the history of this small corner unfolded within the overarching hegemony of a colonial and then postcolonial state. I want to begin, therefore, by providing a brief sketch of the broad trajectory of Zambian history.

From Northern Rhodesia to Zambia

What is now the modern state of Zambia first became a single political unit under British colonial rule.[1] This began with the

1. Andrew Roberts's *A History of Zambia* (1976) provides a good general account of Zambian history from prehistoric times up to 1974. Lewis H. Gann's *A History of Northern*

recognition in the 1890s (by the relevant European powers) of the right of the British South Africa Company (BSAC) to occupy an area north of the Zambezi, although it was a number of years before this formal recognition was translated into effective rule. At first there were two separate BSAC territories, North-Western and North-Eastern Rhodesia. These were combined to form Northern Rhodesia in 1911, and then in 1924, after twenty-five years of company rule, the colony was taken over by the British Colonial Office. Forty years later, in 1964, independence was achieved and Northern Rhodesia became Zambia. As with other colonial borders, those of Northern Rhodesia were primarily the result of struggles between the various European colonial powers as they carved up the African continent amongst themselves. Where particular boundaries were drawn depended on the relative strengths of the different European powers and their perceptions of their strategic needs, rather than on preexisting geographical or social entities.

As elsewhere in Africa, a significant presence accompanying, and sometimes preceding, European expansion was that of the missionaries. The various Christian sects and denominations tended to carve out for themselves separate geographical areas of interest—much as would the different foreign development agencies of a later period. A key focus for many missionary churches was language. The missionaries were not only responsible for providing hitherto oral languages with a written form, often it was they who determined where linguistic boundaries were to be drawn. As when they laid down, through their translations of the Bible for instance, which of the many co-existing, and to differing degrees mutually intelligible, languages within a given region should be considered as distinct languages, and which mere "dialects."[2] The written version of Kaonde and the Kaonde Bible were produced by missionaries of the South Africa General Mission (now the Evangelical Church of Zambia) who first arrived in the Kaonde-speaking region of North-Western Province in 1910, and were still the major local missionary presence at the time of my fieldwork.

From the earliest years of Company rule in Northern Rhodesia there was labor migration: north to the mines of Katanga in the Belgian

---

Rhodesia: Early Days to 1953 (1964) deals specifically with the colonial period. Hamalengwa's *Class Struggles in Zambia, 1889–1989, and the Fall of Kenneth Kaunda* (1992) looks at the whole period 1899–1991.

2. Patrick Harries (1989) describes how this process worked in the case of the emergence of the Tsonga language.

Congo (now Zaire) and south to the mines and farms in Southern Rhodesia (now Zimbabwe) and South Africa. After the Company's original
high hopes of finding mineral wealth (above all gold) in its northern
territories had come to little, inasmuch as the BSAC valued Northern
Rhodesia at all it was as a labor reserve (Roberts 1976:177). Labor migration was "encouraged" by the imposition of taxes, which had to be
paid in cash. The Company also began to sell land to European settlers,
although few were attracted to the tsetse-infested northwestern region.
In the final years of Company rule, however, European prospectors discovered important copper deposits just as new technology to exploit
them was being developed.

In the 1920s, after the end of Company rule, a massive copper-mining
industry developed, which dominated the colonial economy of Northern Rhodesia and has continued to dominate the postindependence
Zambian economy. At Independence copper and cobalt made up over
90 percent of Zambia's total export earnings, and the figure was still
close to 90 percent in the early 1980s (Burdette 1988). The mines cluster
around the railway that runs along the central spine of the country,
linking up with the Katanga mines to the north, and with Zimbabwe
and South Africa to the south (see map). Much of this railway was built
by the BSAC in its initial optimism about Northern Rhodesia's mineral
wealth, and as one link in Cecil Rhodes's dream of a railway from Cairo
to the Cape. Shortly after Independence a further rail link to Tanzania
was built with Chinese aid. All industrial and urban development associated with the growth of copper mining was concentrated along the
original line of rail. This linked the mining areas (which came to be
known as the Copperbelt) with Lusaka, which developed from a small
settlement around a railway siding to become the colony's capital in 1931.
As the mining industry expanded, a number of large towns grew up
around the mines and the railway. In the south of the country there was
some development of commercial farming by white settlers and a certain
amount of small-scale market production of crops, particularly maize,
by African producers. By contrast, North-Western Province and the
other more remote areas were regarded by the colonial state essentially
as labor reserves. The result was a highly skewed economic development
with virtually all industrial development concentrated along the line of
rail and a high dependence on a supply of migrant labor from the rural
areas. Consequently there was both a continual movement between rural
and urban areas and, by comparison with most of southern Africa, a
relatively high rate of urbanization. According to Roberts, by 1932, "it

is probable that more than half the able-bodied male population of Northern Rhodesia was working for wages away from home" (Roberts 1976:191). In 1963, just prior to Independence about 20 percent of the country's population was already living in town and, with the abolition of the colonial state's strict control of migration, by 1969 this had grown to 29 percent (Mwanza 1979: 28), and by 1980 had reached 43 percent (GRZ 1981:3–4).

Although there were various forms of protest throughout the colonial period, the struggle for Independence in Northern Rhodesia began in earnest in the late 1930s as the mining industry recovered from the Great Depression; and the Copperbelt miners were a driving force. It was more of an urban than a rural struggle, and did not involve guerrilla warfare. The major political organization that emerged in the fight for Independence was the United National Independence Party (UNIP) headed by Kenneth Kaunda, who in 1964 became the newly independent Zambia's first president. Eight years later in 1972 all parties except UNIP were banned, the Second Republic was declared, and for almost twenty years Zambia became a one-party state, with Kaunda as its president. The new state was described by Kaunda as being neither capitalist nor socialist but based on the philosophy of Humanism, the tenets of which Kaunda laid down in various publications.[3] Humanism is a highly moralistic—if rather vague as to specifics—set of precepts that claim to reflect an African socialism (Julius Nyerere's African Socialism was an important influence). It draws on both Christian tradition and what are claimed to be the "socialist" traditions of precolonial Africa.

At Independence the Zambian economy was relatively prosperous, due to its copper revenues (immediately after independence the mines were nationalized), and the new government rapidly began making good on its preindependence promises of vastly improved government services, such as health and education. From the mid-seventies, however, there were growing economic problems. The 1970s saw a fall in the price of copper, a sharp increase in the price of oil, and the closing of the border to the south due to Zimbabwe's war of independence. This last factor was particularly serious since not only is Zambia a land-locked country with a poorly developed transport infrastructure, but those road and rail links that were constructed in the colonial period were all geared to links with the south. In the early heady days of Independence Zambia,

3. See, for instance, Kaunda (1967, 1974).

often at the prompting of various expatriate "experts," borrowed extensively—extensively at any rate in relation to its GNP. Increasing interest rates in the 1980s meant that these loans became an ever more onerous burden. In December 1984, for instance, it was estimated that "by 1985 servicing the total debt would require 86 percent of all export earnings" (Burdette 1988:121).

As times became harder, and government services increasingly failed to live up to the early promises, UNIP and Kaunda became ever more unpopular, particularly when the war in Zimbabwe, blamed for so many of Zambia's problems, ended without leading to the long-promised economic improvement. At the end of the eighties, in line with world events, there was mounting pressure both outside and inside the country for an end to one-party rule and for multiparty elections. Bowing to the pressure, Kaunda and UNIP finally ended the ban on parties other than UNIP and agreed to hold elections. In October 1991 there was a general election and the new Movement for Multiparty Democracy (MMD), led by the former Union of Mine Workers' leader Frederick Chiluba, won a landslide victory. Kaunda accepted his defeat with some grace, and Zambia passed peacefully to its Third Republic with Chiluba as the new President. As it turned out, therefore, the fieldwork I did in 1988 and 1989 in North-Western Province was carried out in the dying moments of Zambia's Second Republic. Although at the time it seemed unlikely that Kaunda could survive much longer, no one was predicting such a rapid and peaceful end to one-party rule and the long reign of K.K., as he was always known.

A Rural Backwater

While the storms of history were blowing over first Northern Rhodesia, then Zambia, the northwest of the country was far from being any kind of epicenter. During both the colonial and the postcolonial years, North-Western Province has always remained something of a backwater. As we saw in the last chapter, in the eyes of the colonial state North-Western Province tended to be seen as remote, inaccessible, and inhabited for the most part by benighted souls, clinging stubbornly to "tradition," and willfully deaf to the message of "development." The moralistic tone of so much "development" rhetoric—a moralism common to both colonial and postcolonial variants—tends to

lay the blame for the "underdeveloped" state of their region on individual "Kaonde" themselves, who have unfortunately failed, due to their
attachment to retrogressive "tradition," a lack of proper education, or
whatever, to choose the progressive road of "development." It is true
that North-Western Province as a whole was recognized in the 1980s
(see Jaeger 1981:13–16; ILO 1981:13–27) as being one of the more remote
and poor of Zambia's provinces. It is also true that its people have not
been heavily engaged in agricultural production for the market; but this
is not because those living in the province have deliberately refused to
follow the "development" road. In fact what "development" is often
taken to mean tends, in practice, to boil down to various forms of en-
gagement with the wider economy. And it is the characteristics of North-
Western Province itself, its ecology and the nature of its incorporation
into the polities of first Northern Rhodesia and then Zambia, that have
set the terms on which those living in the province have been *able* to
engage with the wider economy.

Within a country characterized historically by a generally low population density, North-Western Province has always been a particularly
sparsely inhabited region. According to the 1980 census, the province
had 2.4 people per square kilometer, compared to a figure of 7.5 for
Zambia as a whole (GRZ 1988b:14). Geologically, Zambia consists of a
series of flat or nearly flat plateaux, highest in the northeast, reaching
over 2,000 meters in places, and sloping down to just over 200 meters
in the southwest.[4] Most of North-Western Province is around 1200 meters, with a terrain crisscrossed by numerous perennial small streams.
Rainfall is higher in the north than the south of the country, averaging
in North-Western from 1,015 millimeters to nearly 1,520 millimeters.
However, due to the higher rainfall the generally thin soils of the province tend to be more severely leached than those further south. As a
result of the long history of human cultivation, vegetation consists
mainly of rather open secondary forest dominated by fire-resistant trees
with here and there areas of dense virgin forest. The most common form
of vegetation is *miombo* woodland. Much of the province, including
Chizela District, is infested with tsetse fly, which makes it impossible to
keep livestock.

Basic government services, such as schools and clinics, have always
been few and far between; until Independence the few hospitals and

4. The information in the remainder of this paragraph is taken from *Zambia in Maps*
(Davies 1971).

secondary schools there were, were run by missionaries. In 1984 only 16.3 percent of those aged between fifteen and nineteen living in the province were attending secondary school (GRZ 1988b:130). The road network was poor and mostly untarred, and by the late eighties the state-run public transport system (there was no privately run public transport) operated sporadically if at all in the province. North-Western Province's "remoteness" in the colonial and postcolonial period is not something inherent in the physical geography. Its location as a peripheral region is something that began with the way the colonial boundaries were drawn and the BSAC's, and later the colonial state's, orientation of the colony toward Southern Rhodesia and South Africa. This peripheralization was intensified with the development of the Copperbelt and the relegation of much of rural Zambia to the status of a labor reserve furnishing the labor needed both within the colony and further south, particularly by the mines, but also by the white commercial farmers and the colonial economy in general.[5] During the colonial period there was always something of a tension between mining and other interests who were primarily concerned with the availability of labor—and its availability at a sufficiently low wage—and administrators within the colonial state, who, fearful of an ungovernable mass exodus to the urban areas, were anxious that the rural areas should maintain their viability in economic and social terms. The history of North-Western's "remoteness" and "backwardness" is inextricably bound up with "development" elsewhere.

If North-Western Province as a whole was remote and poorly served with basic services in the 1980s, Chizela District was an especially remote and poorly served corner of the province. As I explained in the introduction, it is located within the heart of the region associated with the Kaonde, and, at the time of my fieldwork, throughout the district—as in Kibala and Bukama—Kaonde was the dominant language. English (the primary language of government) was common only in the district center, Chizela town, and only in official government circles did it dominate.

Chizela was a new district, only carved off from the adjacent district of Kasempa in 1980. The township of Chizela was tiny; in 1980 it had a population of 577, which was estimated to reach 1,030 by 1990. This compares with figures for 1980 of between just over 3,000 to just over

5. Karen Tranberg Hansen in her book *Distant Companions* (1989) has drawn attention to the enormous importance of domestic service, a sector that has continued to be important in postcolonial Zambia.

8,000 for the province's other district centers. The provincial capital, Solwezi, was the only sizable urban center, with a population of 15,000 in 1980, which was estimated to rise to nearly 27,000 by 1990 (GRZ 1988b:16). All the other provincial district centers were already administrative centers in colonial times and, unlike Chizela, had a physical legacy of colonial administrative buildings. For instance, all had the serried rank of one-story government buildings with a lone two-story structure rising above them, in the elevated office of which would sit the district commissioner. The British district commissioner might have been replaced by a Zambian district governor, and in front might flutter the Zambian flag not the Union Jack, but the symbolism of authority remained intact. The local embodiment of the state's authority was still perched in his lonely eyrie from which he could survey his domain stretched out below him. In more practical terms, however, Chizela became a separate district too late to benefit from the immediate post-independence boom years. To varying degrees all of Zambia's district centers struggle with a lack of basic infrastructure; shortages of both office space and housing for government officials, a lack of tarred roads, unreliable water and electricity supplies are endemic. In Chizela, the most poorly served district in a poorly served province, these problems were particularly acute.

Having located Chizela in a preliminary way within the larger entity of Zambia, we are now ready to begin mapping out some of the details of the local political landscape and how this was imagined by the people of Kibala and Bukama.

Imagining the State

The people of Bukama and Kibala inhabited, as it were, two coexisting "imagined communities": that of "Zambia," the modern state of which they were citizens; and that of the locally rooted "community of kin." Not that people saw themselves as having to choose between being either Zambian citizens or members of a kin group; both identities were equally part of their social world but they informed and shaped the lives of individuals in rather different ways. People tended, for example, to see themselves as subject to two different authority structures, each with its own spheres of influence. There were certain needs — access to land, help in times of trouble, for instance — that people expected to meet through the reciprocal obligations of kinship; there were others that only the state was seen as able to satisfy, such as those for schools, clinics, and the provision and maintenance of all-weather roads. Both Kibala and Bukama had state-run primary schools and Kibala also had a small clinic. If, as the government was continually urging them, people were to engage in "modern" farming, then they were dependent on the state for the necessary "modern" inputs, such as fertilizer and hybrid seeds, and for the marketing facilities necessary if the produce of that "modern" farming was to find a market.

Mapping out the contours of rural Chizela's political landscape and understanding the character of its political spaces necessarily involves tracing out the complex history of how people's location, first as colonial subjects, then as Zambian citizens, was entangled with their location within the hierarchies of kinship—and how these different clusters of power relations and these different political identities have informed and shaped one another. It should be stressed that this double location as citizens and kin is not peculiar to places like Chizela; it is also to be found in modern industrial societies, even if its significance tends not to be recognized. Current struggles over the role of the state and "family values" in the West, for instance, can be seen as being, at least in part, about the respective obligations of kinship and the state, and where exactly the boundaries between these two domains should be drawn. What is different is the nature of the two domains in rural Chizela and in modern industrial societies (which themselves are far from uniform), and the specific ways in which they are interrelated with one another.

An important part of the reason why this double location is obscured in countries like Britain and the United States is the particular history of the development of the modern bureaucratic state. The history of the institutions and practices of European kinship is an integral part of the history of the development of the modern state precisely because it was out of premodern *European* political institutions and practices that this form of state emerged; and those political institutions and practices had embedded in them their own particular patterns of kinship. Indeed, a key thread in the story of the emergence of the modern state is the assignment of a "proper" separation of the private world of family and kin from the realm of "public" politics. There is, as it were, an established, organic relation of separation between the domains of the state and of kinship in Europe (and those Western countries most shaped by the European tradition), even if in certain respects this separation is in fact illusory. There is, at any rate, a clear naming of this separation, and a hegemonic acceptance of its reality. This was not true of rural Chizela. There, a discourse of political authority based on the relations of kinship, within which it was impossible to decouple legitimate authority from kinship, was still a powerful, and indeed locally hegemonic, presence. At the same time, as people in Kibala and Bukama were very well aware, the ultimate hegemonic presence they confronted was that of the national state.

While there are many differences between the British colonial state that governed Northern Rhodesia and the postcolonial Zambian state, something they have in common is a "modern" bureaucratic way of doing things. From the vantage point of rural Chizela, one dimension of the hegemony of modern bureaucracy in the apparatuses of government was the powerful gravitational pull the bureaucratic model has exerted on the practices of kinship. But these kinship practices have also had their own gravitational field, albeit a weaker one.

To a significant degree, as I hope my account of the emergence of the Kaonde as a "tribe" showed, the headmen and chiefs of Chizela can be seen not merely as having been co-opted by the colonial state, but as indeed having been the creation of that state. This colonial invention of tradition can, however, be overstated. However much they may have functioned as a lowly tier of local government, and may have remade themselves in the bureaucratic image of the colonial government, headmen and chiefs were also the product of local histories and local kinship-based social relations. What the state, whether colonial or postcolonial, has meant as a lived reality in rural Chizela has also been shaped by notions of power and authority derived from the community of kin; kinship thinking has, as it were, colored how the people of Kibala and Bukama imagined the state.

It is the specific character of Kaonde kinship institutions and practices that the next three sections of this chapter are about. In them I explore the Kaonde theory of kinship and the discourse on power and authority that was bound up with it. To put it another way, these sections are about how the community of kin named and explained the social landscape.[6] It is necessary to explain the kinship system and this discourse

6. Kinship was of course a central theme for colonial anthropology, and there is a wealth of material on different Zambian kinship systems in the work produced by the anthropologists associated with the RLI. See, among many others, Colson and Gluckman (1951); Colson (1958); Turner (1957); Richards (1940, 1950); Epstein (1981). More recent work on matriliny in Luapula Province in the postcolonial period is found in Poewe (1981). Moore and Vaughan (1994) questions some of the received wisdom on Bemba "matriliny."

in some detail since grasping their fundamentally different character is not always easy for those (and this is likely to include most of my readers) who have grown up within the hegemony of a discourse on political authority organized around the notion of the citizen.

The political discourse associated with the modern state has at its heart a citizen who is seen as linked to the state and to other citizens through a series of contractlike relationships that define a set of distinct and bounded rights. The Kaonde discourse on political authority named a very different power landscape. This was a power landscape in which the basic units were not citizens but rather a set of different, and fundamentally unequal, kinship statuses bound together in a diffuse but inescapable moral net of general mutual obligation. It needs to be emphasized that this account of authority does not simply define a *different* set of rights; it is a discourse not based on a juridical notion of *rights* at all. Also, this account of authority does not see kinship, as does the modern discourse on citizenship, as something separate and private; rather it is kinship itself that names the key contours of legitimate authority. In the context of 1980s rural Chizela, what this meant was that those who dominated local political arenas "justified and maintained their dominance, and managed to win the active consent of those over whom they ruled" (to echo Gramsci) in part by appealing to the imagined obligations of kinship. The fabric of hegemony was, so to speak, to an important extent woven out of the fabric of kinship.

The overwhelming importance of kinship in rural Chizela could not but strike a westerner such as myself. For people in Kibala and Bukama the primary imagined community was without doubt that of the community of kin; it was kinship above all that named and located individuals within the social world. How difficult it could be for people to conceive of a society in which kinship was *not* all-important was brought home to me by an incident during my first fieldwork trip to North-Western Province in 1980. I was sitting chatting with an elderly Kaonde neighbor trying to explain to her how much less important kinship is to the British than to the Kaonde. Using myself as an example, I talked about how people in Britain did not have anything like her sense of obligation to kin, except to their immediate relatives. My neighbor's eyes opened wider and wider until finally she exclaimed in a tone in which horror and bewilderment were equally mixed, "You Europeans, you're just like fish!" To her the concept of human beings living together in ways unstructured by the hierarchy of kinship with its complex tracery of reciprocal obligation was unimaginable. The very suggestion of it filled her with as much horror as the colonial stereotype of "savage Africa" did Joseph Conrad. For the narrator in Conrad's *Heart of Darkness*, a world without the familiar social structures of the West is a world without restraints in which the id runs free; for my Kaonde neighbor, without the restraining and supportive bonds of kinship what is there to distinguish human beings from brute beasts?

And it was the same in Kibala and Bukama ten years later. The headmaster of Kibala primary school, for instance, asked me if it were true, as many people believed, that westerners also had their own clans and only pretended not to when they were asked about them by Africans. *Why* westerners should be so secretive about their clans was just one of the many impenetrable mysteries of their strange and alien life, although some people suspected that the source of their enormous wealth might have to do with their skill at cutting themselves off from the claims of impecunious fellow clan members. The notion that kinship provided the basic threads out of which social life was woven was in fact one of the "fundamental social evaluations" that Bakhtin referred to as developing "directly from the specific conditions of the economic life of a given group [which] are not usually uttered" and that "have become flesh and blood of all members of that group" (Bakhtin 1988:13). In sum, it was the relation of kinship that provided people, I would argue, with their basic—and most emotionally powerful—model for human relationships in general.

Mapping out this social landscape of kinship necessarily involves explaining Kaonde kinship reckoning and the basic political units within the hierarchy of kinship. Knowing how off-putting many people find discussions of kinship terminology, I have tried to keep this trip through the thickets of Kaonde kinship classification as short as possible. Part of the problem here is that Western readers, socialized into a categorization of kinship based on radically different principles, can find it difficult to think their way into the Kaonde system; all of us, whatever our kinship system, tend to experience our own kinship terminology as transparently representing the "facts" of kinship. It is important, however, that the reader gets a sense of the *kind* of categories into which Kaonde kinship sorted different relatives, and of how these categories fitted together into a particular landscape of power. In the West we have come to think of kinship, and the obligations of kinship, as occupying its own particular domain, which is in many respects seen as separate from, and even opposed to, the domain of governments and states. Kaonde kinship discourse by contrast provided people in Kibala and Bukama with their basic understanding of authority in general. Leaving aside the issue of de facto power—about which people tended to be extremely realistic—the model for legitimate, acknowledged authority was that embodied in the hierarchy of kinship.

Once some of the key contours of the imagined community of kinship have been mapped out, we are ready in the last section of the chapter to begin looking at how this community of kin was incorporated first into the colonial and then into the postcolonial state. The next chapter continues this topic and examines in greater detail how the people of Kibala and Bukama were located politically within Zambia's Second Republic.

Kaonde Kinship and the Matrilineal Core

Kaonde kinship terminology is based on the principle of matrilineal descent; a child belongs to the clan (within which marriage is forbidden) of his or her mother. According to Kaonde oral tradition, the Kaonde have always been matrilineal. The *bishimi* (folktales) I collected certainly presupposed a matrilineal system, and, judging from the colonial archives, the ideology of matriliny has been dominant at least from the earliest colonial period.[7] But whatever may have been the case in the past, in 1980s rural Chizela it was undoubtedly the matrilineal link that was seen as creating the most fundamental bonds between people, and as defining the basic statuses within the community of kin.

Within the Kaonde matrilineage there were eight basic kinship statuses; and for none of them are there simple one-to-one equivalents in English. In the following initial listing of the statuses I have given English equivalents simply because it is necessary to start somewhere, but the reader should bear in mind that these are grossly inaccurate. In the appendix I include a table that provides more accurate glosses as well as diagrammatic representations of the main kinship statuses, which may help to clarify the verbal definitions. The eight statuses were: *inanji* (mother), *mwisho* (mother's brother), *kolojanji* (older sibling), *nkasanji* (younger sibling), *mwana* (child), *mwipwa* (nephew or niece), *nkambo*

7. Melland, the colonial official who wrote the first account of the Kaonde and was first stationed in North-Western Province around 1910, describes the Kaonde as unambiguously matrilineal (Melland 1923:95–96).

(grandparent), *munkana* (grandchild). The basic shape of kinship classification within the matrilineage, and its gradients of power, are represented diagrammatically in figure 1.

The first point to note is that all these kinship terms are classificatory,
that is, they refer to a group of kin rather than a single individual. For
instance, *inanji* (pl. *bainanji*) was a far more inclusive term than *mother*,
being used for *all* of ego's female matrikin in the first ascending generation. In other words, *inanji* included not only ego's biological mother
but all the latter's female siblings and her female matrilateral parallel
cousins from the first to the nth degree.[8] If it were necessary to distinguish someone's biological "mother," she was referred to as "the mother
who bore X" (*inanji wasema X*). The point here is not that there was
any confusion between biological and classificatory mothers, but that in
terms of the bundle of moral obligations associated with the category
inanji, these applied not simply to someone's biological mother but to
all those categorized as *inanji*. The relationship between biological
mother and child was certainly recognized as special, but its specialness
lay in its intensity and strength; it was not seen as involving a different
set of obligations from those of the general category *inanji*. *Mwisho* similarly referred to *all* the male members of ego's matrilineage in the first
ascending generation, including all the male siblings and male matrilateral parallel cousins of all the women classified as ego's *inanji*.[9] In this
matrilineal system, *mwisho*, not father, was the primary male authority
figure.

The second point to note is that of the eight kinship terms only two,
inanji and *mwisho* are gender specific. The two terms for sibling, *kolojanji*
(pl. *bakolojanji*) and *nkasanji* (pl. *bankasanji*), specify whether a sibling
is older or younger but not their gender. *Kolojanji* included all ego's *older*
siblings who shared ego's biological mother, and all those matrilateral
parallel cousins whose *inanji* was *kolojanji* to ego's *inanji*.[10] Similarly,
nkasanji included all ego's *younger* biological siblings and all those matrilateral parallel cousins whose *inanji* was *nkasanji* to ego's *inanji*.[11] Because neither *kolojanji* nor *nkasanji* are sex specific, if a speaker wanted
to indicate the sex, a qualifying adjective was added: *kolojanji wamulume*
(male older sibling), *nkasanji wamukazhi* (female younger sibling). Normally this was only done if the context demanded it, just as English

8. See fig. A.1, appendix.   9. See fig. A.2, appendix.
10. See fig. A.3, appendix.   11. See fig. A.4, appendix.

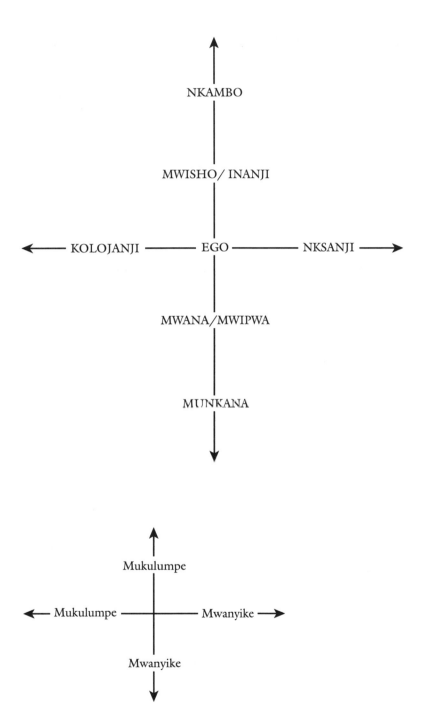

Figure 1. The matrilineal core

speakers refer simply to brothers and sisters without feeling it necessary to specify whether they are older or younger.

In the first descending generation ego's matrikin were different depending on whether ego was male or female. The same term, *mwana* (pl. *bana*), was used to refer to ego's biological children, all the biological children of a male ego's male *bakolojanji* and *bankasanji*, and of a female ego's female *bakolojanji* and *bankasanji*, were also termed ego's *bana*. But whereas a woman's *bana* were her matrikin, a man's were not. A man's biological children belonged to the matrilineage of their *inanji*. According to Kaonde kinship terminology, therefore, strictly speaking a man's children were not his kin (*balongo*). For instance, once when I was talking to Ubaya, the vice-chairman of the Bukama Farm Settlement about the rules of the scheme I asked about inheritance and whether plots could only be inherited by kin (*balongo*). Ubaya replied, "Ee, ne bana" (Yes, and also children). In other words, in the context of a discussion of male inheritance (the assumption was that, unless specified otherwise, the "farmers" of Bukama were male), a man's children would not automatically be thought of as his kin. A man's immediate heirs were his *bepwa* (sing. *mwipwa*). *Bepwa* were the children of a man's "sisters" (*banyenga*), the children, that is, of all his female *bakolojanji* and *bankasanji*; the *bepwa* to whom he was *mwisho*. The relationship between *mwisho* and *mwipwa* was a key authority relationship in local political life. The corresponding relationship between a woman and her brothers' children of course fell outside the matrilineage and seemed to have little significance for people.

In the second ascending generation there was just one term, *nkambo* (pl. *bankambo*), which was used for both men and women and included all those who were *inanji* or *mwisho* to ego's *inanji* or *mwisho*.[12] *Nkambo* was also used for a whole range of kin in the second ascending generation who, although not ego's matrikin, were linked to ego through affinal ties. The second descending generation also had one all-inclusive term, *munkana* (pl. *bankana*), which was used for all children of both sexes, of both ego's *bana* and *bepwa*, and could be loosely translated as "grandchild." Only the *bana* of a female ego's female *bana*, however, were also members of ego's matrilineage, unless, that is, there had been a marriage of cross-cousins.

The basic set of matrilineal relationships stretched a net over the ma-

---

12. See fig. A.5, appendix.

trilineal clan linking each clan member to every other. Whenever two clan members met they would slot each other into an appropriate relationship, *mwisho/mwipwa, inanji/mwana, kolojanji/nkasanji*, and so on. Often people would not know their exact genealogical relationship, but the fact that they shared the same clan meant, by definition, that a genealogical relationship could be assumed. Kinship categories could be very flexible, as they are often for English speakers. For instance, the term *aunt* may be used to refer to the sisters of parents, the wives of uncles, and even women who are merely friends of the family, without there being any confusion in peoples' minds about the different relationships involved. Similarly, kinship terms in Kibala and Bukama had both a precise core of meaning and a far more diffuse and unbounded range of meanings, where the kinship term was being used more as a metaphor or analogy, indicating the kinds of expectations and obligations associated with a specific relationship. For example, when a young and an old villager met who did not know each other, they might well address each other as *nkambo* and *munkana*, indicating by this no more than that this was the kind of relationship in which they stood to each other.

As with any exogamous system, the Kaonde matrilineal clan depended for its reproduction on the "strangers" who married into it. Later I shall have more to say about the kind of structural tensions this involved both within and between households, and some of the ways in which they manifested themselves. Here I just want to describe the basic shape of the Kaonde household as a political and an economic unit. But first let me clarify how I am using this slippery term *household*.

Household is a term that at first sight seems to refer to an obvious and undeniable reality and yet, once one begins to think about what it actually describes in different contexts, is also a vague and shifting creature forever changing its shape. The assumption that the household can be treated as any kind of "natural," unproblematic category, or that it can be taken to be a single decision-making entity, has increasingly come under attack, particularly by feminists.[13] On the one hand, it seems difficult to deny that in some sense all societies have households in that there is some kind (or kinds) of basic unit within which people live. On the other hand, the kind of units households are and what they do can

---

13. This critique is usefully summarized in Henrietta Moore's *Feminism and Anthropology* (1988:54–56). Jane Guyer's 1981 review article remains an excellent survey of the literature on African households.

vary enormously. Are they units of consumption and/or production? Are they units of reproduction and/or the sites where the socialization and education of children take place? What is their role in the political domain? None of the answers to these questions can be assumed. There are no universals, only specific answers for specific contexts; the household is an empirical rather than an analytical category.

One characteristic that is general, however, is that households are always both collective entities and made up of separate individuals. They are sites within which conflictual and supportive relationships are always entwined; disentangling the specific relations of subordination and domination that exist within this dense, and emotionally saturated, knot is not straightforward. It is important neither to romanticize the household—assuming that it can be treated as a single entity with a single set of interests, aims, and within which resources are unproblematically shared—nor, in reaction to such romanticization, to move so far in the other direction as to see households as no more than sites of an unrelenting struggle between warring autonomous individuals. In other words, the notion of the household has to be problematized. We have to start from its double-sided and sometimes contradictory character as an entity that both has common interests and aims and is made up of individuals with different interests and aims. What this means in any given instance can only be discovered through empirical investigation. So, to come back to the specifics of rural Chizela: How did the people of Kibala and Bukama themselves describe the basic units they saw themselves as living within?

The term *household* can be translated into Kaonde as *ba munzubo* (those belonging to the house), and *household head* as *mwina nzubo* ("owner" of the house). The name of the *mwina nzubo* implicitly included within itself all those belonging to that household; he (as in English, the presumption was that households were male-headed unless they were specifically defined as female-headed) was the embodiment of the household as a political entity. It was the male household head who constituted the basic unit within the political pyramid of kinship.

As economic rather than political entities, households were more units of consumption than production (the organization of production is discussed in the next chapter). In practice discovering the household to which someone belonged involved asking by whom was he or she "fed" (*kujisha*). A person might then be described as either being fed by X (*bejisha*), or as feeding themselves (*mwine wijisha*), depending on whether or not they were considered to be part of X's household, or to have their own household. Nonetheless, it was not always true that households were units of consumption in any literal sense. "Feeding" here could be used figuratively in the sense of "being responsible for." Another important characteristic was that the cash incomes of husbands and wives, whatever their source, were not pooled to form a single joint household purse. Each spouse was seen as controlling the distribution of the produce of their own labor and their own income, even if this produce and this income was also seen as subject to a wide range of claims on the part of their spouse and other kin.

Most households in Kibala and Bukama consisted of a married couple and their dependent children, or a single adult. Female-headed households were fairly common in Kibala (12 percent of all households, see table 1) and very common in Bukama (35 percent of all households). The prevalence of female-headed households in Bukama was due, as I explained in the introduction, to its particular history. Female-headed households by definition had no adult male, and it was usual for a brother, an uncle, or some other male kinsman to act for husbandless women in the sphere of public politics. Although many men might have aspired to polygyny, only a small minority had two wives, and no more than a handful had more than two. In any formal *political* context a man and his wife or wives would constitute a single household, although in terms of their day-to-day *economic* organization spouses tended to constitute relatively autonomous units, each engaging in his or her own productive activities. This autonomy was especially marked in the case of polygynous men, with each wife having her own fields, her own granaries, her own kitchen, and so on. Normally a household never contained more than one adult male. Virtually the only exceptions were cases where one man was considered either mentally or physically incompetent.

The next level in the political hierarchy above that of the household was that of the *muzhi* (village). Each *muzhi* was seen as consisting primarily of a core of matrilineally related households; and each had a headman (*mwina muzhi*, lit. " 'owner' of the village"), who was normally the most genealogically senior of the *muzhi*'s male matrikin. The name of a *muzhi* referred both to a particular matrilineal segment and to its headman. The relationship between headman and household heads was analogous to that between a male household head and his dependents. In both there was the acknowledgment of a generalized authority that was also diffuse and nonspecific. The *muzhi* was in fact the household writ large, with the headman, as it were, standing for all those belonging

Table 1   *Male and Female-Headed Households in Kibala and Bukama*

	Kibala	Bukama
Polygynous households		
Two wives	14	3
Three wives	1	1
Polygynous households as % of male-headed households	7%	9.6%
Total male-headed households	206 (88%)	52 (65%)
Female-headed households	29 (12%)	28 (35%)
Total households	235	80

NOTE: These figures are based on surveys I carried out in 1988. In Kibala my survey of household composition was based on 28 of the 31 settlements.

to it (the *bena muzhi*), for whom he was able, and indeed expected, to speak.

Muzhi was first and foremost a political category that referred to a social rather than a geographical location; its primary meaning was a particular group of matrikin, *not* a physical settlement. Nonetheless, at any given time each *muzhi* was also associated with an actual geographical site. If someone said, "I am going to X," mentioning the name of a village, everyone would understand that he or she was going to that particular place. The inhabitants of this physical embodiment of the *muzhi* would normally include, in addition to the headman and his matrikin, a number of people who had married into the village or chosen to live there for some other reason. Within this kinship-ordered political universe, however, these outsider individuals were excluded from the *muzhi*'s own political hierarchy. "Belonging" to a particular *muzhi* had a number of different meanings. Individuals had a specially deep tie to the village of their birth mother (*inanji wamusema*); this was their primary village. However, they also belonged to some extent to the villages of other of their matrikin, and even though they did not belong to their father's kin group, in some weaker sense they also had ties there. For anyone in Chizela the wide range of meanings *muzhi* could have, and its shifting reference to people and places, did not create any problem, since the context would define which meaning was appropriate. For the Western reader, however, it is important to stress that the community constituting a village did not all live in one place and that individuals might be members in some sense or another of many different villages.

The way new villages, in the sense of physical settlements, came into being was normally through a particular group of kin within an existing village splitting off and forming their own autonomous settlement with its own headman. When this happened the old and the new villages would see themselves as linked by the same kinship ties as existed between their respective headmen, uncle (*mwisho*) and nephew (*mwipwa*), or older (*kolojanji*) and younger sibling (*nkasanji*), for instance. This particular relationship would then be frozen, defining the relationship between the two villages in perpetuity. Within a locality such as Kibala, most of the villages were linked in this fashion in a net of hierarchical relations. On becoming a headman, a man would take the name of his village and subsequently he would always be called by this name; a crucial part of what he was succeeding to, in fact, was a particular location within the kinship hierarchy. In other words, in inheriting the name of his predecessor a headman by definition also inherited all his predecessor's kinship relationships to other villages. Succession to headmanship was in principle adelphic, with the most senior male of the *muzhi* (in the sense of kin cluster) becoming the new headman on the death of the old. In practice, however, in the 1980s genealogical seniority in itself did not decide who would succeed but rather provided a field of candidates, all of whom were male matrikin of the late headman; and judging by the colonial records this seems to have been true since at least the early colonial period. Which of this field of candidates actually succeeded was decided by the senior members of the matrilineage (women as well as men) on the basis of individual candidates' competence. Interestingly, it seemed to be agreed that there should be a lengthy period, often one or two years, before a new headman was formally chosen. One way of looking at this time lag is as a space within which de facto power struggles had a chance to work themselves out. In other words, only when it had become clear who of the potential successors actually commanded the greatest support would the formal process of selection take place. Very occasionally, it seemed, a woman (usually the widow of a headman) might be recognized as a village "headman" in her own right. There was one such woman in Kibala, but this seemed to be more the recognition of a de facto situation than a genuine succession. Really, people told me, this woman and those living with her were part of another, male-headed, village; it was only because of quarrels between her and her male matrikin that she lived in a separate settlement.

Above the headmen were the chiefs (*bamfumu*). Each *muzhi* was seen as owing allegiance to a particular chief and in the vicinity of Kibala and Bukama this was Chief Chizela. In talking about the various settlements in Kibala people would distinguish between those that were "proper" villages (*muzhi mwine*), and those that were actually part of another village even though they were living in a distinct and separate settlement. In the 1980s a *muzhi mwine* was a village where the headman had been installed with the "proper" ceremony and that was recognized as a distinct village by the local chief. The authority of a chief over "his" villages was, on the one hand, defined in the same all-encompassing way as that of the household head over his dependents and the headman over the members of his village; on the other hand, it was also vague and generalized. This was an authority seemingly accepted unquestioningly in principle but in practice virtually unenforceable—a reality recognized by the chiefs, who sensibly made no attempt to control the day-to-day lives of their ostensible subjects.

Having provided this overview of the building blocks of the kinship hierarchy, we are now ready to move on to look in more detail at the idea of social order embodied in this hierarchy and at its discourse on legitimate authority—in other words, at how it named the basic contours of power of the social landscape.

A Discourse on Authority

Within the Kaonde community of kin, as should already be apparent from the kinship terminology, the key ordering relationship was that between older (*mukulumpe*) and younger (*mwanyike*). *Mukulumpe* and *mwanyike* were the two terms of a single hierarchical relationship whereby, by definition, *mukulumpe* (older and hence senior; pl. *bakulumpe*) had authority over *mwanyike* (younger, junior, and hence subordinate; pl. *banyike*). The closest equivalents to *mukulumpe* and *mwanyike* in English are *elder* and *junior*. Like *elder* and *junior*, *mukulumpe* and *mwanyike* are relative terms meaning "older" or "younger" that were normally used only in reference to people, not things, and that could also be used to refer to a particular category of people. The net of matriliny that linked each clan member to every other and enabled fellow clan members to immediately slot each other in to an appropriate relationship automatically defined who was *mukulumpe*, who *mwanyike*.

Bakulumpe (elders) was also the term for both men and women—the term is non-gender specific—who had reached full social and political maturity. *Bakulumpe* were the decision makers; they embodied mature wisdom and experience, while *banyike* represented youthful irresponsibility. *Bakulumpe* were responsible and could be trusted to be discreet, while *banyike*, as young people themselves said, had "light tongues" and were inherently untrustworthy. Of course these are stereotypes, but stereotypes that people used to order their world. However serious and sensible a young person might be, he or she was likely to feel awkward and uneasy, particularly in a public or formal setting, about assuming the authority proper only to a *mukulumpe*. In any such settings it was *bakulumpe*, not *banyike*, who were expected to speak. *Mukulumpe* and *mwanyike* were also relative concepts, so that even a small child was *mukulumpe* to his, or her, younger brothers and sisters, while an elderly person was still *mwanyike* to his, or her, older siblings. In the course of the various interactions of daily life individuals were continually shifting in and out of being *mukulumpe* and *mwanyike*. Even the status of an acknowledged *mukulumpe* had a certain relativity. There was no single rite of passage that transformed the immature adult into a *mukulumpe*; becoming a *mukulumpe* was an incremental process that happened gradually as the individual moved through the various life stages: marriage, having children, establishing an independent household, having grandchildren, and so on. Within any given social context, however, all those involved were always hierarchically located vis-à-vis one another by clear *mukulumpe/mwanyike* relationships. The classificatory nature of Kaonde kinship terminology meant that the genealogical relationship between any two people—ideologically, if not in practice, fixed and unalterable—automatically defined the proper hierarchical relationship between them; one was always senior (*mukulumpe*) and one junior (*mwanyike*). The *mukulumpe/mwanyike* relationship provided, in fact, a basic ordering framework for every aspect of social life—from the most informal, two women meeting on the path to their fields, to the most formal, the selection of a new headman.

The hierarchical (*mukulumpe/mwanyike*) relationship lay at the heart of the Kaonde discourse on legitimate authority, as indeed it does in the discourses on authority to be found throughout rural Zambia. The basic hegemonic assumption that all human society is rightly and inevitably based on this kind of hierarchy of status and power was so taken for granted in rural Chizela that it was not even perceived as being an assumption; it was seen simply as a basic fact of nature. This "fundamental social evaluation" is, however, radically opposed to the assumption, so hegemonic in the modern discourse on citizenship and the state, of a "natural" justice based on the fundamental legal equality of individuals. There was an interesting moment in Kabompo during the 1988 IRDP replanning sessions when the incompatibility between the acceptance of certain "natural" and inescapable hierarchies, and the belief in egalitarianism—and the profoundly unsettling effect of having one's deepest beliefs brought into question—suddenly emerged with an unusual clarity. To me this moment illustrated in a very concrete way how the hegemonic, being beyond dispute, does not need to be explicitly stated but exists as an implicit presence defining the parameters of debate.

The topic being discussed by a group of young northern European expatriates and various Zambian colleagues was the progress, or lack of progress, of local co-operatives. In defending a decision not to provide support to a group of young men (a number of whom may well have been in their thirties) who wanted to form a co-operative a local Zambian official asked rhetorically, "But how can you expect young people to do anything on their own?" The shudder of collective horror that ran through the assembled ranks of young expatriates was palpable; this was blasphemy against the sacred doctrine of egalitarianism, which for those brought up in Western societies is a basic plank in their belief structure, particularly in the case of those who choose to work for something like an IRDP. But the belief that there is a natural hierarchy that places older and hence more senior people in a position of authority over those younger and therefore junior tends to be just as deep and unshakable in the minds of most rural Zambians. It is not merely that the people of Kibala and Bukama believed in the importance of hierarchy, rather the possibility of any kind of orderly human society *not* organized on the basis on such a hierarchy was, as it were, virtually unthinkable.

In Kibala and Bukama the basic model for *all* social relationships was that of the *mukulumpe/mwanyike* relationship whereby the older and senior had a general all-inclusive authority over the younger and junior, who in return for deference and the acknowledgment of their subordinate status could, in a similarly generalized and nonspecific way, legitimately expect protection, support, and help. However, while this model was hegemonic, since the obligations involved were seen in such generalized and diffuse terms, the space for negotiation was large. Similarly, while various moral claims may have been accepted unquestioningly in principle, all kinds of evasions were possible when it came to their more tangible implications. People in Kibala and Bukama—young, old, male or female—may rarely, if ever, have questioned the principle involved, but they did continually question its significance in particular cases. Was this particular headman *abusing* his authority? Was that particular *mwanyike* expecting *more* than was reasonable?

A crucial component of this authority relationship was *mushingi*, normally translated as "respect." It was *mushingi* that described the proper relationship between *mukulumpe* and *mwanyike*. An oft-repeated complaint, made particularly but not exclusively by older people, was young people's lack of respect for their elders. I asked one elderly man, for instance, how the Kaonde used to live, to which he responded by lamenting the absence nowadays of respect:

We Kaonde people used to live very differently. In those days elders were given a lot of respect [*mushingi*]. We are not given that respect. It seems the world has changed, they say Zambia now. This is how we lived in those days: we lived in villages with respect. Have you seen people respected nowadays? In those days we used to be given breast meat as gifts [i.e., if a hunter killed an animal]. The young people used to bring us breast meat. . . . The young people are saying in Zambia there is no need to respect an old person. . . . In those days when we approached the elders we would kneel down and clap [still the normal respectful way of greeting an elder], but these days they just come and stand with their hands in their pockets. (Banyinyita, Kibala, 12.viii.88, TK)

Respect, as this complaint illustrates, involved both the observance of a proper deference in speech and behavior that physically expressed subordination *and* the giving of material goods such as meat. Of course, this quotation cannot be taken as evidence that in the past the young did indeed show this degree of respect to their elders, but it does tell us something about the *ideology* of respect (*mushingi*) and how the power relation for which it was a marker, was perceived. Not to show respect brought shame (*bumvu*); and shame not only to those failing to show respect but also to their kin, who should have taught them better manners. Fear of doing or saying something shameful, of *bumvu*, was a powerful internalized sanction against any flouting of the local *mukulumpe/mwanyike* relationship and all that flowed from it.

And it was not only the young who were expected to show respect to their elders; elders, and those in positions of power generally, were also supposed to show a certain respect to those subordinate to them. This was a reciprocal relationship. Not surprisingly the importance of elders and headmen themselves showing respect tended to be stressed by younger people. My young male research assistant, for instance, put it this way: "A person can be respected if he has also got [i.e., shows] *mushingi*" (Mukwetu, Bukama, 20.xii.88, TE). The reciprocity of the *mukulumpe/mwanyike* relationship meant that just as elders were supposed to receive goods and services from their juniors, so juniors, provided they were properly deferential and accepted their subordinate status and the legitimacy (in principle at least) of the claims of elders, could themselves legitimately demand help and support (both material and nonmaterial) from those elders.

It needs to be emphasized, however, that *mushingi* was not about any kind of precisely defined jural rights; this was not a legal or contractual relationship. Rather it provided sets of expectations—albeit expectations carrying a powerful moral charge—on the basis of which individuals, in the context of specific issues, continually negotiated in their day-to-day dealings with others. The concept of *mushingi*, as it were, gathered together a loose set of moral precepts that in a very general way delineated how people were supposed to behave, and to which people would appeal to strengthen some concrete demand. At its core there was, as it were, a kind of platonic, ideal *mushingi* relationship from which the specific precepts emanated. It was this absolute, if misty, moral core that was evoked when, explicitly or implicitly, people demanded that they be accorded proper *mushingi*.

The central assumption of this Kaonde discourse on kinship and authority was that inherent in the very meaning of kinship were reciprocal relationships locking kin together in a dense and inescapable net of obligations. These obligations were at one and the same time essentially ill-defined and unbounded, and morally binding and indissoluble. These were not relationships that people could *choose*; they were not relationships freely entered into by individuals possessed of an autonomous existence outside their kinship location. Indeed, within this discourse it was difficult to imagine individuals separated from their kinship location; it was a particular location on the map of kinship, which, above all, defined who exactly an individual was. An interchange from an interview I had with an elderly headman, Mukulu, indicates something of how inescapable the responsibilities of kinship were seen as being. I had asked Mukulu about a headman's responsibility if a member of his village had to pay compensation:

Mukulu: If he has lost [i.e., a case] you as a village headman can pay for your child.

Crehan: ... Is the person then supposed to pay you back, or to work for you?

Mukulu: No, you just pay for him because he is your child. ... Where can he get it to pay you back? After all he is your child, you are the same.

(Kibala, 7.viii.88, TK)

Let me stress again, however, that what I am talking about here is an *ideology* of kinship. Mukulu's sentiments do not allow us to make any assumptions about how exactly he would have behaved in an actual case. In fact I found that it was often those who had some of the worst reputations as hard-nosed and ungenerous who were the most ready to launch into lyrical rhapsodies about selfless devotion to kin. What Mukulu's answer to me does tell us about is the assumptions within which particular claims and counterclaims were likely to be framed. Claims on a relative could be made both on the basis of being subordinate, a *mukulumpe* had an obligation to help a *mwanyike*; and of being senior, a *mwanyike* should respect a *mukulumpe*. The outcome of a specific claim in a specific context, however, would always have depended very much on the interplay of precisely those specifics.

But if it was the *mukulumpe/mwanyike* relationship that shaped the way people thought about social relations in general, how did gender fit into the picture? The answer is very simple: men had authority over women. Overriding the various hierarchies of matrilineal classification was a simple gender hierarchy that made men *mukulumpe* and women *mwanyike*. It is the basic structural components of this gender hierarchy that the next section explores. Once again, how precisely these underlying structures played out at the level of the lives of actual individuals depended on many different factors; the power relations of gender were always intertwined with other power relations. Let me stress that all I am attempting to do here is to map out certain underlying contours that give a particular shape to the power landscape within which individual women and men had to chart their own courses.

Husbands and Wives, Brothers and Sisters

In all my time in North-Western Province, whenever the subject of the relationship between women and men came up both women and men would stress that women must show respect (*mushingi*) to men. Subordination to men was a reality in which women were immersed from the moment of their birth. Not that this made women cowed victims; they were very conscious of the range of claims they had on their husbands and male matrikin and would insist on these in no uncertain terms. But these very claims, particularly those from wives that husbands should also show them proper respect—by providing them with the "clothes" that were their due, for instance—depended, as with the claims of other *banyike* (subordinates) in this kinship-based hierarchy, on their reciprocal willingness to show respect to husbands and kinsmen. I have never in any of my fieldwork trips heard any woman question the basic assumption that men have authority over women. In the case of husband and wife this authority included the legitimacy, in certain circumstances, of a husband beating his wife. At the same time women would continually accuse particular men, especially husbands, of abusing their authority in specific instances: a husband had shamed his wife by beating her *in public*, he had used unreasonable force, he had beaten her while she had a child on her back, and so on.

The assumption that men have authority over women was reflected in the kinship term used for a man's "sisters"; and, as I explained above, in this classificatory system the category of "sister" included a wide range of matrilateral parallel cousins. While *kolojanji* (elder sibling) and *nkasanji* (younger sibling) did not distinguish between male and female siblings but only between older and younger, there was another term, *nyenga* (pl. *banyenga*), which referred to all of a *man's* female siblings, irrespective of whether they were older or younger. There was no similarly inclusive term, however, for either a woman's female or male siblings. The point here is that men were seen as having authority over all their "sisters," older or younger. In terms of political authority a man was always *mukulumpe* to *banyenga*. The absence of a corresponding term for a woman's male siblings reflects the general absence of women as formally acknowledged actors within the political hierarchy. Older women were certainly recognized as *bakulumpe*, and as having some say in community decisions, but they were very clearly not acknowledged players in any formal political setting. This exclusion tended to be physically marked on such occasions as when women would be seated together in a group at some distance from the main body of men. There were a few older women who might speak up, but often the women's main vocal participation would take the form of interjections of which, formally at least, the men seemed to take little notice.

But while women were *always* subordinate (*mwanyike*) to men in some general sense, their subordination to their husbands and to their male matrikin were of very different kinds. The matrilineal principle of Kaonde descent provided a particular structure to gender relations. While the implications of this structuring may have varied over the colonial and postcolonial period, depending on the larger political context, there are certain aspects of the basic location of women vis-à-vis their husbands and male matrikin that have remained constant. In terms of her day-to-day life a married woman's primary subordination was to her husband. The nature of this subordination—at least at the level of ideology—is indicated by the English translations given by Wright of the normal Kaonde words for husband and wife. *Mwata* (husband) is translated as: "lord, husband, chief"; *mukazhi* (wife) as: "female, wife" (Wright n.d.). Similarly, a woman used the respectful second person plural when addressing her husband, while a husband used the second person singular, which was normally used when addressing children and subordinates (*banyike*). The nature of the relationship between husbands and wives is discussed at length in chapter 5, but crucially, at its heart, there was a fundamental economic interdependence. The primary division of labor in rural Chizela was one based on gender; women and men needed access to each other's labor, and the way this access was obtained on a daily basis was above all through marriage. Women were also subject to the authority of their senior male matrikin, but the nature of this authority was very different to that of a husband. The interdependence of male and female matrikin centered not on day-to-day subsistence needs but on the reproduction of the matrilineage itself.

The principles of Kaonde matriliny meant in fact that there was a fundamental split in male authority over women. On the one hand, there were a woman's matrilineal kinsmen, concerned with her reproductive potential; and on the other hand, there was her husband (who was of course not a member of the same matrilineage), concerned with her day-to-day productive capacities. Although, according to Kaonde ideology, a woman was always under some kind of male authority, the difference between the dependencies binding men and women together as husbands and wives, and as matrikin, brought into being a space for women to play off husbands against male matrikin. A constant through both the colonial period and postcolonial years of the Second Republic was the acceptance (by men as well as women) that men had an obligation to protect their kinswomen against unreasonable treatment by their husbands. Since a man's own biological children belonged to their mother's lineage and it was only through the children of his "sisters" (*banyenga*) that his own kin group (*muzhi*) was reproduced, this expectation had a very solid foundation. It was the crucial dependence of men on their "sisters" in this regard that underlay women's claims of help and support from their "brothers." As the proverb had it, "Eat with the chickens [i.e., children of *banyenga*], the guinea fowl [a man's biological children] will fly away to their homes" (Janga na banzolo, bankanga batumbuka, ke baye kwabo).

For a woman, all her *permanent* claims on men were on members of her matrilineage. The link between matrikin could never be dissolved; and since marriage did not involve the incorporation of a woman into her husband's kin group and the severing of her links with her own natal kin group, a woman remained embedded within the world of her male and female matrikin. In the past, it was claimed, a newly married woman would stay in her natal home, and for a considerable period her husband would either live with his in-laws or visit her but continue to live elsewhere. Only after some years, frequently once a number of children had been born, would a man take his wife to live in his village. Even though there has been a clear shift to virilocality in the course of the colonial and postcolonial years, with women increasingly moving to their husband's home on marriage or very soon after, in the 1980s some women, particularly those whose husbands had more than one wife, still remained living with their matrikin for considerable periods.

Matrikin, both male and female, provided women with a crucial long-term security. If, after a woman had moved to her husband's home, her husband died, left her, or was simply becoming, as local women put it, "difficult" (*bashupa*), she always had the option of retreating to one of her matrikin. Kaonde marriage involved—at least in theory—a period of labor service performed by the man for his wife's parents, and although the groom would also give some small sum of money or presents to his in-laws, in the event of a divorce there were no large payments of bridewealth that had be repaid. This meant that a woman's relatives had no material interest in ensuring she stayed with her husband. Very importantly, since a headman built up his village (*muzhi*) by attracting his kin to settle with him, a woman could always rely on one or more of her male matrikin being happy to welcome her if she wanted to leave her husband. But while a woman's male relatives may have provided her with a refuge, living without a husband could have its problems. For while her male kinsmen had a generally acknowledged moral obligation to build her a house, provide her with fields, and generally supply her with the basic goods a husband would normally be responsible for providing, enforcing such claims could be difficult. What tended to happen in the 1980s was not that a man would refuse to help his "sister" (*nyenga*), but that he would endlessly procrastinate, and a woman could find herself having to make do with some abandoned half-ruined house or a temporary grass shelter for a long period. There were few sanctions for such a woman to apply; unlike a wife, she could not withhold any of the crucial day-to-day services on which a husband relied. In other words there could be a wide gap between the acknowledgment of claims *in principle* and their translation into actually getting a new shelter built or a field prepared. A woman also had claims on the labor of her sons-in-law (again the classificatory nature of the system meant that an older woman would usually have a fair number of men she could call on in this way), but again she had few direct sanctions she could apply. However, uxorilocal marriage, which people claimed was more common in the past, would probably have given women greater power vis-à-vis their sons-in-law.

It was within the matrilineage that men too had permanent and indissoluble claims; it was his matrikin on whom a man could rely. This was an attitude summed up in the proverb, "When you travel go and see your mothers; a woman [i.e., wife] is a stranger and tomorrow she will desert you." For both women and men marriage, it seems, had an inherent fragility; a wife or husband could always leave. The ease and frequency of divorce is something that both local people in the 1980s and the colonial record describe as an enduring feature of Kaonde culture. The woman who lived closest to me in Bukama may have been something of an extreme case but not all that extreme. She was forty-one years old and currently married to her eighth husband, having had ten children by six of her husbands. The de facto power of headmen and their ability to be effective players in political life, as opposed to their de jure authority, depended on their ability to attract their kin to settle in their villages. While a woman's children "belonged" to her matrilineage in general, there was no rule as to which of her normally large array of matrikin she or her children should live with. It was accepted that in the case of divorce normally "children go with their mother," although once children were old enough to decide for themselves it was very much up to them where they chose to live. Male matrikin were always, therefore, at least in a structural sense, in competition with one another to attract their kin, and particularly their kinswomen, to their village.

Whether in the context of the matrilineage or in that of marriage, there was in both Kibala and Bukama an unquestioned male hegemony; women seemed to accept that in some general sense they were subject to the authority of their husbands and their male kinsmen. Within the arenas of political life, for instance, the formally recognized actors were normally male, and it was assumed that on formal "public" occasions women would be represented by their husbands or male kin. Women, particularly older widowed or divorced women, might occasionally occupy positions of political authority in their own right, but normally where a woman was located in the hierarchy of authority and power depended on the men, husband and matrikin, to whom she was attached. The authority of a chief or a headman, for instance, cast its glow over his wife or wives, particularly a senior wife. Similarly, being a close matrikinswoman of a chief or a powerful headman gave a woman undoubted prestige. In general the status and respect accorded a woman strengthened as she had children and grew older. A relationship that, according to Kaonde ideology, involved a particularly high degree of respect (*mushingi*) was that of mother-in-law, and there was a formal relationship of avoidance between a woman and her sons-in-law. In other words, while there was a general male hegemony, it is important to stress that this did not mean that all women were identically located. Here, however, my concern has been simply to map out the main power contours underlying gender relations as these were named by the political discourse associated with the community of kin.

Aside from gender, the other main contour of inequality within this discourse was that of age—a basic hierarchy reflected in the *mukulumpe/mwanyike* relationship. And here women could never achieve the same full *mukulumpe* status that was possible for men. In the case of men, one of the requirements for a man to be accepted as being an acknowledged *mukulumpe* (elder) was that he have access to the services of a woman. In other words, he needed to be married. No man who had to fetch his own water, cook for himself, and so on could hope to be respected as a full *mukulumpe*. Young unmarried men, and even young married men could be seen as in some sense a subordinate group, and as *banyike* they were not expected to play a major role in any formal political arena; but, of course, young men could expect in time to become part of the senior male elite, although they were likely to have to wait until they were in their mid-thirties or even longer to achieve this.

The *mukulumpe/mwanyike* relationship was at the heart of the whole hierarchical edifice of headman and chief. It was kinship with its inescapable hierarchies and its all-embracing but highly generalized and nonspecific relationships that provided the basic model of power, and it was the language of kinship that people used to talk about authority and power; it was through kinship that authority was named. But how was the hierarchy of headmen and chiefs located within the overarching hierarchies first of a colonial and then a postcolonial state? It is this question that the final section of this chapter begins to explore.

Chiefs and Headmen: Colonial and Postcolonial Transformations

The weakness of Kaonde headmen and chiefs is one of the refrains in the colonial reports right from the beginning of the colonial period. One irritated colonial official in 1913 (only fourteen years after colonization), for instance, discussing the dispersed nature of Kaonde settlements and the reluctance of people to move closer together, remarked that one of the reasons for this was "the apathy of headmen, a great many of whom seem to think that if a man was likely to cause trouble the further away he was the better."[14] From 1915 there is a note that "The Bakaonde are not accustomed to and do not like strong headmen, and with a few exceptions the chiefs and headmen are not very anxious to govern."[15] What needs to be stressed here is the following: firstly, as I argued in chapter 2, Kaonde chiefs and headmen probably never had exercised the kind of day-to-day control that colonial officials assumed to be synonymous with political authority; and secondly, that colonization and the imposition of *pax Britannica* also radically undercut the old authority structures. No longer were chiefs and headmen the only source of protection in an otherwise lawless world. Rather than representing authority itself, they were now dwarfed by the overarching might of a colonial state that had usurped whatever real powers of direct physical coercion they might once have possessed. Thirdly, however, the basic character of Kaonde political authority, as I hope my account of Kaonde kinship and its discourse has made clear, was fundamentally different from that of a modern state like Britain. Both its coercive, repressive dimension and its hegemonic, persuasive one represented a different, and far more personalized, kind of power— one not easily transferred to the bureaucratized and impersonal system that to British colonial officials defined good government.

From the beginning of colonial rule, however, the thinly stretched administration, with its handful of officials posted in rural areas, was anxious to co-opt local authority figures. Taking it for granted that all African societies were "tribal" and that this essential "tribal" identity itself defined the nature of chief and headman, the only question for the

14. ZNA, KDD 5/1, *District Notebooks, 1902–1964.*
15. ZNA, ZA/7/1/3/6, *Annual Provincial Report, Kasempa, 1915.*

colonial administration was how best to make use of these preexisting and "authentically African" entities. By 1920 we find one colonial official who, after noting that headmen and chiefs "have continued to render such assistance as one could expect from them and no more," adds complacently, "Roadmaking and tax payment are now merely regarded as matters of routine, and in these duties the Headmen do render considerable assistance."[16] But of course, whatever the reality of Kaonde headmen (*mwina muzhi*) and chiefs (*bamfumu*) prior to colonialism, that reality was the product of a particular history and a particular political context. In the quite different colonial context their substantive reality was transformed, even if this was masked by a formal continuity. The colonial administration was continually wanting to have it both ways: docile and obedient colonial servants who were also recognized as authentic and legitimate by local people. The same colonial officer who praised the headmen's help with road building and tax collection went on to note a little less happily,

Were the Divisional Headmen less obviously servants of the *Boma* I think their usefulness would be greater. They do not appear to regard themselves, or to be looked upon by the public as servants of the Chief which is their proper position.

Seven years later, in an attempt to enhance their status, the ten recognized divisional headmen in Kasempa were "provided with fez caps and with messengers or mailmen's cast-off great-coats."[17] It is difficult, however, to imagine that this would have lessened local perceptions of them as "servants of the *Boma*." Then in 1931 the role of chiefs and headmen in the colonial administration was strengthened with the introduction of Indirect Rule and the establishment of local native authorities. Once again the puppets created refused to show much evidence of independent life. As a comment from 1933 put it,

About three years have now elapsed since Native authorities were appointed for the first time, and they have never yet assembled of their own accord for discussion or deliberation, even though the idea has been placed before them by various officials on various occasions. . . . With one important exception (viz. Watchtower activity) . . . none of the authorities seem to have found it necessary to give any orders other than those that were suggested to them by the District Commissioner at the time of their appointment to be authorities.[18]

16. ZNA, ZA/7/1/4/6, *Annual Provincial Report, Kasempa, 1920.*
17. ZNA, ZA/7/1/11/6, *Annual Provincial Report, Kasempa, 1927.*
18. ZNA, ZA/7/1/16/2, *Luangwa and Kasempa Province, 1933.*

Their incorporation into the administrative hierarchy linked chiefs and headmen into the powerful coercive apparatus of the colonial state, albeit in a peripheral and ambivalent way. In theory at least, disobeying a chief or headman could bring down the wrath of that state on an offender's head. Their legitimacy as the authentic heirs of precolonial autonomy was likely to be undermined, however, if they were seen as no more than colonial stooges. In 1921 one colonial official, after noting that "control by chiefs and headmen has decreased and is decreasing, each year more speedily," made the following comment about the death of one chief. "Chief Kalilele died in January at a good old age. He was quite frank in his opposition to the white man, but yet was one of the few chiefs who seemed to exercise any real control over his people."[19] It is tempting to replace the "but yet" with "and consequently."

By the time of independence in 1964, the meaning of both chieftainship and headmanship had been redefined by more than sixty years of colonial rule. After all, only the very old by that point would have had any personal experience of how things were prior to colonialism. In addition both the colonial administrators and the "tribal" office holders had an interest in stressing the formal continuity—a continuity that lent the system of Indirect Rule whatever legitimacy it had—rather than the actual substantive transformations.[20] Independence and the replacement of the colonial administration by a Zambian one did not alter the fact that Kaonde chiefs and headmen were now inextricably embedded within formal state institutions in a way they had not been prior to colonization. After independence a House of Chiefs was established that was envisaged as a form of second chamber to the Zambian Parliament, but this was never a very significant player in the national arena. Although chiefs were stripped of much of the local juridical power they had had under Indirect Rule, local chiefs retained their own courts, to which many local disputes continued to be brought, particularly those concerning accusations of witchcraft. In formal terms, chiefs and headmen during the Second Republic existed essentially as a parallel and clearly subordinate hierarchy of authority in a sometimes uneasy, and not very clearly defined, relationship with UNIP and its government. The story as regards the substantive, as opposed to the formal, reality is

19. ZNA, ZA/7/1/5/6, 1920–21.
20. See Channock (1985) for an extended discussion of the complicated interactions between the colonial state and "tribal" authorities that resulted in the invented tradition of "customary law."

more complex with wide regional differences.[21] Let me stress again that my account here is limited to the situation in Chizela and Kaonde chiefs and headmen.

So far I have stressed the rupture that colonialism represented, but this is not the whole picture. The old kinship-based hierarchies did not lose all their power, even if they were now part of a far wider world in which there were other competing forms of authority. Not only was there the overarching might of the colonial administration, there were also, for instance, the various forms of spiritual and practical missionary authority, as well as the whole other world of the mines and the towns to which so many men (and some women) migrated for work. So what kind of authority did chiefs and headmen continue to exercise, and what were the spheres in which it was effective?

As I have argued in my account of the Kaonde discourse on authority, this was a theory of power in which dominance was justified with reference to the inescapable moral norms that defined the community of kin. The hegemony of kinship authority—the way, that is, it constructed consent—was based on the notion of a fundamental and beneficial reciprocity binding together senior and subordinate (*mukulumpe* and *mwanyike*). According to the ideology, this was an authority that wove a social fabric out of morally right and mutually beneficial obligations. With colonization and the loss of the power of direct coercion, the *moral* dimension of chiefly authority and that of headmen became ever more the essence of this authority. There is perhaps a parallel here with the common phenomenon throughout Africa whereby conquering people continued to acknowledge and respect the spiritual power of displaced autochthonous chiefs. Certainly in the 1980s the authority of Kaonde headmen and chiefs was above all a moral authority. A chief represented the pinnacle of the pyramid of kinship: he (or very occasionally she) was the ultimate *mukulumpe* representing the widest net of authority. Chiefs, for instance, were described as owning the land; the local chief was *mwina kyalo* (the "owner" of the country). The term *mwina*, however, has a wider and more flexible range of meanings than *owner* does in English; here the sense is rather "has authority over."[22] While people

21. See van Binsbergen (1987) for an analysis of Zambian chiefs in the postcolonial period.

22. Wright's Kaonde-English word list (Wright n.d.) gives the following meanings for *mwina*: "owner of" (e.g., *mwina kabwa* [dog]), "adherent" (e.g., *mwina Kilishitu* [Christ]), "citizen" (e.g., *mwina kyalo* [country]); for *mwina muzhi*: "headman, villager"; for *mwina nzubo*: "host, householder." *Mwina*, therefore, includes ownership of something like a dog-

recognized that in practice a chief's rights had been circumscribed by the state, the chief was still described as having an ultimate moral authority over everything that happened within their area. For example, I asked the chairman of Bukama's co-operative society if the chief had a role in the society, and he told me yes. However, when I pressed him on what this role was, it emerged that in practice the chief had nothing whatsoever to do with the society. Yet to come straight out and say that there was anything that was outside the jurisdiction of the chief as "owner of the land" would not only be a sign of great disrespect (a lack of *mushingi*), but in terms of an underlying moral authority would also be untrue. When I asked Chizela's district governor about the role of the chief in allocating large areas of land for farms to people coming from outside the area, his answer revealed some tension and ambivalence about the reality of the chief's powers:

We have allowed our chiefs to operate in this country so we have to give them some powers, so somebody wants to put a farm in such an area he will have to go and see the chief, but the chiefs are aware about our policies, they have been told that we want people to go into intensified farming. Now where there is open land and it is free from human habitation, it should be given to those who are interested in farming. (Chizela District Centre, 26.xii.88, TE)

When I went on to ask if this meant the chief's consent was something of a formality, the district governor said in effect yes, since all the land in Zambia is ultimately vested in the president.

One aspect of a belief that, no matter what the formal legal position might have been, the chief was still in some sense the owner of the land was the belief that chiefs were the ones with the most powerful *bwanga* (medicines and skills associated with the realm of *balozhi* [witches] and *bulozhi* [witchcraft]), and that anybody who fell foul of a chief risked some kind of "mystic" punishment, such as sickness. How far a chief's power of this kind was purely defensive against *balozhi*, and how far a chief himself might practice *bulozhi*, was hedged around with ambiva-

---

(and *mwina* would also be used in relation to owning inanimate objects, such as a hoe), and the authority of a headman (lit. "owner of the village") or chief. In addition, it could also be used for membership in a community such as the Christian Church or a modern state, or being a member of a village. It is only the context that makes it clear whether *mwina muzhi* means "member of a village" or "village headman." Significantly, *mwina* does not distinguish between the rights over "property" (i.e., something that can be owned and that has no rights vis-à-vis its owner) and authority rights over people.

lence — not least because accusing such a powerful figure of using *bulozhi* was fraught with danger. It seemed to be generally assumed in rural Chizela, however, that *all* positions of power and authority within the local community were, almost by definition, entangled with *bulozhi*. The pervasive fear of *bulozhi* in this context can be seen more generally, I would argue, as stemming from a sense that in order to occupy any position of power or authority a person must have the acceptance of the local "owners" of the land, those, in other words, in whom inheres the general moral authority of *mukulumpe* vis-à-vis *mwanyike*. This applied not only in the case of the old hierarchies of chiefs and headmen, but extended to the new UNIP ones. In chapter 6 I look in detail at *bulozhi* beliefs.

Some Zambian chiefs have succeeded in establishing themselves as significant figures of power in the new postcolonial Zambia, but this was not true of any Kaonde chiefs as of 1990. Local chiefs and headmen were, however, thoroughly enmeshed in the political hierarchies of the postcolonial state, just as the concrete realities into which the Zambian state was translated in Kibala and Bukama were threaded through with strands deriving from the moral universe of kinship. It is these realities with which the next chapter is concerned.

CHAPTER 4

Political Locations II:
Citizens and Kin

We visited the school on the education of the masses on voting for the forthcoming presidential and general election.

> Entry in Kibala school log book, signed
> by various government officials and
> Chief Chizela, 8.iv.78

By [i.e., because of] your visit sir, the road from the turn off to here has been graded and we request you to be visiting us once or twice a year.[1]

> Minutes of Kibala Ward meeting, 21.viii.87

A tradesman does not join a political party in order to do business, nor an industrialist in order to produce more at lower cost, nor a peasant to learn new methods of cultivation.

> Antonio Gramsci,
> *Selections from the Prison Notebooks*

This chapter is about how the state, as embodied in the specific form of Zambia's Second Republic, was lived as a day-to-day reality in the rural Chizela of the 1980s. In it I explore some of the concrete ways in which the state was both a coercive power and engaged in the construction of hegemony. I also look at the complicated inter-

---

1. This is from a speech written by Sansoni and recorded in the ward minutes in English. It was delivered (first in English, then in a Kaonde translation by one of the teachers) on the occasion of a visit by a high-ranking politician (MCC [Member of the Central Committee]) to Kibala.

twining of the discourses of citizenship and kinship, at the kind of political landscape this created, and at how this landscape was gendered. I want to begin this mapping of rural Chizela's political terrain with a brief account of the revived Kaonde ceremony of Ntongo as I witnessed it in 1988.

Ntongo

Ntongo is a firstfruits ceremony in which each village headman takes a calabash of beer made from the newly harvested sorghum to the chief to whom he owes allegiance. The roots of the ceremony lie in the precolonial past, but during the colonial period it was either, as some people told me, forbidden, or more probably simply lapsed. It was revived in 1986, according to Chief Chizela, at the prompting of UNIP: "UNIP said our old customs like *Ntongo* should begin again" (Bukama, 2.xi.88, TK). The modern Ntongo needs to be seen not as the assertion of a surviving primordial Kaonde identity, but as a particular performance of "Kaondeness" within the arena of the postcolonial Zambian state. However much it may have drawn on some notional "tradition," it was a modern event belonging to the moment in which it was taking place, and was a product of that moment. The meaning of "being Kaonde" in the 1980s was inextricably bound up with being a Zambian citizen, and as such could not but be caught up in the struggles of the Kaunda regime to sustain not merely a coercive power but also a genuine hegemony.

Kaonde chiefs may never have been very powerful, but in common with chiefs in much of rural Zambia they have continued to be seen locally as possessed of an ultimate *moral* authority within their region— an authority that UNIP was anxious to appropriate. One form this appropriation took was the encouragement of local "tribal" ceremonies, which were seen as helping to build an "authentic" Zambian identity that would both acknowledge the multiple precolonial regional "traditions" and also locate them firmly within the modern postcolonial state. Part of what these ceremonies conducted within the arena of the national state were about was the attachment of local and particular chiefly legitimacies to the wider legitimacy of "the Party and its government."

Part of the pressure for the revitalization, resurrection, and in some cases creation of "traditional" ceremonies undoubtedly derived from the importance of these in the competition between different Zambian "tribes." Officially, tribalism was denounced as an evil that "the Party and its government" was bent on rooting out wherever it was to be found. Inevitably, however, competition over scarce resources involves competition between different regions, and one way in which this expresses itself is in various forms of tribalism. Impressive and authentic "tribal" ceremonies have become an important assertion of "tribal" identity, particularly since the advent of television means that there is now a huge new audience to which the performance of "tribal" identity can be given, an audience that is national rather than local. Increasingly the form and character of a traditional ceremony is shaped to an important extent by its final destination, the nation's television screens. And the format used to locate the different "traditions" on the grand map of the national mosaic, particularly when the medium is television, is not a product of individual, local "traditions" or even a national Zambian one. Rather the format here draws heavily on the narrative devices and forms of representation developed in the West within the genre of documentary ethnographic film.[2] As a consequence what qualifies as "authentic" and traditional, even within Zambia, tends to be filtered through a Western prism of "the genuinely African." This is yet another example of what hegemony can mean in practice.

The Ntongo I attended in 1988 was the third since the ceremony's resurrection. It was held one afternoon in June at Chief Chizela's capital just outside Chizela township. The ceremony had not achieved the crucial accolade of being televised for the National Broadcasting Service but its staging as an event had clearly been influenced by other televised ceremonies. It did, however, have something else that has become a regular part of "traditional" Zambian ceremonies: the specially produced T-shirt printed with the ceremony's name and date, and a silk-screened photo of the chief. Those attending included, in addition to those headmen acknowledging allegiance to Chief Chizela, all the local dignitaries from UNIP, the Member of the Central Committee (MCC), the provincial parliamentary secretary, and so on. Much of the long afternoon was taken up with speeches by the various notables, all of which were first delivered in English and then translated by an interpreter into Kaonde.

---

2. Crawford and Turton (1992) collects together a particularly interesting set of articles on film and ethnography.

The proceedings were opened with a dance by a well known local diviner dressed in a leopard skin. Most of the village headmen in attendance wore Western-style suits, usually far from new but carefully preserved for such formal occasions. A number of men on this hot afternoon wore heavy, worsted three-piece suits. The district governor, dressed like the other party notables in an elegant safari suit, then delivered his speech, stressing unity and how the people of Zambia are one no matter where they may live. It was then the turn of the MCC, whose performance illustrates the way the Party's rhetoric—in general a modernist one stressing the importance of "development"—was often interwoven with a different rhetoric appealing to notions of "authentic" Zambian "tradition." He began by donning a *chitenge*—the two-meter length of cloth normally worn by women but also sometimes by village men when they dance—over his safari suit and launching into a UNIP "song of unity" to which the audience was invited to sing along, which a few duly did, though with a conspicuous lack of enthusiasm. While singing the MCC danced up to the chief and made the traditional offering, an action that within the local chief/headman hierarchy would be a clear statement of subordination on the part of the one making the offering. The fact that the MCC could do this without there being any danger of its being taken as anything more than a purely symbolic gesture of recognition of "our common Zambian heritage" indicates just how much chiefs have been stripped of any real power. Having, as it were, linked himself to Kaonde "tradition," the MCC then began his speech proper, a prominent theme of which was UNIP and the coming presidential election. Kaunda (K.K.) was the only candidate for the presidency, and there was no possibility of his not being elected. Nonetheless, faced with Kaunda's rapidly declining popularity, the UNIP machinery had been charged with ensuring that people did actually cast a vote and that there would be the proper impressive number of "yes" votes for Kaunda. The MCC told his audience how important the coming election was, and how pleased he was to see that Chizela District was solidly behind K.K. He also stressed the importance of "traditional" ceremonies such as Ntongo in encouraging the development of agriculture.

The response of the sizable audience who had gathered to watch the proceedings was difficult to gauge. The attendance of party and government officials at all important public occasions was accepted and expected, just as they were expected to deliver the same well-worn homilies that they always repeated on their periodic rounds of local ward meetings. Speeches within the public arena, whether by representatives of the state or anyone else, were expected to follow certain rhetorical forms. When local people questioned visiting politicians they would normally use a highly deferential mode of address (patterned on that of the *mukulumpe/mwanyike* hierarchy) even when they were trying to press certain demands. This deference was reflected in a speech of welcome given to the MCC in 1987 and recorded in the minutes of the Kibala ward record. Prior to listing a long series of complaints and demands, there was a fulsome preamble part of which ran as follows:

Today is an important occasion in that we are able to share ideas and also to carefully and properly map out a future and right course for the Party's activities in Kibala ward. This is a step in the right direction since you will educate us on many matters concerning the Party and its government on which perhaps we up to now had been ignorant. (Minutes of Munyambala Ward meetings, 21.viii.87 [recorded in English])

For a westerner, and particularly a Britisher, it is difficult not to hear at least a hint of irony here, but this is probably to respond ethnocentrically. Occasionally someone, often someone who had been drinking, would ask questions of a visiting dignitary in a more straightforward and less deferential way. But this always seemed to give rise, after the important personage had departed, to a lot of head shaking and condemnation of this shocking breach of manners that would bring shame (*bumvu*) on the whole community. Perhaps the most important effect of all the UNIP speeches to the grass roots was that just by their physical presence, and their repetition of the expected phrases, politicians and bureaucrats reaffirmed the reality of the state. They were tangible proof that "Zambia" did indeed exist.

Not that the sighting of officials at such events was the only evidence people had of the state; the state, as embodied in UNIP and the apparatuses of government was most certainly a real presence in Kibala and Bukama. People understood very well the hegemonic power it represented, symbolized, for instance, in the official registration cards that everybody was supposed to carry, and virtually all did. While the bureaucratic hierarchy of UNIP and the kinship hierarchy of chiefs and headmen did not in reality occupy distinct spheres, local people nonetheless made a clear distinction between them. Despite the colonial overtones everyone in rural Chizela continued to use the term *Boma* to refer to the world of officialdom associated with the modern Zambian state. Also normally included within the category "Boma" were the IRDP and *magermani*. In Chizela local people made a clear distinction between Chizela, which meant to them Chief Chizela's capital, a small settlement located just outside the district center, and the district center itself, the town of Chizela. Nobody in Kibala or Bukama would ever say, "I am going to Chizela" to mean they were going to Chizela town; they would say, "I'm going to the Boma."

The officials might have been Zambian rather than British, but to most of those living in rural Chizela in the 1980s the world of the Boma still represented a distinct and different universe, and one that often seemed to be in opposition to their own world. Even if the Boma was no longer associated with a colonial state, it still represented the concrete reality of the state at the local level. It was still the embodiment of all those things that the government in Lusaka tried to get local people to do, like producing more maize for the national market, building their own schools and clinics; and everything that it tried to prevent people from doing, such as unlicensed hunting, distilling spirits, or spending part of the year living by their fields out in the bush. Not that the Boma was only an oppressive presence; it also represented a state that, as local people saw it, had clear obligations towards them, its citizens. It *ought* to provide schools, hospitals, and roads, not to mention the marketing facilities essential if the grain they were continually being urged to produce was to be sold. The Boma was all those official institutions such as the District Council and the Department of Agriculture that controlled so many of the key resources on which villagers depended. There was no doubt in people's minds as to the value of those resources or to the reality of their dependence on the Boma.

At one meeting organized by the IRDP that I attended, for instance, an IRDP official explained to those assembled how they should organize themselves through various self-help schemes so that projects begun by the IRDP would continue after the program was phased out. As usual, after the speeches questions were invited from the audience. One of the small minority of women present expressed a certain skepticism, although her question was framed in properly deferential terms, in line with the conventions of the *mukulumpe/mwanyike* hierarchy. The LIMA groups were still young, she said, and if the IRDP abandoned them now, how could they manage? Local people had no idea how to produce fertilizer, for example (Chizela, 23.vi.88, NE). Those living in the rural areas and those belonging to the Boma can be seen as engaged in an ever continuing dialogue of claims and counterclaims. It was, however, the language in which the Boma voices spoke, and the Boma's naming of rural reality that was hegemonic. It is what those Boma eyes saw when they looked at the rural areas, and how they named those who lived there, that is the subject of the next section.

UNIP at the Grass Roots

If what the people of Kibala and Bukama saw when they looked toward the world of officialdom looming in authority over them was the "Boma," what the politicians and government officials saw when they looked toward the rural "masses" was likely to be "villagers," whom they of the Boma had a duty to mobilize, lead, educate, and generally control. Politicians, government officials and the educated elite often used the term *villager* in a disparaging sense to mean someone who, rather than embracing the ideals of progress and development, clung stubbornly to an outmoded and backward-looking tradition. To make it clear where I am speaking of "villages" and "villagers" in the negative tones of the Boma, I have used quotation marks. The pejorative Boma tone echoed through an interview I had with Chizela's district governor. It was apparent, for instance, when the governor was explaining to me how his main concern as regards the Bukama settlement scheme was the amount of marketable surplus its farmers were producing. As so often, it seems that the farmers here are assumed to be male.

Mainly we want to look at the results every year, what are they producing. If the production goes down then we have to go in to say, "Gentlemen, what's happening? You are turning these places into villages." (Chizela District Centre, 26.xii.88, TE)

And the answer to this problem? In the eyes of those in the Boma it was above all *education*, as the district governor went on to tell me with particular reference to the failure of "villagers" to increase the area cultivated each year and generally engage in accumulation: "Unfortunately, as I was saying, we are still having problems because some people are still having this village thinking. We need to be continually educating." (26.xii.88, TE)

In the day-to-day struggles between the Boma and those in the rural areas, with local people asserting their claims on the state and the politicians and government officials striving to implement government policy—such as greater production for the national market—this cry for education was continually heard from those on the Boma side of the divide. The dominant image of the relation between the state and those in the rural areas was that of teacher and pupil. The state was seen as an educator leading "villagers" out of the ignorant dark of backward thinking into the shining day of development. This is how the district governor put it when I asked him to define development:

You [KC] have seen these people in the rural areas, you have been in Kibala, you have been in Bukama: first of all we have to develop their minds, to conscientise them, to make them know how to live a better life. That is also development. . . . This is how I look at development, it is some sort of movement from a primitive level to an enlightened level. You see? . . . Some people would like to go on scratching a piece of land; one *lima* as long as it is enough for the person to eat that person is happy, but that is not good. We want them to produce more, let them eat and the surplus should be sold so that they can meet other commitments. (26.xii.88, TE)

Inextricably bound up with the notion of the backward "villager" was its opposite, the progressive farmer, a tireless warrior in the struggle for development, who was defined by all that the "villager" was not. When government officials and the like used the term *farmer* they normally meant not simply someone whose livelihood is derived from the cultivation of a piece of land, but specifically one who sold at least some of his or her crop to the national market and whose cultivation was based on "modern" and "scientific" methods, such as the use of fertilizer. As we shall see in the next chapter this clear opposition between the categories "villager" and "farmer" was reproduced in the distinction that the people of Kibala and Bukama themselves made between ordinary cultivation (*kujima*) and "farming" (*mwafwamu*). This Boma definition of farming had the effect of excluding the majority of Chizela's rural inhabitants from being thought of as farmers, consigning them to the ranks of those who act as a brake on "development," an inert mass of "villagers" to be educated. For instance, the Solwezi district agricultural officer told me when I first arrived in North-Western Province in 1988 how out of Chizela's total rural population (something over 10,000 in 1980 [GRZ 1988b]) his department was actually working with 2,700 people, little more than a quarter. These, he explained, were those belonging, in his words to "active farm families." He went on to tell me in the same interview how there were some very enthusiastic farmers in Chizela District because "farming has not been long in Chizela" (NE).

In other words, local sorghum-based cultivation with its long history simply did not count as farming.

While "the masses" may not have supinely accepted the Boma's view of them, the Boma and its naming of social realities nonetheless exerted a powerful hegemonic force throughout rural Zambia. So that even if local people had their own ways of seeing things, in their dealings with state institutions and officials it was difficult for them to escape Boma definitions of reality; if "the masses" wanted the state to hear them, they had to use the names and the language recognized by the state; and they had to speak from where the state located them. But even more insidious and difficult to overcome is the power of a hegemonic discourse to make its definitions of reality the *only* definitions, and its names the *only* names—as when people in Kibala and Bukama apparently accepted that their ordinary sorghum cultivation was not "real" farming (see p. 162).

The people of rural Chizela made a clear, if implicit, distinction between the world of the Boma and their own world structured around the community of kin. As long as they remained in the latter they felt at home and comfortable, and would resent Boma interference, but once they felt themselves to be on the Boma's territory this confidence tended to evaporate. The attitude was rather "the Boma is a foreign country: they do things differently there; and strangers in that country have no choice but to abide by its rules." To avoid being misunderstood, let me stress that I am using spacial *metaphors* here. The Boma world was also very much a part of Kibala and Bukama. Not only were there people living there, particularly the teachers and other government employees, who were seen, and who saw themselves, as belonging to the Boma world; even within individuals themselves there could be this divide. In certain areas of their lives or in certain contexts a teacher, for example, might identify with the Boma and speak with the Boma's voice in exhorting local people to send their children to school, while in others, such as his own forays into the officially condemned fish trading, he might think of himself more as a member of the local community. Even those who were clearly not part of the Boma world might well use the pejorative language of the Boma to criticize the shortcomings of their neighbors or fellow kin, describing them as "uneducated" and backward, for example. Let me also stress that what I am concerned with here is a separation that existed primarily at the level of discourse—a separation that people used *to name* the basic reality within which they lived their lives but that did not necessarily correspond in any simple way to a dichotomy in that reality itself.

During the period of the Second Republic it was UNIP that provided the organizing framework for the Boma. The government was UNIP, a relationship summed up in the slogan that was heard everywhere, "the Party and its government." And it was the Party's structure that constituted the country's administrative structure.

At the base of the administrative pyramid was the ward. Kibala with its thirty-something settlements constituted one ward, while Bukama was part of a larger ward. Each ward had a committee elected by all its UNIP members, the key members of whom were the chairman, vice-chairman, secretary, and treasurer. According to the UNIP constitution each ward was also supposed to elect a number of other officials, such as a publicity secretary, but in Kibala, and in this it was probably representative of many remote rural wards, the precise composition of the ward committee and the manner of its selection were determined by the ward's chairman, vice-chairman, and secretary decided was necessary or possible. In addition to the ordinary UNIP members there were also youth (men up to the age of 35) and women's sections. Since the ward chairman was elected solely by UNIP members, only a minority of the ward's inhabitants were involved—and an even smaller minority of women. In Kibala in 1988, for instance, there were a total of 329 UNIP members: 148 men, 46 women, and 135 youth (all men) out of a total adult population of close to 800.[3] In all local political arenas, positions of power within the ward tended to be monopolized by older men. Although in theory a ward chairman could have been a woman, in practice this was virtually unheard of and there were no female ward chairmen in Chizela District. It was the ward and the ward chairman who provided local people with their primary representation within "the Party and its government." In the late 1980s the main decision-making body at the district level was—at least in formal terms—the district council, and it was the local ward chairmen who made up its voting councillors. Decision making within the Second Republic always remained highly centralized, however, and in practice rural councils had very few real powers, particularly since they had almost no income of their own. Chizela District Council was particularly impoverished.

The ward chairman was both the primary UNIP representative *within* his area and at the same time the main representative *of* his area within

3. The UNIP membership figures are taken from the Munyambala ward secretary's records, the population figure from GRZ (1988b:28).

the formal structures of government. This dual role necessarily involved a certain amount of conflict since the definition of UNIP's role down among "the masses" was rather different depending on who was doing the defining. For those looking down from the Boma a key theme, as always when officialdom contemplated "villagers," was the mobilizing and educative function of local officials. From this vantage point the responsibility of ward officials was, as Kibala's ward secretary, the teacher Sansoni put it, "to encourage people to do farming, to educate them as to what their role is as citizens of Zambia and to teach them the modern methods of farming" (Kibala, 2.vii.88, NE). Or, in the words of the district governor, the ward chairman's role was

to organise the Party in his ward and to get involved in development projects. Now here we have agreed that we have to get some of these things done on [a basis of] self-help in view of our financial problems, now it is for the ward chairman to mobilise the people and come up with self-help projects . . . the ward chairman has to be very, very active in mobilising, but the most important thing is to make sure the Party is well understood in his area. (Chizela District Centre, 26.xii.88, TE)

In sum, the Boma expected the ward chairman as UNIP representative to explain and implement the policies laid down by the Party, and to propagate "modern" notions of citizenship and "development." At its most basic this could translate into simply ensuring that there was some kind of formal party structure at the village level. Kabaya, Kibala's ward chairman (a less sophisticated man than Sansoni and not as well versed in Party rhetoric) explained that what was important was

to persuade people to build houses so that it is easy to allocate branches and sections—if you do this even the Government will recognise you. Also to sell [Party] cards to local people and address public meetings. (Kibala, 7.ix.88, NK)

As the Boma saw it, grassroots party organizations were there to carry the word of "the Party and its government" down into the dark reaches of "village" ignorance; and ward chairmen were first and foremost *their* representatives charged with the task of imposing a Boma view of things on "villagers."

As might be expected, what the people of Kibala and Bukama themselves wanted and expected from their ward chairman was not always the same as what the Boma wanted and expected. They tended to put far less stress on the educative function of ward chairmen. Also, not surprisingly perhaps, how people described the role of ward chairman tended to be very similar to the way they described that of headmen in the past. During the colonial years headmen had indeed had just this Janus-faced role of state representative at the local level and representative of the local within the state.[4] Two of the LIMA group chairmen in Kibala defined the role of the ward chairman as follows:

The chairman's work is: one, to supervise the whole ward, are the people doing well? Two, to see how they are cultivating, does everybody have food? Three, have they built good houses? Four, to see how they are living, are they staying together in harmony and peace? (Mulonda, Kibala, 14.viii.88, TK)

The ward chairmen are there to help the people in their areas, and to help them with cultivation. To help them live in peace without fighting. . . . Ward chairmen are doing the same work that was done by [chiefs and headmen] in the past. (Tyemba, Kibala, 15.viii.88, TK)

It would seem that at least to some extent UNIP's administrative hierarchy had been mapped onto the older hierarchies of headman and chief, or at any rate onto these as they had come to be understood during the colonial period. This perceived continuity with the older chiefly hierarchy was similarly reflected in one elderly man's explanation of how Kibala became a separate ward: "We brought up the matter as to why Kibala who is a great chief had not been given a ward" (Kibala, 23.viii.88, TK).

Although the ward chairman was not a paid functionary of the state, as local representative of "the Party and its government" he had a responsibility to see that government policy was carried out. The coercive dimension of this was very clear to local people, however much the official rhetoric might frame it as "education." In their daily life people were continually confronted by the state as a repressive presence. Local hunters were hedged around with laws telling them when they could and could not hunt, what methods they were allowed to use, and that they must buy licenses before killing animals. Even if these regulations were normally ignored, the game guards charged with enforcing them had become yet another hazard of the always dangerous business of hunting. Similarly, when local women wanted to take advantage of one of the few sources of income available to them, selling alcohol, in theory

---

4. See Barnes, Mitchell, and Gluckman (1949) for some reflections by RLI anthropologists on this reality.

this was subject to state regulation. Many women brewed grain beer for sale, and some also distilled it into a fearsomely strong spirit, *lutuku*. Although the regulations seemed rarely if ever enforced, the distilling of *lutuku* was illegal and known to be so. Even the brewing of beer was supposed to be controlled by headmen (a legacy of their colonial role) and ward chairmen. Periodically word would come down from the Boma that there was too much beer brewing, and that this was preventing people from working in the fields and must be curtailed on pain of a fine by the local court. And for a short period women might be frightened off brewing.

Another point at which the state confronted local people—especially those attempting to run some kind of business—as a tangible and coercive presence was the price inspector. Until the late 1980s the price of many commodities, including all the industrially produced goods local shopkeepers brought back from town, were state regulated with party officials being given the task of ensuring that shopkeepers did not charge more than the permitted markup. Those found doing so could be fined or even have their trading licenses revoked. Enforcement of the price regulations depended on complaints of overcharging being taken by local people to UNIP officials in the district center who would then visit and check on the traders accused. Both the ward chairman and the most prominent entrepreneur in Kibala had had uncomfortable experiences with price control inspectors (this second case is dealt with in more detail in chapter 6). In practice a ward chairman seemed only to adopt an actively coercive role when directly pressured to do so by the Boma, and even then, as with the regulation of brewing, this tended to remain at the level of impressively fierce, but ultimately empty, rhetorical pronouncements. After all, not only had he to live with those subject to such prohibitions, and their likely anger, he also needed their votes if he were to be reelected.

In addition to representing UNIP within the ward, the ward chairman was also the primary representative *of* the ward within the wider party structures. In theory, it was through their ward chairman that people could articulate their demands and make claims on the state. A ward chairman was expected to fight for the interests of his community and to secure for them the maximum possible share of government resources. As Mulonda put it when I asked him about the role of the ward chairman in the Boma,

When the ward chairman goes to the *Boma*, his responsibility is to take a report[5] to the District Governor telling him what is needed in the ward. The chairman should tell the District Governor about all the problems in his area and persuade him to help the people there. (Kibala, 14.viii.88, TK)

But while local people may have seen their ward chairman as some kind of representative of their interests within the world of "the Party and its government," for them UNIP was not an entity that articulated their specific interests or struggled for them. For people in Kibala and Bukama what UNIP represented was not so much a political party as a particular manifestation of the state itself. They would doubtless have agreed with Gramsci that "a peasant does not join a political party to learn new methods of cultivation." It is true that there was a lot of official rhetoric along the lines of the following formulation from the section on co-operatives in the Fourth National Development Plan.

The overall objectives of the Co-operative Programme 1989–93, is to improve the standard of living and quality of life of the people of Zambia, especially the disadvantaged groups in both rural and urban areas, including women and youths through the successful practice of participatory democracy, equitable distribution and mutual self-help. (GRZ 1989:423)

But however much talk there might be about "participatory democracy," local people had no illusions about the nature of the underlying power relations. They never forgot that, in Gramsci's words, "there are rulers and ruled"; and as far as they were concerned, it was the Boma that wrote the rules while they were the ones who were ruled. Of course, they had plenty of ways of evading the Boma's rules, particularly when these concerned something like hunting which was felt most definitely not to be "a thing of the Boma," but it is important not to confuse the ability to evade particular rules with the overturning of basic hegemonic power relations.

Beginning with the colonial period there has always been an underlying opposition between the state and local communities as regards access to resources of one kind or another and the nature of the respective claims the state and "the masses" have on one another. This opposition may often have expressed itself in hidden and unacknowledged ways, but these were struggles nonetheless, struggles stemming from a genuine structural opposition. The official channel through which local communities were supposed to have access to the ear of the state and

5. Mulonda himself used the English term *report* here.

its decision-making processes was that of the UNIP ward, making the ward chairman a potentially key figure. It was he who was supposed to take local claims on the state into the decision-making arenas of "the Party and its government" and press for them. In reality, however, the powers of ward chairmen to act as lobbyists for their community were very circumscribed. In theory their role as voting members of the District Council should have given them a certain leverage, but since the District Council itself was such a powerless body, little could be achieved through it, especially by a lone ward chairman.

At the same time it was possible for a skillful ward chairman to use his formal and informal links with the Boma to secure for himself and his close associates preferential access to scarce state-controlled resources. Demand for the maize flour sold by the state monopoly often outstripped supply, and there was always a problem transporting it from the district center; an effective ward chairman could ensure that a supply (often for resale locally) reached him. Similarly, he could "persuade" the marketing lorries to visit his area. In a situation of scarcity, in which *all* state services were in chronically short supply, wards were necessarily in competition with one another. In line with the ethos of hierarchy and the *mukulumpe/mwanyike* relationship, it was accepted that those, like ward chairmen, in positions of authority were perfectly entitled to benefit personally from their office; what was important was, firstly, that they were *effective* in their struggles with the state, and secondly, that they did not monopolize the benefits. Local people demanded some "trickle-down effect," even if they accepted that the amount trickling down would be concentrated among the power elite and would be pretty exiguous beyond that.

What little real de facto power ward chairmen had vis-à-vis the Boma stemmed primarily from the potential threat that "the masses" might withdraw their support from "the Party and its government." Not that this threat was articulated explicitly either by local representatives or Boma officials, but it lurked as an unspoken presence in all relations between Boma and "the masses." Zambia may have been a one-party state in the 1980s and organized opposition to UNIP may have been forbidden, but the government still needed to exert a hegemonic and not merely a coercive control. The legitimacy of "the Party and its government" rested on the assumption that in some sense it represented the interests of "the masses." And indeed once it became clear—as was already happening during my fieldwork—that UNIP and Kaunda had lost the trust and goodwill of the vast majority of Zambians, the whole one-party edifice rapidly crumbled. UNIP's rhetorical definition of itself as "the militant vanguard of revolutionary peasants, workers, students and intellectuals"[6] necessarily assumed an implicit contract whereby the Party received the support of "the masses" in return for which the Party looked after "the masses'" interests. While both politicians and "the masses" understood that the rhetoric should not be taken too seriously, it did provide an important framework for the continual struggle between local people and politicians over their competing claims on one another. From the local community's perspective the basic character of their relationship with "the Party and its government" was essentially that of a *mukulumpe/mwanyike* relationship; it was their acknowledgment of the legitimacy (in principle at least) of the Party's claims on them that gave them their claims on the Party. And just as a headman (*mukulumpe*) who failed to provide the members of his village (*banyike*) with the expected help and support was liable to find himself deserted, once the Party disappointed too many local expectations it too was liable to find its "masses" absenting themselves, as was already happening in the late 1980s.

To lobby effectively for his ward, a ward chairman needed to be a skilled operator in the political world beyond his community. Although the politics of patronage were an important element in this world—as indeed, whether overtly or covertly, they also are to varying degrees in modern bureaucratic states—the *formal* structures of power and the language of power were bureaucratic. Local ward chairmen, who came out of a political environment dominated by a discourse of power explicitly based on the *mukulumpe/mwanyike* relationship of patronage, were often very skillful clients, but they nonetheless remained enormously disadvantaged in the Boma world. This was true not least because the language of officialdom was English, which very few in rural Chizela (almost none of whom were women) spoke and even fewer felt confident in. Since it was UNIP policy not to post officials to their home areas, within the Boma world English was a genuine lingua franca as well as the official language of government. In addition, even if "the Party and its government" were anxious to maintain some level of local support, those in a distant rural backwater like North-Western Province were certainly not an important constituency. As far as the UNIP politicians

6. GRZ, UNIP Constitution, 1988a.

and bureaucrats were concerned, Chizela "villagers" had little with which to bargain.

Ward chairmen had to operate both in the Boma world and in their local community. They needed to be able to work within the bureaucratic structures of the Party and government, with their committees, minutes, points of order and their rhetoric of impartiality and equality, *and* within local hierarchies with their idiom of kinship and *mushingi* (respect), which took for granted an inevitable and necessary inequality. Kibala's ward chairman, Kabaya, was generally recognized as lacking the skills necessary to navigate in the Boma; he did not speak or understand English and had failed to win government resources for his ward. Nonetheless, he had been elected not once but twice. When I asked people about this, one reason I was given was his powerful standing within Kibala's kinship hierarchy. It was a basic reality of Chizela politics that no one stood any chance of being elected as ward chairman unless they had the support of local authority figures within the kinship hierarchy. In line with the powerfully held belief that chiefs and headmen as owners of the land exercise a pervasive mystic control, one of the mechanisms by which the dominant kin group in an area seemed able to exclude others from positions of power was *bulozhi* (witchcraft), which I discuss in detail in chapter 6. Just as *bulozhi* had always been an element in the power of headmen and chiefs, it also inevitably played a part in the struggles within the community over the new political power structures. One of the forms it commonly seemed to take was a pervasive fear on the part of those not favored by the established authority figures in the area, particularly the chief, that if they were to put themselves forward for office this would at once lay them open to attack from those authority figures' powerful *bulozhi*. Similarly, people were fearful of what might happen to them if they did not vote for the candidate designated by the chief or the other powerful elders (*bakulumpe*); going against their wishes in this way would necessarily represent a serious lack of respect (*mushingi*). A number of people I spoke to mentioned fear of *bulozhi* as a significant element in Kabaya's election.

Another important factor in Kabaya's success was that local people did not have the kind of knowledge that would have enabled them to judge in an informed way whether or not a potential candidate had the appropriate skills. Most people simply did not know how things were done in the Boma. When I asked Tyemba why Kabaya had been elected despite not speaking English, even though it was clearly stated in the

UNIP rules that anyone standing as a candidate for ward chairman must be proficient in English, he replied:

We just saw it happen. Because at first he was in UNIP, standing on ant-hills and selling UNIP cards. Because people did not realise they thought he was very good. They did not know that things are changing. They thought in the [District Council] meetings they talk in Kaonde just like we do.[7] (Kibala, 15.viii.88, TK)

Tyemba's statement here should not be taken too literally however. When I asked people if they thought it was important that the ward chairman should be able to operate in English, they all said yes. Rather Tyemba was speaking figuratively both to criticize elements in the community he saw as less sophisticated—an example of how the Boma scorn for "uneducated villagers" was not confined to the world of official-dom—and to describe a more general unfamiliarity on the part of local people with how things are done in the Boma. While people may have been well aware of the importance of English, since so few of them understood or spoke English it was difficult for them to judge a candidate's language competence. Kabaya, I was told, had represented himself as knowing at least some English.

Another problem was that the pool of people with the necessary skills was so small. In both Kibala and Bukama, apart from a few men too young to be taken seriously as political actors, the only people at ease in English and in the Boma world were the handful of teachers and other government employees, but they were not local men. Anyone without kinship links in Kibala, no matter how competent, had little hope of being elected ward chairman. In the ward of which Bukama was a part, for instance, the vice-chairman of the ward was a man who had settled in the area after many years of working in town and was widely acknowledged as being exceptionally proficient not only in English, but in the ways of the Boma—all of which, it was admitted, was in marked contrast to the ward chairman himself who was something of the same stamp as Kabaya. But this vice-chairman was a Bemba whose wife was from Chizela but who did not himself have any kinship links in the area. Local people, I was told, were happy to have him as vice-chairman, and for him to accompany the chairman acting as interpreter (not simply in terms of the language), but they were not prepared, it

7. This was not peculiar to Kibala; there were about four ward chairmen out of Chizela's fifteen who were in Kabaya's position.

seemed, to have a stranger as their representative. A key factor in Kabaya's successful election, I was told, was the mobilization of his numerous relatives in Kibala. The election of ward chairmen can be seen in fact as another instance of how state structures had to some extent been reshaped to conform to the established—and in local terms hegemonic—hierarchies of the community of kin.

While the local community and the Boma may not have seen eye to eye on many points, there was one on which they were in full agreement: formal politics was the business of men. All the recognized decision makers—the headmen, chiefs, ward chairmen, government officials, development planners, and so on—were almost always male, and everybody assumed that they would, and should, be. The final section of this chapter maps out some of the gendered contours of the political landscape, and looks at the location of women within this overwhelmingly male political world.

The Political Location of Women

As far as I could tell, the women I talked to in Kibala and Bukama did not have anything like coherent and explicit, alternative *female* accounts of the world in which they lived with which to explicitly challenge the dominant male hegemony. While they often complained about men—particularly when no men were present—they seemed to accept the existing gender hierarchy as "natural" and unalterable. This is another example of hegemony as a dominant group's ability to make their way of naming social realities the *only* way, and to repress potentially counterhegemonic understandings—a power to stifle alternative accounts that tends to be especially effective when individuals are asked to verbalise their experience in a public setting.

In general the articulated accounts given by the people of rural Chizela—and I stress *articulated*—of "the way things are" looked at the world through the eyes of senior men. From this vantage point men and women were seen as necessarily and inescapably bound together in a mutually beneficial interdependence, which wound around them a diffuse net of reciprocal moral expectations. The nature of this interdependence meant that while there were many legitimate demands that rural women could make of their menfolk, the *legitimacy* of these demands depended on women accepting that there were also legitimate demands that men could make of women. The general shape of men's demands on women and women's demands on men, although not their precise demarcation in concrete cases, was laid down by the general norms of the sexual division of labor. For people in Kibala and Bukama, these reciprocal obligations between men and women were inherent in the very names "women" and "man"; they defined what it meant to be a woman, and to be a man. Part of what this meant for women was that it was only from *within* the existing sexual division of labor that they could make demands on men. For women to challenge the accepted allocation of tasks between the sexes would have been, in a sense, to deny their identity as women. It would also have been tantamount to questioning the legitimacy of their expectations of access to the labor of husbands and male kin. The problem as local women saw it was not the sexual division of labor per se, but how to make men fulfill their obligations as these were defined, albeit in a very general way, within that division of labor. As far as I could tell women did not seem to question the general male hegemony itself, or how this hegemony defined "being a woman." Women, as well as men, seemed to accept that part of what being a woman meant was serving men. As little girls who were sitting doing nothing were likely to be reminded by their mothers, who would ask them sharply, "So, do you think you're a man?"

An important factor constraining the participation of women in formal politics was that the division of labor between men and women included not only a division of labor within the realm of production, but also an allocation of responsibility within the political domain. The whole sphere of "public politics" was associated with men; it was not "women's business." This inevitably had the effect of inhibiting women and constraining their participation in formal political events, though it is important not to overemphasize women's exclusion. Women were normally present at such events, and some of the older ones (those, that is, who had attained recognized *bakulumpe* status) could indeed be highly vocal presences. The only public events in which women played a dominating role, however, were those in which *only* women participated, for instance, a special church service for women or, in the past, girls' initiation ceremonies.[8]

Away from the public spheres of rural life when there were no men around, women tended to be less deferential but they still seemed to

---

8. In neither Kibala nor Bukama did I find any evidence of *kisungu* (girls' initiation) still being practiced.

content themselves with ridiculing male pretension. While such mocking subversion may be seen as an implicit refusal to acknowledge the desirability and benignness of the dominant account, in no sense can this kind of ridicule be seen as amounting to a claim that relations between men and women could be other than they were. While individual women often came into conflict with particular men, husbands, sons, and so on, the tactics used by women tended to be those of passive resistance rather than confrontation. Wives were enormously skillful, for instance, in the art of prevarication. Faced with a demand by her husband with which, for whatever reason, a woman was reluctant to comply, a wife had all kinds of ways of not doing what she was asked without ever refusing outright.

An incident in Kibala illustrates a common pattern of private ridicule/public deference. One day when I was walking with a female research assistant we came across two old women busy in their fields. We started chatting and I asked about the role of men in cultivation; one of the women, Kyela, snorted and said very emphatically, "men just eat, women cultivate." Since she seemed an interesting woman with decided opinions I was anxious to talk further with her, and we arranged a time when I hoped we could sit and talk at our leisure. But when I turned up at the appointed time, I discovered that it had been decided that her husband should be present. It was he who was sitting in pride of place next to the chair that had been put out for me, while Kyela was sitting some way off; and I had no choice but to interview her through her husband, most of the time with him answering for her. The opinionated old lady I had met in the fields was unrecognizable in this respectful and deferential wife. In Chizela, as Kyela well understood, it was men, not women, who were the main actors on any formal occasion: the hearing of court cases, the adjudication of disputes, church services, and encounters with anthropologists. The right to speak for the community in such public arenas was indeed central to the very definition of being a senior male (*mukulumpe*).

Women did have a very clear sense of their location within the prevailing hegemony, and that this gave them a legitimate set of claims on their husbands and male kin. But this was a political identity, I would argue, firmly located within the domain of kinship and the hierarchical structures of the *mukulumpe/mwanyike* relationship. Central to this political identity was a basic premise that the relationships between individuals are always relationships between brothers, husbands, wives, mother's brothers, sisters, and so on, all of whom are linked together in irreducibly hierarchical ways. In other words, it is assumed that the most fundamental of the socially recognized relationships that establish the basic network of claims people have on one another are woven out of the strands of kinship; and that the ordering of these strands is necessarily and inescapably hierarchical. According to this view of political life, it is impossible to tear individuals out of this kinship fabric to make of each an autonomous *citizen*, whose rights, as a citizen, transcend their gender and their kinship location.

But, of course, the people of Kibala and Bukama *were* citizens of the Zambian state. As with any other modern state, political rhetoric in Zambia is underlain, firstly, by the assumption that the basic units within it (its citizens) are autonomous (and genderless) individuals; and, secondly, that all citizens are equal. Those who wish to operate in the formal political arenas of the state have no choice but to adopt the dominant egalitarian rhetoric. The problem for the women of Kibala and Bukama was that they did not have an articulated account of how things were for them as women that based itself on these kinds of egalitarian claims. Implicitly, it is true, their stress on their particular claims as women could be seen as the germ of a critique of the assumptions inherent in the rhetoric of citizenship. However, in the absence of the articulation of this germ into a coherent and systematic account capable of challenging the dominant hegemonies of the local community and the state, it was difficult for women's struggles to rise above the level of individual passive resistance.

If the women of Kibala and Bukama were in general relegated to the margins of public politics, their marginalization was especially pronounced in the case of encounters between the local community and those belonging to the world of the Boma. Both women and men took it for granted that those who speak on such occasions will be men. Women could speak on issues specific to women, such as "development" initiatives aimed exclusively at women, but men spoke for the community as a whole; theirs was the voice of authority, and a voice that women themselves tended to adopt, particularly in public contexts when men were present. It was this voice, for example, that tended to be adopted by those older women who did speak up on public occasions.

A practical reality that made it even more difficult for women to speak was the language used in encounters between the community and the Boma. Not only was the primary language English (even if there were normally also translations into Kaonde), but the idiom used was a bureaucratic one. Those unable to speak English and unversed in the mechanics of modern bureaucracy were, therefore, especially disadvantaged. While it is true that this applied to the vast majority of Kibala's and Bukama's inhabitants, there were at least a few men—usually those who had learned to operate in a modern bureaucratic world while working in town—who were reasonably comfortable operating in this world. There were no women. The assumption that it was men who were the community's "natural" decision makers, and it was they who should speak for the community as a whole, necessarily contributed to women's general lack of ease in such encounters.

Given the acceptance, by women as well as men, that on the public stage it is men who act, what then was the role of women in such public arenas? One way in which local women undoubtedly were a significant presence—and this was perhaps their major presence in such contexts—was insofar as men were well aware of wives' and kinswomen's de facto power to resist certain demands on them. Men, for instance, did not have free access to the labor of their wives. While there were a range of goods and services that husbands could expect their wives to provide, any demands on a wife's labor that fell outside the accepted range were likely to be contested, or at least to be the subject of negotiation. For instance, many women did not work on their husbands' LIMA plots. Those women who did, it was generally agreed, could expect a share of any profits.

There was, however, a formally designated space for women's voices within UNIP: the Women's League. The three types of UNIP membership, ordinary, Youth, and Women's, corresponded to three of the main cleavages in rural society: older men, young men, and women. The relationship between the three kinds of members was also an accurate reflection of the taken-for-granted assumption that power was the prerogative of those who were neither youngsters (*banyike*) nor female, that is, older men (male *bakulumpe*). A significant difference in the situation of women and youth is, of course, that women, unlike young men, do not automatically in the course of time become senior males. The UNIP category "youth" (which included men up to age 35) corresponded very closely to one meaning of *mwanyike*. When UNIP spoke, its "normal" voice was a male one. Youth and women were, so to speak, special interest groups, whose interests within UNIP were to be represented by the Youth League and the Women's League. But what were the reality of these organizations within Kibala and Bukama?

Every ward was supposed to have its own Youth and Women's Leagues (made up of the local "youth" and "women" party members) with a Women's League chairwoman and Youth League chairman; each league within a district having a representative who was a voting member of the District Council. It was through this representative structure that, in theory, women and youth could speak with their own voices within the formal political arenas of the state. It was not, therefore, that "women" and "youth" were excluded from the Party, but their participation was carefully contained within *separate* organzations whose purpose was defined by the hegemonic male UNIP voice. Whatever may have been the effectiveness of the Women's and Youth Leagues nationally, in neither Kibala nor Bukama did either have any real presence even to the extent of holding meetings, let alone actually doing anything. Nonetheless, at the time of my fieldwork there were Women's League chairwomen in both Kibala and the ward to which Bukama belonged.

Kibala's Women's League chairwoman was called Zamina. In the late 1980s Zamina and her husband were one of the more prosperous households in Kibala. Both of them had joined the LIMA scheme as soon as it was initiated in Kibala in 1980. I had hoped to interview Zamina on her own, but predictably it turned out to be a joint interview with her and her husband. It was he in fact who did much of the talking, concentrating his full attention on me while Zamina sat off to one side husking maize. He explained to me how his wife had become the local Women's League chairwoman in Kibala. Although she had not had any formal education, and could not speak any English nor read or write in Kaonde, "in discussions with Boma people she conducted herself like someone who has been to school," and so when "the people in the Boma asked the ward chairman to elect someone as the Women's League chairwoman" (Kibala, 31.viii.88, NK), Zamina was elected. This election was clearly not the result of spontaneous organization among local women. Zamina, I could not help suspecting, had probably been made an offer she could not refuse. She herself complained to me how reluctant women in Kibala were to come to UNIP meetings, seeing them as a waste of time. When I went on to ask her what she personally thought was the value of these meetings, she told me, using the standard rhetoric of education, that she wanted to learn about the things that were happening in the Party.

UNIP itself defined the role of the Women's League and other women's organizations very much in the terms of education and mobilization. As, for instance, in the party constitution, according to which the Women's Affairs Committee was to formulate "policies for the development of women and children in political, social, cultural, economic,-

scientific and technological development" (UNIP Constitution, GRZ 1988:66). The coupling of women and children here is worth noting. The constitution does not seem to have in mind an organization that is concerned with women organizing *themselves*.

Underlying the thinking of UNIP, the Zambian government, and expatriate development organizations has been the implicit assumption that "women" are a specific and separate category within an otherwise genderless political domain. The powerful effects of such a hegemonic assumption are enhanced precisely because its unstated and taken-for-granted nature prevent it from being explicitly challenged. In line with this assumption, a key strategy that has been promoted as a way of reaching women, and meeting their specific needs, is the women's club. Both the Women's League and foreign donors have encouraged the formation of such clubs. The model for these women's clubs in terms of their organization and what they do is one originating from outside the local community. There is always a bureaucratic structure involving a chairwoman, treasurer, and secretary, and it is these English terms that are used. The impetus to establish a club has normally come not from rural women themselves, but from someone like a government employed community worker, a party official, or a foreign aid worker.

The activities engaged in have tended to be based on very traditional notions of the activities appropriate for women. One of the teachers in Kibala, for instance, saw the encouragement of women's work by the Kibala ward secretariat[9] (of which he was a member) as meaning "knitting and so forth" (Kibala, 10.ix.88, TE). Apart from knitting, other activities seen as appropriate for women were such things as sewing, cooking, learning about nutrition, making vegetable gardens, candle making, and soap making. This view of the role of women can be seen as deriving in part from Western missionary models of the good Christian wife and mother, but it was also in tune with the local male hegemony, which stressed women's general subordination to men and tended to agree with the missionaries that the primary role of wives should be attending to the needs of husbands and children.

In Kibala, Zamina told me, there had been a women's club, but by the time of my fieldwork it no longer existed. The club had been founded

9. The ward secretariat was an organization set up by the local IRDP that was supposed to help coordinate the different IRDP activities at the ward level and provide a channel through which problems could be forwarded to the appropriate local government body. The four members of the ward secretariat in 1988 were all male.

by a former health assistant responsible for running the Kibala clinic. Once he was transferred, the club stopped functioning. When I asked Zamina what the club had done, she told me they had "knitted socks and some hats" (Kibala, 31.viii.88, NK). Given the fact that the impetus for women's clubs, at least in rural northwestern Zambia, does not seem to have come from rural women themselves, it is not surprising that the women I talked to did not explicitly challenge the form these clubs took. For many women they were simply irrelevant; and for those who *were* interested in being a member of such a club, the idea of transforming their structure and content would probably have seemed as absurd as that they should suggest the transformation of UNIP or the Zambian state. The women's club was a thing of the Boma, and it was the Boma that wrote the rules. As far as the women of Kibala and Bukama were concerned, they were faced with a simple choice: accept the club as it existed and make whatever use they could of it or ignore it. Women were always interested, for instance, in any possibility of gaining access to children's clothes, which were always in desperately short supply. At the same time, however, it is possible to discern certain *implicit* challenges.

Zamina, for instance, did not explicitly challenge the accepted model of the women's club, but she also referred to the hopes that she and a number of the women had had that the club might have become the nucleus of a co-operative that would have been able to acquire a small hammer mill for grinding grain. The co-operative is an institution that has been much favored by UNIP and foreign donors, and at the time of my fieldwork the IRDP had a scheme for supplying local groups with hammer mills on credit, the idea being that the group would repay the loan out of the profits it made. I will have more to say about the Kibala and the Bukama co-operative societies in the next chapter. The key points in this context are, firstly, that the idea of a hammer mill was particularly attractive to the *women* of Kibala since it was they who were responsible for the arduous work of pounding grain for the daily *nshima* with a mortar and pestle. There were no hammer mills in the vicinity of Kibala, and pounding was a task that regularly took up many hours of a woman's time during a week. But, and this is the second point, there was no possibility of local women actually being able to raise the initial capital necessary for such a venture.

The stereotypical response to my questions about the role of women's clubs, as in the case of other local-level UNIP organizations, was that they "educated" people (see Zamina's response above). In reality, however, a major attraction of such organizations has probably been that in some rather vague and general way they have appeared to provide a channel, or at least a potential channel, to the powerful wider world beyond the local community. It is also important not to overlook the vested interests of the elite women who have always dominated Zambia's official women's organizations, and who were anxious to retain their officially sanctioned role as women's representatives.

Another significant group of women belonging to the Boma world were those who were employed specifically to work with women, as community development workers, women's project officers, and so on. They also had their own interests and their own understandings of what women want. They were usually women with a secondary school education, and sometimes some further training. They were of course literate in English and at ease in a bureaucratic world; and their socialization into this world meant that they had also been socialized into the whole rhetoric of "development" with its stress on the centrality of "education" in the "development" of "villagers." In addition, these women's very livelihood depended on them accepting both the basic premises of a separate women's sphere and the naming of what it is that women want and need in the terms articulated by the hegemonic male-accented voice of UNIP.

In theory women's clubs and the Women's League could have acted as a means through which local women were able to lobby for their interests in the formal arenas of power beyond their community, but they have not in fact done this. They have never directly challenged the structures of male power, either within their own communities or more generally. For instance, they have not questioned the accepted norms of the sexual division of labor, which, as I describe in the next chapter, were precisely what made it more difficult for women than for men to take advantage of new economic opportunities, such as selling crops to the national market. Nor have they argued for government policy and development programs in general to be specifically designed so as to enable women to benefit from them. The emphasis has always been on "educating" and "developing" women in line with an externally generated model. As the UNIP constitution put it, the role of the Women's Affairs Committee was, among other things, to "work out ways and means of instilling in women a sense of responsibility towards their work, families, country and the Party" (GRZ 1988:66). Women's organizations, therefore, have no tradition of operating as campaigning organizations. And yet, there were no other organizations in rural Chizela that provided any recognized space for women, and particularly nonelite women, to speak as women in the formal arenas of the state.

Embedded in the political institutions and practices of rural Chizela were two entangled but different discourses. One, associated with the world of the Boma, was structured around the notion of citizenship and the rule of law, before which all individuals are equal. The other was one that derived from the community of kin. This latter discourse was based not on the notion of autonomous individuals and equality, but on individuals who could not be torn out of their specific location within the overlapping, and always hierarchical, maps of kinship, age, and gender. In different ways both these discourses assumed a male vantage point that named *for* women what their role in public politics should be. The discourse of kinship and the *mukulumpe/mwanyike* (senior/junior) relationship of hierarchy recognized women as having their own interests and legitimate claims on men, although it also defined formal politics as essentially the responsibility of men. The discourse of citizenship, with its claim to transcend gender, in practice tends everywhere to translate into "the citizen" being assumed to be male unless specifically identified as female,[10] in the same way that households are assumed to be headed by a male, unless, that is, they are specially marked as *female*-headed households. Within this apparently gender-blind discourse of citizenship and equality, that is in reality so strongly male accented, for women to draw attention to how the status quo disadvantages women and privileges men tends to be seen as the sectarian pleadings of a "special interest" group.

10. Among a number of feminist critiques of conventional notions of liberal democracy are Phillips (1991, 1993); Pateman (1970, 1989); and Young (1989). See Sassoon (1987b) for some explorations of the implications of this for women in modern industrialized societies.

CHAPTER 5

Economic Locations: Men, Women, and Production

The wife grows food to feed our bodies. I grow food to sell for money to clothe our bodies. So we just combine; she grows food for my consumption, and I get the money to clothe us.
LIMA group chairman, Kibala, 14.viii.88

      The economic landscape of rural Chizela, like the political landscape described in the previous two chapters, was one in which women and men were located very differently. This chapter traces out some of the basic contours of this economic landscape, paying particular attention to the ways in which these were gendered. Central to my mapping here is the exploration of two key forces that have played a major role in the shaping of rural life: monetization and commoditization.

Kinship and Commodities

      While it can be assumed that communities in rural Chizela were never, even in the precolonial past, completely self-sufficient and always engaged in exchanges of various kinds with their neighbors, before the slave and ivory trade brought guns, cotton cloth, and other trade goods into the region there were probably relatively few goods that were not produced locally. Kaonde men smelted and worked iron and made the bark-cloth that, together with the skins of the animals they

143

hunted, provided clothes and other coverings. In general, it seems safe to say that in this period the bulk of the necessities of daily life would normally have been produced and consumed outside market relations.

Gradually, however, a range of imported trade goods began to establish themselves as ordinary, everyday necessities; they became the way people *expected* to satisfy certain needs. This process began in the precolonial years of the slave trade when cotton cloth began to displace bark-cloth, and guns to replace spears. Through such changes the region began to be linked in *structural* ways to the often distant places from which these goods originated. It was these kind of structural linkages that began the process of turning whole regions, such as present-day North-Western Province, into rural peripheries locked into unequal (although not unchanging) relationships with other more powerful economic regions. This process was accelerated with colonization and the development of a migrant labor system that sucked vast amounts of male labor out of the rural areas while simultaneously providing a flood of cheap mass-produced goods on which the wages of those migrant laborers could be spent. Not only did industrially produced hoe blades, metal cooking pots and water containers, blankets, and ready-made clothes increasingly come to replace locally produced iron, clay pots, bark-cloth, and animal skins; there were also a whole range of new goods such as the bicycles, Bibles, and soap that now became an established part of rural life. At the same time, those who could afford them began to favor cement and other imported building materials for house construction, and iron sheets rather than local grass for roofs.

With various imported goods increasingly being seen as necessities, access to some kind of a cash income became ever more necessary. Economic life in 1980s Kibala and Bukama was certainly monetized; nonetheless, there was still a significant difference between rural life and town life as regards the *degree* of monetization. Production in Kibala, and even on the Bukama farm settlement scheme—particularly the production of food—was still to a significant extent geared around the production of use-values for the producers' own consumption, or for nonmarket forms of distribution. That is, rather than being bought and sold, goods were distributed through a network of acknowledged claims of kin either to particular use-values or more generally to a share of any surplus produced. These were claims embedded in the very definitions of marriage and kinship. Also very important, it was still primarily through such nonmarket relationships that people gained access to land and to labor. How those living in Kibala and Bukama saw the uneven process of monetization within their communities varied considerably, as the following three extracts from my interviews illustrate.

The first comes from Sansoni's response when I asked him about the differences between urban and rural life. Sansoni, the teacher who had spent most of his life in town, began by saying,

In the town most of the things that are found there, they need money. If you want to buy some cassava, you have got to produce something to get it, but here in the rural areas you can go to your relative, and he will give it to you free of charge . . . in town you cannot live without money so it requires that every day you must have money in your pocket to enable you to make a living, but in a rural area you can live for one year without touching a iong[1] but still you can manage to survive.

He went on to explain that it has taken him time to adjust to rural life.

Before I used to feel bitter because I was used to the town life whereby there are not so many people who come to bother you . . . the thing that has caused a change [in Sansoni's attitude] is that if you become stingy in an area like where we are, Kibala, people will begin giving you names, they will be saying "that man is selfish, he doesn't want to share things with other people", sometimes they will be saying "no, he is proud because he is educated, that's why he does not want to share things with other people". (Sansoni, Kibala, 1.ix.88, TE)

Then there was Banyinyita. An elderly man with little formal education, Banyinyita had grown up in Kibala returning there in the early sixties after working for a number of years in town. He, like Sansoni, stressed the lack of monetization of rural life.

Because of the hunger we had last year. This is what made me cut trees for a new field. I said these things [i.e., being part of a local pit-sawing cooperative initiated by the IRDP] will make me die of hunger. Who will be moving with a bag of money in their pocket? Having a bag of money in the house, am I in town? Here in the village I do not want a bagful of money. I want my wife to do well [ie. produce more grain]. Let her pound and pound, and the children will eat and become happy. (Banyinyita, Kibala, 12.viii.88, TK)

Kyakala was another elderly man with little formal education who was living at Bukama. He had worked as a migrant laborer on the mines

---

1. At independence the currency adopted was the kwacha (K), 100 ngwee (ng) making up K1. At the time of my fieldwork the approximate value of the kwacha was U.S. $1 = K8.

for some years but had spent the majority of his life in the rural areas. Unlike Sansoni and Banyinyita, what Kyakala wanted to stress to me (at least in this context) was how much town ways of thinking and behaving had spread to the rural areas. I had asked him why he had moved to the settlement scheme. His answer was in part a lament for what he saw as the breakdown of the old morality and the new overwhelming dominance of money.

If you stay in the village where do you find money? These days you can only expect your own child to give you things or assistance. In those days every member of a village was a child of the headman. . . . But it's different these days, even your *mwipwa* [sister's son, a man's heir in the matrilineal Kaonde system] will only help if you pay him money. . . . The difference is simply that these days people are more interested in money. You cannot send [i.e., on an errand] your friend's child without giving him money as a payment. In the past people were not interested in money; they were only interested in eating [i.e., production for direct consumption] and helping their elders. The difference I have seen nowadays is with money. Unless one has money one cannot expect anyone else to help him. That is why even we old people are here in farms [i.e., Bukama] just hoping to make a little money to buy a cake of soap to wash with. . . . These days even children are not concerned about their parents because they are just interested in wealth. That is why you find even very old people still dragging hoes just to make a little money for their future. If you have no money nobody will come to your aid. These days if even your child killed an animal you do not expect him to send you a piece if you have not money to pay for it. In the olden days someone who killed an animal first thought of the headman or his parents for fear of being punished. (Kyakala, Bukama, 21.xii.88, TK)

Whether or not Kyakala is romanticizing the past is not the point here; what is is the underlying assumption in *all* the passages quoted that there exist two quite different ways of organizing the flow of goods and services: one based on market principles, money and exchange-value, and one based on a web of reciprocal obligations between kin, out of which the very names of kin categories are woven. At the heart of what the names *mwisho* (mother's brother) and *mwipwa* (sister's child) meant was this inescapable reciprocal obligation. Another important characteristic of this kinship-based flow of goods and services was that it often involved access to specific goods and services, such as a piece of meat from an animal killed or being able to send a young child on errands. In other words, what was involved was access to *particular use-values*, not easily substitutable for each other. Sansoni and Banyinyita may have wanted to stress to me how little monetized rural life is compared to the way things are in town, and Kyakala the extent of monetization in modern-day rural Zambia, but all three were agreed that there were two different, and often incompatible, mechanisms of distribution and access to resources operating. One of these mechanisms relied on money and the exchange-value of goods, while the other depended directly on the relationships between people created by kinship. Let me emphasize that what I am drawing attention to here are the kinds of relationships seen as underlying the processes by which individuals obtained access to resources and the social product was distributed. In both Kibala and Bukama the actual transactions of day-to-day life were a complex tangle of both kinds of relationship. In mapping out the broad economic contours I have attempted to trace out the way in which the different strata laid down by market and nonmarket relations in practice continually interacted with one another to create a complex mosaic. Running through this mosaic were complicated, and strongly gendered, patterns of inequality and hierarchy.

Let me also stress that what I have tried to do in this chapter is to map out the basic economic landscape within which the people of Kibala and Bukama found themselves in the 1980s. The paths that particular individuals carved out for themselves within that landscape cannot of course be read off from its contours in any mechanical way, but nonetheless those contours helped shape individual trajectories. It is those shaping effects on which I have focused rather than the rich diversity of individual paths.

A crucial dimension of economic relations in rural Chizela was the significantly different location of women and men. And this was true both in the case of monetized relations and those organized through kinship. The economic landscape of Kibala and Bukama in 1988 was a deeply gendered one. Just as men and women were assigned different roles within the political domain, so too were they allotted different tasks in economic life, or, to put it more precisely, certain tasks were associated with women, while others were associated with men. There were tasks seen as female tasks, and tasks seen as male, even if in practice women might sometimes carry out male tasks, and men female ones. In addition, the effects of monetization and commoditization were themselves gendered. Where production had become commoditized, for instance, as when crops were grown specifically for sale to the national market, women tended to be systematically disadvantaged. In general, whether it was a question of generating a cash income by selling labor or the produce of that labor, women tended to have fewer, and less profitable, options than men. Of course, just as the communities themselves were not homogenous and undifferentiated, neither did the women of Bukama and Kibala constitute a single category; but nonetheless there were certain general ways in which the location of women was systematically different to that of men, and it is on the basic pattern that I want to concentrate in this chapter. Inevitably this has meant a certain flattening of the differences between women, but a proper examination of these would require yet another chapter.

I want to begin by looking at the particular nature of the economic interdependencies that defined Kaonde marriage—in other words, the basic interdependencies to which both women and men in Kibala and Bukama would normally refer when I asked them about the meaning of marriage. I say *Kaonde* marriage here because in this predominantly Kaonde region it was the Kaonde notion of marriage, including its ideological stress on a sorghum-based cultivation system, that was dominant. However, although the specifics of the interdependence of wives and husbands may vary, a similar general interdependency could probably be found throughout much of rural Zambia.

Kaonde Marriage

The primary division of labor in rural Chizela was one based on gender. There was very little specialization of labor; with a few exceptions, such as hunting, healing, and divining, adult men and women were expected to know how to perform virtually all the tasks appropriate to their sex and age. At the same time, it was accepted that their levels of skill would vary. Each sex had its own range of allotted tasks. Men were responsible for clearing the bush and making fields, women for the bulk of day-to-day cultivation; men built houses, women cooked and "kept" house. The whole texture of daily life was, so to speak, woven out of a basic interdependence between men and women; if adults were to live a life in accordance with local norms, men needed access to women's labor, and women to men's. And the primary relationship through which this access was obtained on a day-to-day basis was marriage. The most powerful claims as regards meeting daily subsistence needs were those of a wife on her husband and a husband on his wife (or wives). It was a husband's duty to make fields and build a house for his wife (or wives); it was a wife's duty to "feed" her husband.

Failure to fulfill these responsibilities—which were considered quite as central to marriage as sexual services—was grounds for divorce. It was in fact marriage and its reciprocal obligations that played the central role in organizing the large part of production that was noncommoditized. It was above all as husbands and wives that adults met most of their basic consumption needs that they were unable to produce themselves.

In their daily lives husbands and wives, as it were, continually confronted each other with claims to various goods and services; the legitimacy of each spouse's claims depending on the honoring of their own reciprocal obligations. A woman who did not feed her husband could not expect him to provide her with clothes; a man who did not clear fields for his wife could not complain of her empty granary. It should be stressed that what was involved here were not the carefully defined and bounded terms of a legal contract, but rather a series of general and somewhat vague moral precepts. In any given context the precise meaning of these precepts could be endlessly argued about; they created, as it were, a moral reservoir to be drawn upon to defend or oppose particular behavior or actions. The household was necessarily, therefore, a site of struggle. Sometimes the struggle might be open and explicit, sometimes implicit and unacknowledged, but whatever the nature of the struggle it was always informed by this reservoir of moral assumptions. Households were not, of course, only sites of struggle; the mutual benefits of interdependence so stressed in the Kaonde ideology of gender relations were also a structural reality. To see how this complicated interdependence played itself out in the day-to-day lives of actual households, it would be necessary to look at the specific histories of particular households. My concern here, however, is simply to identify some of the key forces shaping those ultimately unique histories.

One important reality was that the interdependence between women and men, and their need for each other's labor, was far from symmetrical. In general, men's tasks tended to be one-off ones, such as making a field or building a house, which could then be used for a number of years. Women's tasks by contrast tended to be those of day-to-day reproduction, tending the crops in the field, food processing and preparation, collecting water, and such like. Men, therefore, needed access to women's labor on a *daily* basis. An adult man who had to collect his own water, cook his own food and so on would be seen either as rather pitiful and ridiculous, or, if he appeared to have made a conscious choice to live like this, as eccentric. Although unmarried men could appeal to their female matrikin for help with certain female tasks, such as pounding grain for *nshima*, from time to time, it was only a wife who would perform the routine "domestic" tasks on a regular basis. As a result a man *had* to be married if he was to be accepted as a responsible adult (*mukulumpe*) who would be taken seriously as a player in the formal arenas of political life.

But while a man needed access to female labor on a daily basis, a woman could manage with only periodic access to male labor. The stereotypical formulation for the reciprocal obligations involved in marriage was that a wife "fed" her husband while a husband "clothed" his wife. By implication the term *clothe* here included not only actual clothing, but also the provision of a range of tools and implements, such as hoes and the harvesting and winnowing baskets, which a woman needed to fulfill her responsibility of "feeding" her husband. In addition, a husband was expected to provide his wife with fields, a house, a cooking shelter, and granaries. As regards her day-to-day subsistence, however, it was perfectly possible for a woman to live without a husband and to live a life that did not contravene local norms. It was unlikely, for reasons I will come to, that a woman on her own would be prosperous, but her daily routine of working in the fields, pounding grain, preparing food, fetching water and firewood, and so on would follow the same basic pattern whether or not she had a husband.

When I asked local men about polygyny and its advantages and disadvantages, the stereotypical answer I was given began: "A man with more than one wife eats better than a man with one." Whereas in industrial societies marriage tends to be seen as centering on the mutual fulfillment of sexual and emotional needs, in Chizela the sexual and emotional dimension of marriage was seen as only one strand, albeit an important one, of a relationship that was seen as being equally, and even predominantly, about the meeting of basic material needs. This difference was brought home to me one morning when I was walking to Chizela District Centre with Mukwetu and another local man, Wilson. The conversation turned to Ubaya, the only man in Bukama apart from Chief Chizela to have three wives. In tones of wonder mixed with disbelief Wilson told us how he had been walking past Ubaya's place at about 6 a.m. and had seen him sitting in front of his house eating *nshima*. Enviously Wilson and Mukwetu told me how Ubaya regularly ate *nshima* and relish three times a day: in the morning, the middle of the day, and the evening. Even the more prosperous in Kibala and Bukama usually only ate *nshima* twice a day, at lunchtime and in the evening, and many only had one *nshima* meal a day. To eat *three* such meals a day represented an almost sinful indulgence. Wilson went on to explain to me how each of Ubaya's wives would cook once a day, one in the morning, one at midday, and one in the evening. Mukwetu and Wilson then agreed that this was the benefit of having a number of wives—there was always *nshima* ready to eat—and explained to me that this was why Ubaya had married three women. For men, not only was marriage the expected way of satisfying a whole range of basic consumption needs, it was often the *only* way of satisfying these needs. Even if the increasing monetization of economic relations in the rural areas meant it was possible to buy various kinds of labor, male access to female labor still depended very much on marriage.

But if men tended to fantasize about having more than one wife, women were decidedly less enthusiastic about the prospect of sharing a husband. For a woman, being a co-wife meant having to compete not only for sexual attention, but for her husband's labor, and the money and goods with which he "clothed" his wives. Very important, a co-wife did not have the same power to put pressure on her husband by withholding her labor since he would just go to one of his other wives. There was very little economic cooperation between co-wives; normally each would have her own fields, her own house, and her own cooking shelter. Women were extremely critical of a man who failed to provide all of these for each wife, describing it as not showing proper respect (*mushingi*) to the wives, as shaming them. From what I observed in Chizela, most women tried to prevent their husbands from taking other wives, and there were often bitter fights over a husband's attempts to do so. Those women who did become co-wives seemed prepared to accept this either because, like Ubaya and Chief Chizela, the man in question was particularly prosperous or of high status; or because they had decided that even a share of a husband was better than no husband. Ubaya and his three wives were seen as something of a prodigy in Bukama because they all seemed to live together in such harmony, and apparently had done so for many years. Mukwetu assured me, and this seemed to be a general belief, that Ubaya must have very powerful medicine (*muchi*) to be able to maintain such harmony. (In the next chapter beliefs about *muchi* are discussed in detail.) There was another polygynist, Abraham, who, it was agreed, did *not* have the necessary medicine, and his problems illustrate the kind of struggles that polygynous marriage often involved, and the different power resources of husbands and wives.

The Unhappy Polygynist

Abraham, an elderly man and the chairman of the Bukama settlement scheme, had two wives; one he had married in 1960 and one in 1975. Both wives had had numerous children by him. My time in Bukama coincided with the beginning of the cultivation year when work on the fields should have been starting in earnest. But despite this for most of my stay Abraham and his two wives were absent. Like some others in Bukama, Abraham was also the headman of a village that had its primary location elsewhere, and he divided his time between there and Bukama. Normally however, people told me, he would spend the majority of his time on the settlement scheme. Since I was anxious to interview Abraham as the scheme chairman, I continually asked when he was likely to arrive in Bukama, and continually I was given the answer "soon" or "any time now," but still he failed to appear. He would occasionally turn up briefly when there was a specially important meeting, but only to return to his village, some twenty kilometers away, immediately after the meeting was over. After some weeks of this I was finally told why Abraham was finding it so hard to return to Bukama: his wives were being "difficult."

Abraham and his wives were very fond of beer, and whether in Bukama or in his village all three of them tended to spend a good deal of time at beer drinks. Although both wives lived together with Abraham in Bukama, only the senior wife, Finesi, was currently living with him in his village; the junior wife, Niva, preferred to stay in the nearby village of one of her matrikin. Particularly in the case of polygynous unions it was quite common for wives to live with their matrikin, receiving periodic visits from their husbands, rather than moving to their husband's home. It seemed that neither of Abraham's wives (who were on very bad terms with each other) were particularly keen on living in Bukama. Then one night when Abraham made one of his regular visits to Niva he found her with a man in *delicto flagrante*, and after this he decided he had better stay with her to make sure she did not stray again. This continued for some time until Abraham began hearing reports that Finesi was now taking advantage of his absence to "play" (*kukaya*) with other men, as the local term had it. Abraham was therefore faced with two recalcitrant women, in two separate places, neither of whom could be persuaded to accompany him to Bukama to begin cultivating, and neither of whom, it seemed, could he compel to do so.

In general Kaonde women in the 1980s seemed to have a considerable degree of freedom as regards whom they married, and whether or not they stayed married. Divorce, whether initiated by wife or husband, seemed to be frequent and relatively straightforward; in the last chapter

I cited the case of my neighbor in Bukama who had had eight husbands, and children by six of them. Within marriage, however, all the women of Kibala and Bukama seemed to accept that there must be at least an outward show of deference by women toward their husbands. For a woman not to show respect (*mushingi*) would bring shame (*bumvu*) on both her husband and herself. But while it may have been accepted by women as well as men that a husband was senior (*mukulumpe*) and a wife junior (*mwanyike*), getting a wife to submit in practice was not always easy, as the case of Abraham illustrates. And, as I have already argued, within the accepted hierarchy women would struggle for what they saw as their just claims. For instance, as I noted in chapter 3, while I never heard a woman claim that a man did not have the right to beat his wife, women would say that he should not beat her *in public*, or so as to draw blood, or when she had a baby on her back and so on. In any given instance, therefore, a woman and her relatives could usually find some reason why a particular beating was unjustified. Another factor that probably helped to keep marital violence within some kind of bounds was the public scrutiny to which almost anything done by anybody was subject. In the small communities of rural Chizela it was hard to keep anything private and, as with parents' chastisement of children, there was a clear understanding of what constituted reasonable punishment of an erring wife, even if the limits tended to be clearer in the case of others than when it was oneself.

The use of physical force, and the threat of its use, was an important reality in the relationship between husbands and wives, but as with any well-established relation of domination, for much of the time it remained in the background, an unspoken presence emerging only when the more subtle fetters of male hegemony proved inadequate. At the same time, if a woman wanted to leave her husband, there was relatively little he could do about it, particularly given the absence of large bride-wealth payments and that men as well as women accepted that when a marriage ended the children stayed with their mother. Precisely because divorce did not involve a women's matrikin having to refund a husband anything, a woman could always rely on finding sympathetic matrikin with whom she could settle.

The fact that a woman could leave a husband and take her children with her defined certain limits to a husband's power. A man's designated heirs might be his sisters' children, but there tended also to be strong bonds between fathers and children. During the colonial and post-colonial period there has been a growing emphasis on the role of the father as the assumed head of household and on the basic nuclear family of mother, father, and children, at the expense of matrilineal family structures and the authority of *mwisho* (mother's brother). It is difficult to know how different things were in precolonial times but the tendency of state institutions and laws—whether of the colonial or postcolonial government—to take as their basic units male householders and the nuclear family has undoubtedly been an important force encouraging a greater recognition of the links between fathers and children.[2] In addition, the new possibilities for individuals to create and hold onto personal wealth of one kind or another, whether this wealth comes from wage-labor, market production or business enterprises, has led to some individuals, particularly the more successful ones, trying to prevent their wealth flowing out to their matrikin and keeping it within the more clearly bounded unit of spouses and children.[3]

Whatever the reasons—and whether or not things were different in the past, or merely seem so because the matrilineal ideology obscures the real relations that existed between fathers and children in the past—in the 1980s there was a recognition of the bond between fathers and children that represented something of a contradiction within the overarching matrilineal hegemony. Many fathers perceived themselves as making considerable investments in their children, particularly in terms of the costs associated with modern education in government schools, and in return looked to their children to provide them with support in their old age. Although children in Chizela, once they had reached an age where they were capable of making decisions for themselves, had considerable freedom of choice in deciding where to live, in people's minds the fundamental tie was still that to mother and matrikin. If divorced fathers wanted to attract their children to them, then they had to be able to offer them "a better life" as it were, which usually meant certain material inducements. In other words, what actually happened after a divorce tended to be that children would go with their mother unless their father was able to offer them something more attractive. Older men, therefore, tended to be reluctant to divorce women with

2. See Channock (1985:172–91, and passim) for discussion of the patrilineal bias of the colonial lawmakers.

3. Berry (1993) discusses some of the different ways the competing pressures of either concentrating resources within a restricted family group or using them to mobilize wider networks have worked themselves out at different times in southern Ghana, southwestern Nigeria, central Kenya, and northeastern Zambia.

whom they had had numerous children even if the women were proving "difficult."

Another reason that made older men more hesitant about divorce was that, unless they were able to offer considerable material inducements, they were likely to find it difficult to find another wife. However much it might be agreed that age was a reason for respect (*mushingi*), Chizela women did not seem to consider age in itself particularly desirable in a husband. In addition, a number of older women claimed to prefer living alone to taking on all the extra work entailed in having a husband, even though living without a husband probably meant living in greater poverty. For older men, however, lack of access to female labor not only meant that they had to carry out for themselves demeaning female tasks, it also robbed them of a key part of what defined a male elder (*mukulumpe*). In the case of an older woman, the respect (*mushingi*) she was given and the amount of authority she had seemed to depend almost entirely on her own personal qualities. Whether or not she was married seemed to be irrelevant except to the extent that not being subordinate to a husband may have made things easier for certain powerful women.

What was necessary for a Kaonde woman to be accepted as adult was for her to have her own fields, and in particular her own sorghum field. The expectation was that it was a woman's husband who provided her with these fields. Although a woman's responsibility to "feed" her husband implied more than simply the provision of food, ideologically at least it centered on the provision of the Kaonde's preferred staple, sorghum; what a wife "fed" her husband was sorghum. The cultivation of sorghum was, as it were, the symbolic heart of the interdependence between women and men; and this cultivation was described by both women and men as primarily the responsibility of women. This is not to say that men's role in sorghum cultivation was denied, but ultimately sorghum was seen as a woman's crop; it fell within the *moral* domain of women. This female moral domain was also seen as concerned with cultivation for subsistence, that is, the production of food as a basket of use-values for direct consumption rather than for sale. The cultivation of sorghum was, it seems, regarded as something that *ought* not to be part of the world of the market and cash transactions, even if in practice sorghum was sometimes sold, paid labor occasionally employed, and new fields prepared for money. The following quotations from two Kibala men provide a male gloss on the interdependence between men and women in cultivation.

The wife grows food to feed our bodies. I grow food to sell for money to clothe our bodies. So we just combine; she grows food for my consumption, and I get the money to clothe us. (Mulonda, Kibala, 14.viii.88, TK)

Crehan: In the case of a sorghum field which husband and wife have cultivated together, does it belong to the wife, or the husband, or to both of you?

Kijila: Traditionally a sorghum field belongs to the woman. We [men] just help them to make sure they finish in time for the cultivation of other crops, like maize. When we come to LIMA [crops] and soya beans, these automatically belong to me.

(Kibala, 19.viii.88, TK)

I will come back to the relationship between the cultivation of sorghum and that of the crops grown for sale, but first I want to focus on sorghum.

Everyone I talked to in Chizela agreed that sorghum was the quintessential Kaonde crop, and its shifting cultivation the basis of the "traditional" Kaonde way of life. This sorghum-based cultivation system also included a variety of subsidiary crops, such as maize, millet, and a range of vegetable crops, but sorghum was its ideological heart, and here, following local usage, I have taken sorghum as standing for the system as a whole. The primary role of men in sorghum cultivation, as described by both women and men, was the initial bush clearing and preparation of fields (*kutema*). And the primary context within which a man cleared a field for sorghum was as a husband preparing a field for his wife. One of the criteria people used, at least in conversation, to define when a young man was old enough to marry was whether or not he had the necessary physical strength to undertake the arduous labor involved in *kutema*—felling mature trees with a hand axe and stacking them carefully in rows so that they would burn well and provide the bed of fertile ash in which the sorghum would be planted.

A woman without a husband could appeal to one of her male matrikin or a son-in-law to clear a field for her. This was recognized by both men and women as a legitimate moral claim, and was indeed how most of the women I asked who did not have husbands had acquired their sorghum fields. In practice, however, getting a man other than a husband actually to clear a field, rather than merely promising to do so, could require considerable persistence on the part of the woman, and sometimes even payment. The way monetization was creeping in here was characteristic. Because it could be so difficult to get this kind of kinship obligation fulfilled, women with the necessary cash (often someone who had recently moved from town where they had managed to acquire some small stock of funds) would sometimes prefer to pay. However, this cash payment might well be combined with the pressures of kinship. What was seen locally as a "fair" price for such a task tended to be extremely low, so that a man might only be prepared to take it on, even for money, *because* the woman was his kinswoman. Also, the payment might well be less than he would have expected had she not been kin, and he was likely to be more ready to accept that he might have to wait a long time for his money. While it had become accepted, as by Kyakala (see above, p. 146), that nowadays you often had to pay people, even kin, to do things, it was also accepted that "payment" might well take the form of a long-term, and hard to collect, debt. To a certain extent it was as if the new monetary transactions had been partially absorbed into the older and more diffuse obligations of kinship. Another way of seeing this complicated reality would be as the principles of the market and the law of supply and demand struggling to assert themselves within what was still in many respects the overall hegemony of a moral universe of kinship.

Once prepared, the responsibility for cultivating a field shifted to the woman for whom it had been cleared. As one old woman put it, with an expressive wave of her hand, when I asked her about the role of the man once a field has been burned, "He is gone [*waya*]" (Inamwana, Kibala, 26.vii.88, NK). This was one of the areas, however, where women's perceptions were sometimes different from those of men. Some husbands in Kibala and Bukama did work hard in their wives' fields, but as the quote from Kijila suggests, even by men this labor input tended to be seen as "help" that enabled a woman to carry out *her* responsibility of feeding husband, children, and herself in the coming year. In general, apart from whatever "help" her husband might decide to provide, a woman could expect her dependent children to give her some assistance with the routine tasks of cultivation such as weeding, planting, and bird scaring. Access to the labor of children was an important resource for women, and since children living with their mothers depended on them for their food, mothers had some degree of coercive power. There was a strong moral expectation (at least on the part of adults) that children should work in the fields of those who fed them, even if in practice there was often a good deal of struggling over this obligation. Struggles were particularly common between women and their adolescent sons, who were chafing to break out of the female domain of their mothers and enter the higher-status world of men. There could also be a tension between whether children should be working in the fields or going to school.

Women might also get some help on their fields from their kins-women. Adult daughters and their mothers, for instance, quite often helped one another, especially if they lived close by; or a granddaughter might be sent to help a grandmother. But although husbands, dependent children, and other kin might give varying amounts of help with culti-vation, women were quite capable of carrying out these tasks alone, and often did. As I walked around Kibala and Bukama I would pass field after field in which a woman, often with a baby on her back, was work-ing alone. A key point here is that it was almost always through claims based on marriage or kinship that women were able to mobilize labor on their sorghum fields; it was very rare for a women to *pay* for labor on these fields.

Nonetheless, however hegemonic the notion that kin *ought* to help each other, this alone was not always sufficient to mobilize labor. Build-ing up the kind of strong links that transformed the abstract principles of kinship into active flows of goods and services required work. Kin ties needed to be nurtured, as a number of *bishimi* (folktales) reminded people; those who are hard and unfeeling toward their kin are likely to find themselves deserted in their hour of need. This, after all, was a system based on reciprocity—not immediate or precisely specified rec-iprocity, but reciprocity nonetheless. Such a system depends on people having the confidence that ultimately those who are currently benefici-aries will eventually, in some form or another, be benefactors. At the same time it is also important that people do not attempt to quantify or itemize the details of this reciprocity too precisely.

Once the sorghum was harvested it was stored unthreshed in small granaries close to the fields. Each woman had her own granary (or gra-naries) in which to store her food crops. She would then collect grain from her store as and when she needed it. It was generally accepted by men as well as women that a woman's sorghum was hers to distribute, and there was a strong prohibition against anyone other than a woman herself taking grain from her granary. This did not mean, however, that it was her private property to do with as she pleased. Not only did she have to feed her husband and children, she also had powerful obligations to help any of her matrikin who were short of food; as long as there was grain in her granary she could not deny needy kin. This moral im-perative made the subject of just how much grain someone had a touchy subject, since the only acceptable reason for refusing help was an empty granary. The excuse of an empty granary was understood by everybody as a polite form of denial that was not necessarily strictly true. It was her husband, however, who had the most powerful de facto claims on a wife. He might well put pressure on her to sell grain, or to use it to brew beer for sale, and this pressure—which could involve physical force, or at least the threat of force—was difficult for a woman to withstand.

The claims of a husband on his wife's surplus were a particularly gray area in an area of moral obligation that was generally gray and undefined. It was clear that a wife should feed her husband, and that in general she was subject to his authority, but whether that meant that a husband could *demand* that a wife's grain be sold, either directly or in the form of beer, tended to be decided by the particular dynamics of the specific relationship of actual wives and husbands. What needs to be emphasized is the basic recognition that men obtained access to their basic staple food *through* women. Women's de facto control here was strengthened by the fact that it was they who carried out the processing of the sorghum and other foodstuffs; it was they who threshed and pounded the grain to turn it into flour; it was they who cooked the *nshima* and brewed the beer. There was also the art of prevarication, which was such an important thread in the fabric of village life generally and which was a basic weapon in a wife's arsenal; without openly defying their husbands, women knew all manner of ways of putting them off. Marriage often involved protracted battles of will in which male "authority," while never denied, could prove extremely difficult to enforce at a more concrete level.

The perceived location of sorghum cultivation within the domain of women, and a husband's inescapable dependence on his wife to "feed" him, was symbolically encapsulated in the harvesting of the sorghum. There were many tasks, such as fetching water, pounding, and cooking, that were seen as demeaning for adult men, but which men might do if there were no woman to do it for them. The final cutting of the ripe sorghum heads prior to their transportation to the granary, however, was something that was not only supposed to be done by women but, according to Kaonde ideology, *could only* be done by women. Men without wives—whether these were young men who had not yet married, or older men who were widowed or divorced—simply did not grow sorghum; and the answer I was always given if I asked why some man had no sorghum field was "He has no wife to harvest it." And this was an ideological norm that seemed to be adhered to in practice. Apart from once during my Kasempa fieldwork,[4] I never came across any man without a wife who grew sorghum. This one exception harvested his sorghum together with his only son, a teenage boy who lived with him, performing the domestic tasks that would normally be done by a man's wife. This man had lived without a wife for many years and was something of a recluse who was generally regarded as antisocial and an eccentric. When I pointed out to local people this exception to the rule they just shrugged and indicated that the man's general eccentricity was explanation enough.

Not only was sorghum cultivation located within the moral domain of women, it was also seen as *not* belonging to the modern world of agricultural officers, development planners, and production for the market. Neither the way women acquired sorghum fields nor how they obtained "help" on those fields nor the basic distribution of the harvested grain were seen as the kind of relationships that it was appropriate to organize through market mechanisms; these were relationships that were seen as primarily and properly organized through marriage. It was not so much that people saw the incorporation of sorghum into the world of market relations as transgressing some moral norm, but rather that it was so inextricably embedded in the nonmarket relations of marriage and kinship that people, as it were, simply could not imagine it outside those relations. Suggesting such a thing would have been analogous to suggesting to someone in the U.S. that relations between parents and children really ought to be organized on rationalist capitalist principles. In Kaonde eyes, the cultivation of sorghum was not about the production of commodities and exchange-value, it was about the production of food directly as use-values. It is true that exchange-value could be said to be struggling to emerge as economic relations in rural areas become more monetized and commoditized; but even though a certain amount of sorghum was sold, in theory at least, this was supposed only to be the surplus left over once the producing household's basic consumption needs were met. Sorghum was not grown *in order to be* sold. In local eyes sorghum was not a cash crop. As one elderly man told me, "We used to grow sorghum for our own consumption, but now we grow maize for money . . . " (Kibala, 14.viii.88, TK)

The development of "growing of maize for money" in Chizela Dis-

---

4. See Crehan (1987).

trict in the 1970s and 1980s was part of a more widespread expansion of maize production by small-scale producers in a number of the more remote provinces, where there had previously been little production of crops for sale to the national market. This expansion of production was dependent, however, on government support of various kinds, including the supply of inputs such as subsidized fertilizer and the collection of the harvested maize from local producers. Predictably, these support services have not been able to survive the new hard-nosed economic "realism" that has become so hegemonic a part of the economic "common sense" of the 1990s. The withdrawal of these services has led to this small boom in maize production collapsing as quickly as it developed.[5] In the late 1980s, however, the "growing of maize for money" was seen by both those living in the rural areas, and those in the Boma charged with their "development" as absolutely central to that "development." While a number of people in Kibala and Bukama may have had reservations about the practical value of this "development" in bringing about any real improvement in their lives, they had no doubts about its place in Boma thinking. A lack of "development" was how the Boma named their condition, just as the Boma named as central to its task the carrying of the gospel of "development" to backward "villagers." Given this hegemonic naming, those named as "villagers" had no alternative when dealing with the Boma but to use its language of "development." Indeed, this hegemony meant that local people had no other terms in which to talk about these kind of linkages with the wider economy. The "growing of maize for money" was a thing of the Boma, and even when struggling over the respective responsibilities of local "farmers" and government, those local "farmers" would frame their claims in the language of "development," just as during the colonial period people had used the discourse of the "tribe."

The production of maize for the national market, seen in the 1980s as such a key element in the "development" of rural Chizela, provides a good example of the kind of substantive realities into which commoditization and monetization can translate at the level of people's day-to-day lives. It also shows how strongly gendered these processes are. The next section explores this example, looking at the place of "growing of maize for money" within the local economy, and at how this economic opportunity was named. At the end of the section I also look briefly at

5. See the articles in Crehan and von Oppen (1994) for a discussion of various aspects of this maize boom.

three other foodstuffs, beer, fish and game meat. In the course of the colonial and postcolonial years all of these have—with little help from any "development" program—become ever more important as commodities. That is, they have come increasingly to be produced specifically for sale.

Kujima and "Farming"

The idea of producing crops for sale was not new in the Chizela of the 1980s, but cultivation for the market tended to be seen as something quite distinct and different from the ordinary cultivation of sorghum. This difference was marked in the term local people used to refer to it: *mwafwamu* (the English word *farm* with the addition of the appropriate prefixes and suffixes incorporated into Kaonde). The normal Kaonde term for cultivation or agriculture is *kujima*, the root meaning of which is "to hoe." *Mwafwamu* was seen as quite different from *kujima*. The way the two terms tended to be counterpoised by local people is illustrated in this exchange I had with one elderly LIMA chairman:

Crehan: You said that there are no women members in your [LIMA] group. What are the reasons for this?

Tyemba: They do not like to do farming [*nkito ya mwafwamu*] . . .

Crehan: Is it that the women here just want to cultivate sorghum?

Tyemba: That's it, they don't want to cultivate farms only sorghum.

(Kibala, 15.viii.88, TK)

In this book I use *kujima* to refer to the sorghum-based cultivation system I have described, and "farming," in quotation marks, to refer to the newer, market-oriented pattern of cultivation that used purchased inputs and cultivation methods laid down by agricultural extension agents, and that usually required access to credit from state agencies—in other words, what was referred to locally as *mwafwamu*. The basic differences between *kujima* and "farming" are summarized in table 2. This table shows clearly the high level of dependence of "farming" on services provided by the state, both as regards the production process itself and to ensure access to a market. While the sale of small surpluses

Table 2   *Kujima and "Farming"*

	Kujima	"Farming"
1.	Cultivation practices based on local skills and knowledge.	Cultivation practices based on recommendations by Agricultural Extension agents.
2.	No credit involved.	Credit from government-funded credit schemes normally used to buy inputs, and sometimes labor.
3.	Irregular, unmeasured plot, *chitimene* system, plot not stumped.	Measured rectangular plot, *chitimene* system not used, plot stumped.
4.	Seed (mainly sorghum, some maize), not purchased, local varieties.	Hybrid seed (maize, soya) purchased through Dept. of Agriculture.
5.	Seed broadcast.	Seed planted in rows.
6.	No fertilizer used.	Fertilizer used, purchased through Dept. of Agriculture.
7.	Hoes and harvesting knives the only tools used.	Tractor (if available) rented for ploughing.
8.	Female plot owner seen as having main responsibility for cultivation.	Registered plot owner (more often male) responsible for cultivation.
9.	Wage labor rarely employed.	Some casual wage labor employed.
10.	Grain stored in locally built granaries.	Grain stored in sacks purchased through Dept. of Agriculture.
11.	Bulk of grain used by producer's household, any surplus sold from producer's home at "customary" prices fixed informally.	Grain bought by government agency at nationally fixed prices. Collected from a limited number of government-determined collection points.

had long been an inherent part of the local economy,[6] the local demand—at least on the part of those with the necessary cash—was insufficient for the newer larger surpluses of "farming." Sale beyond the local community required transport, and in this remote, sparsely populated region with few roads transporting sizable amounts of bulky grain needed some kind of state-subsidized transport.

The main crop associated with "farming" was maize. Maize has long been an important subsidiary crop in *kujima*. Since it ripens earlier than sorghum, it helped to shorten the hunger period, experienced by almost

6. The colonial archives, for instance, have numerous references to sales of produce. See, for instance, ZNA, sec. 2/134, *Kasempa Annual Report on Native Affairs, 1935–1937*; sec. 2/936, *Kasempa Tour Reports, 1940–47*, Tour Report no. 5, 1940; sec. 2/155, *Provincial and District Organisation, Western Province, 1948*; sec. 2/136, *North-Western Province Annual Reports, 1953*.

all households, when the previous season's sorghum had been finished and the new sorghum was not yet ripe. After the introduction of the LIMA program in the late 1980s, however, the production of maize as a cash crop for sale to the national market increased rapidly. Chizela District was part of the area covered by a German-funded Integrated Rural Development Project (IRDP) that operated from the late 1970s to the early 1990s. A central element of this IRDP was the LIMA program. This consisted of a package of measures involving input supply, technical advice and marketing, which were designed to increase the production of small-scale producers, enabling them to sell to the national market. Although the scheme originally envisaged a range of crops in addition to maize, in Kibala and Bukama as in most of the project area, in practice, apart from some soya beans, LIMA meant maize.

Inherent in the IRDP there was always an interesting tension: Just who controlled the allocation of resources? Was it the expatriate experts or was it the Zambian government? And if it was the latter, *which* government institutions?[7] As an *integrated* development program in theory, the IRDP was supposed to work *through* local government institutions; in reality the German and other foreign experts working for the project always tended to exercise an ultimate control. It was they who had determined that the IRDP's primary "target group" should be the small-scale producer rather than "emergent farmers," a priority not necessarily shared by local government officials. As the district agricultural officer in Chizela stressed to me, for instance, "in the case of the IRDP, what I would very much say to them is that instead of just concentrating on the small-scale farmer they should also even help those progressive farmers, or emergent farmers" (Chizela, 27.xii.88, TE). Even when a Zambian was appointed as controller of the IRDP in the mid-eighties the German project advisor continued to exercise a considerable degree of control over the project's budget. The Zambian officials themselves tended to have few illusions about the nature of the power relationship. As the Chizela district governor put it,

The IRDP confined themselves to the small-scale . . . so these complaints [that other IRDPs have done more], have been there, that the IRDP has not done enough, but as beggars you have no choice, you have to thank, you have to thank for even the little some countries can do for us. (Chizela, 26.xii.88, TE)

7. See Crehan and von Oppen (1988) for a detailed account of the struggles within North-Western Province's IRDP.

Similarly, at one District Council meeting when one of the ward chairmen was insisting that "the Germans" had come to work for the Zambian government, the same district governor tried to inject a little political realism, muttering with some irritation how this kind of misunderstanding was an example of "village mentality." A key point to emphasize here is that wherever ultimate control over the IRDP may have been located, the program was never a neutral presence. As a potential source of what were by local standards a huge quantity of scarce and immensely valuable resources, the IRDP could not but represent a powerful intervention into local political arenas.

In the interests of efficiency the delivery of services to those participating in the LIMA program was organized on a group rather than an individual basis, and to this end local producers were formed into what were called LIMA groups. In Kibala there were five groups, the largest having eighteen members and the smallest six. In tsetse-free areas the IRDP had instituted a scheme that provided groups with oxen and ox carts to help with local transport. Chizela, however, had tsetse.

The most prominent "farmer" in Kibala, Temwa, embraced the LIMA program enthusiastically, and his account of the opportunities and problems of LIMA provides a view of how it looked to a male "farmer" anxious to expand his market production.

We were in luck when the Germans came. . . . I started farming and I saw that things were just moving in the right direction. . . . Even women were saying "Let's cultivate and make some money." . . . I said, "Indeed, cultivation is good." The Germans continued helping us with loans. The good thing about the Germans is that they came to help the poor. If a person lacks money, it is a good thing to give them a loan so that in the future they can stand on their own. When I started making money, I stopped getting loans. I used my own money to buy fertilizer. I would buy some food and call people to come and help me [i.e., give people food in return for agricultural work]. (Kibala, 24.viii.88, TK)

Transport, however, was always a major problem for Temwa, especially once he began producing eighty to ninety 90-kilogram sacks of maize. The marketing lorries of the North-Western Co-operative Union (NWCU, the provincial body responsible for buying crops for the national market) would come to Kibala to collect the LIMA crops, but they would only pick up from one of the designated collection points. Temwa talked to me at some length about his transport problem—my status as an influential outsider with access to the ears of those in power should be remembered here; this was in part an appeal. But nonetheless, his account reveals very clearly both the dependency of small-scale producers—and not only the small-scale—on a range of services, such as marketing, which they cannot possibly provide themselves; and also the kind of struggles in which they have to engage, and *expect* to engage in, to secure such services. It also illustrates the way claims on the government tended to be couched in a developmentalist and patriotic rhetoric.

It was a problem for me to transport my bags. . . . I cleared the road [the kilometer or so from Kibala school (where any visiting vehicles usually arrived) to Temwa's home] and said that if people want to help me they will come and collect the bags from here. They[8] refused, telling me I must take my bags to the same place as the rest of the group. Now the bags were just too many, I said to myself, "What can I do?" I went there to implore them [*nakapopwejile*][9] and they came and collected those bags. I did not stop farming, I produced [the next year] 90 bags of maize. They again told me to take the bags of maize to the group [collection point]. Then I fought hard until they moved the collection point near to me. . . . Then the IRDP changed its policy and refused to collect from individuals [beginning in 1986 the IRDP cut down on the number of collection points]. I failed to transport my maize. I went there again to plead with them, saying that I had a lot of bags of maize and I could not manage to take them to the [new] collection point. There is a good road [i.e., the one cleared by Temwa] on which the maize can be transported. Help me so that I will also be encouraged to grow more food if the lorry will come and collect it from near here. I can produce 100 to 200 bags of maize. They refused to collect the maize but they were telling us to grow more food. President Kaunda is always calling on people to grow more food. . . . The only way that Zambia can go forward is by grasping the hoe and tilling the land. . . . The problem of collecting the maize continues. . . . There is no transport. If they had given us even oxen, but there are no oxen. Even they could have given us wheelbarrows, there are no wheelbarrows. People cannot carry 100 bags on their head and make a profit. Someone has to find people to transport the maize and pay them. . . . In 1988 I have not grown enough because of transport. I only produced 15 bags . . . maybe the Government will find another way of helping us . . .

8. The "they" with whom Temwa struggled over this issue were essentially the local representatives of the Department of Agriculture, the agricultural extension worker, and the IRDP. In other words, "they" were all those who dwelled in the world of the Boma, the "they" that those in rural Chizela saw as controlling access to so many vital services.

9. The term Temwa used here, *nakapopwejile*, comes from the verb *kupopwela*, which is used for the clapping that forms such an important part of Kaonde greetings and of all expressions of respect, gratitude, and so on. It is used particularly when inferiors are showing respect for superiors, such as commoners to chiefs. The meaning that is especially relevant here is "to beg" or "to implore."

they should help us so we are encouraged to grow more food. (Kibala, 24.viii.88, TK)

If sorghum and *kujima* were associated with women, "farming" and LIMA were seen by both women and men as primarily a male affair; and the large majority of those who engaged in production for the market on any significant scale were men. Out of the total of sixty-three LIMA group members in Kibala in 1988, thirteen were women.[10] The statements by the two male LIMA "farmers," Kijila and Mulonda, that I quoted above—"The wife grows food to feed our bodies. I grow food to sell for money to clothe our bodies"; and "When we come to LIMA [crops] and soya beans, these automatically belong to me" (see p. 156)—reflect the assumption that "farming" properly belongs to men. The point here is not that it was seen as wrong for women to engage in "farming," but that their first responsibility was for the crops that would feed the household. If a woman could manage to do this *and* do some "farming," that was fine. Mulonda indeed stressed that some cash crops could be grown by women: "Even a woman has the right to grow soya beans" (Kibala, 14.viii.88, TK). Soya beans were considered particularly suitable since they were planted late so that their cultivation did not interfere with that of the main food crops. The other side of women's responsibility for *kujima* is, of course, that married *men* who decided to engage in *mwafwamu* could rely on their wives to provide the household's basic food needs, take responsibility for childcare and generally do the day-to-day work of servicing the household, which left husbands free to concentrate on cultivation for the market. The problem for women, therefore, was not that they were forbidden to engage in cultivation for the market, but that *in practice* it was often difficult for them to do so.

And women's *kujima* obligations were not the only barrier to their participation in the LIMA scheme. Another problem for women was the need to engage with the highly bureaucratic world of government and IRDP officialdom. This was a literate world, policed by endless forms (usually in English) that operated according to rules and conventions that local women, most of whom were illiterate even in Kaonde, let alone English, found alien and intimidating. It is true that this was

---

10. It was difficult to ascertain how active these groups were. A number of them seemed to have little existence beyond a list of names, but the relative exclusion of women is nonetheless significant.

also an intimidating world for many men in Chizela, but women faced the extra problem that, as we saw in the last chapter, it was also a space that was named by the prevailing hegemony as essentially *male*. The "proper" way for women to participate in this formal arena was via men, husbands, brothers, headmen and so on.

An instance of the difference, in practice if not according to the rules, between the way the LIMA scheme operated for men and for women was in the way the loan system was organized. During my stay in Kibala I watched the local agricultural assistant register "farmers" for loans for the coming cultivation season. It was he who filled in the forms and told registering loanees where to sign or put their thumbprint. To obtain a loan it was necessary to have the signature of two local guarantors. For the men registering this seemed to be no more than a formality. The man registering would simply call on a couple of the crowd of men standing round, all of whom were known to one another, and with the odd grumble they would add their signature or thumbprint. One elderly LIMA chairman, Mulonda, who had been called to sign several times did once demur, arguing that one particular man was perhaps taking on more than he could handle with two *lima* and it would be better if he were just to register for one. Mulonda was, however, brusquely told by the agricultural assistant that he had already written down "two *lima*," and in the face of the authority of the already written, Mulonda dutifully added his signature. In the case of women, however, whatever the official rules may have been, if the woman were married—and most women who registered for LIMA were married—then it was assumed by the agricultural assistant and everyone else in Kibala that one of the guarantors had to be her husband.

The development of "farming" (*mwafwamu*) can be seen as a particular example of a commoditization of cultivation geared around the production of crops specifically for sale to the national market. Local people themselves recognized this as something significantly different from the long-established practice of selling surplus crops produced as an integral part of the ordinary cultivation for consumption, as is shown by the clear distinction they made between *mwafwamu* and *kujima*. Maize, however, was not the only foodstuff that had become important as a commodity. Three others that had come to be seen as ways of generating a cash income were beer, fish, and game meat. From relatively early in the colonial period people had begun producing these for sale, and in the 1980s all of them were important both in terms of bringing cash into the local economy and in the local circulation of that cash. In all these cases this commoditization owed little to any "development" program. Even more than in the case of maize, however, these commodities were highly gendered: beer was produced and sold by women, while both fish and game meat were produced and sold by men.

The brewing and selling of beer was one of the main ways women managed to earn a certain amount of cash. Like the cultivation of sorghum, brewing was located clearly within the domain of women; providing beer for her husband and those to whom he wished to serve it was seen as one of the duties of a wife. And not only was brewing defined as a normal female task, it also fitted in well with their ordinary domestic responsibilities, and moreover there was always a local market for it, even if not an unlimited one. Women have been brewing grain beer, sometimes to celebrate a special occasion, sometimes for a communal work party (*mbile*), and sometimes just out of hospitality, ever since precolonial times. During the colonial period, however, women began also brewing beer for sale, apparently taking the idea from the bars of the urban areas. It has also become common for women to buy grain, either maize or sorghum, specifically to brew beer. In the 1980s beer brewing was so thoroughly commoditized that beer that was not brewed for sale or for a work party (later in the chapter I will have more to say about *mbile*), but simply to be offered to relatives and neighbors, had become the exception. The customers to whom the beer was sold were overwhelmingly male. In part beer brewing can be seen as a means through which women obtained a share of male incomes; even a husband would be expected to pay for the beer he consumed when his wife had brewed it for sale. The amounts of cash that women could earn through the sale of beer, at least in Kibala and Bukama, tended, however, to be considerably less than those that could be earned through *mwafwamu*.

Just as beer was seen as belonging to the domain of women, so fish and game were defined as the business of men. Like beer, both were important foodstuffs in precolonial times, and small-scale exchanges of meat or fish for grain seem to have been common. Then during the colonial period these exchanges started to become monetized. In the case of fish, the sale of dried fish to the urban areas developed early in the colonial period, more or less as soon as there were urban areas to sell to, and has continued to be an important source of income for many men. The great advantage of dried fish is its high value-to-weight ratio and its relatively good keeping qualities, both of which ease the problems of transport. Large and valuable bundles of fish can be transported quite long distances by bicycle. Temwa, the local entrepreneur who was so active in the LIMA scheme, got his start, as we shall see in the next chapter, as a fish trader.

Game meat too seems to have begun to become a commodity relatively early. Successful hunters—and only someone with a proven record of killing game was acknowledged as a hunter (*kibinda*)—always seem to have been few in number. This was one of the very few areas in which there was a genuine specialization. One of the great advantages of game meat (which like fish was often dried) as a commodity, which has remained fairly constant over the years, is that it is both a prestigious, highly valued food and it is in relatively short supply. Even though much of the hunting in the 1980s contravened the game laws—something that made its transport beyond the local area a risky business—there were always plenty of buyers for game meat, including Boma officials who would make special trips to the rural areas to buy meat. A hunter did not have to advertise that he had meat; word would quickly spread that this scarce and highly prized commodity was available, and he would usually soon have more eager customers than he had meat for. Apart from avoiding the game guards, the main problem sellers of meat faced was fending off the demands from kin for free meat, or for a specially low price.

The commoditization of beer and game meat had certain interesting similarities. Both beer and game meat can be seen as always having had a significantly social character in that these were foods that their producers expected to distribute among kin and neighbors. Prior to the commoditization of meat and beer, both, although not sold, were produced to be shared. A hunter who had killed an animal would normally have shared the meat, and been *expected* to share it, with his kin and neighbors, just as a woman did not brew for herself or even her household alone. A common occasion for the brewing of beer in the past was when a hunter had been successful, particularly if he had killed a notable animal such as an elephant or a lion. Significant here is the fact that both beer and game meat do not keep well and have to be consumed relatively quickly. In both cases, it seems this nonmonetized sharing transformed itself rather easily into selling, and into brewing and hunting being undertaken specifically to raise cash; even if, as in Kyakala's lament for the passing of the old ways, people would recall nostalgically a time prior to this commoditization.

A significant commonality in all the cases of commoditization I have considered was the importance of gender. Each commodity, whether maize, beer, fish, or game meat, was associated either with women or men. It was women who sold beer, men meat and fish, while, as we have seen, LIMA crops were seen locally, even if not in the eyes of the German architects of the IRDP, as primarily the business of men. The transformation of various goods into commodities represents a central thread in the story of monetization and commoditization but it was not the only thread. Another important part of this story was the commoditization of labor.

Commoditization and Labor

The buying and selling of labor has long been an established part of rural life in Chizela. Ever since the earliest days of colonialism local people have left the area in search of paid work, and a proportion of the money earned has always, in one way or another, found its way back to the migrants' home areas. The extent and pattern of the flow of migrants has varied over the years,[11] but the money that has flowed back into the rural areas, however little in absolute terms, has always been a significant element in the local economy. Since Independence there has in addition been the handful of rural-based, salaried government employees: the teachers, health workers, agricultural assistants, and so on. There was also some local employment of casual labor, which had led to the term *mupisweki* (piecework) entering the Kaonde language. It had become possible for men and women—particularly those who were widowed or divorced, or who had yet to marry—to *buy* certain of the goods and services that previously would have been provided by a spouse or some other kin.

Just as in the case of the commoditization of goods, however, the effects of the commoditization of labor power have tended to be significantly gendered. Whatever the form in which labor power has been sold, and whether as sellers or buyers of labor power, women and men have found themselves located somewhat differently.

As was discussed in chapter 3, the colonial migrant labor system mainly sucked huge numbers of men out of the rural areas. After Independence more women may have migrated to town, but even by the

11. Ferguson (1990b) argues that the pattern of labor migration, even in its colonial heyday, was always more complicated than the classic model would suggest.

time of the 1980 census they were still significantly outnumbered by men (GRZ 1981:7; Davies 1971:46). As the country's economic situation deteriorated in the seventies and eighties employment opportunities in general shrank, but for women things were even harder than for men (see, for instance, ILO 1981:31, 35–36). For most rural Zambians, particularly those in the more remote regions, the one road out of rural poverty and into a salaried job was that of education, although by the late eighties even jobs for the educated were becoming increasingly hard to come by. Salaried government officials in rural Chizela were overwhelmingly male, and those few who were women usually had jobs perceived as having to do with women, such as community development officer. In Kibala and Bukama all the twelve salaried government workers (nine teachers, two agricultural assistants, one clinical officer) were men.

Simply to acquire an education was more difficult for girls. Not all children in Kibala and Bukama went to school. A 1987 survey for the Ministry of Health, I was told by one of the teachers at Kibala school, had estimated that 78 percent of Kibala's school-age children were at school. Of those children who did attend school only a minority completed the full seven years of primary school, and of those the vast majority were boys. In 1988, for instance, Kibala primary school had forty-five children in Grade 1, of whom slightly more were girls than boys, but there were only twenty-eight children in Grade 7 and only six of these were girls. The small percentage of students from North-Western Province who passed the final exam well enough to be selected for secondary school were also mainly boys. An extra hurdle for those few girls (usually like their male counterparts in their late teens if not older) who did make it as far as secondary school was avoiding becoming pregnant, which for them, but not for the schoolboys often responsible, meant an end to their school career. The net result of all this was that there were far fewer educated rural women than men—something that had a considerable effect not only on their chances of finding any kind of salaried employment, but also on their ability to participate in the arenas of "modern" political life.

Women and men were also differently situated as regards local casual employment (*mapisweki*). Most male tasks tended to be one-off, periodic ones, and there were always men, particularly young unmarried ones, who were willing to clear fields, build a house, and generally to carry out such male tasks for money. Women without husbands, who could not persuade their male kin to help them, could—if they had the money—often buy the services they need. But just as in modern Western societies, the bulk of the day-to-day repetitive tasks associated with women (often servicing the needs of husband and children) did not seem to transform so easily into commodities as did the tasks performed by men. Given that local men tended to have readier access to cash than women, there was the somewhat paradoxical situation that while men were more likely to have the money to buy the services of women, they could only do this to a limited extent, whereas women tended not to have the necessary money. But those women who did, if they were prepared to pay what were seen in local eyes as scandalously high prices, had little problem in buying all the male labor they needed.

The fact that men had greater access to cash than women was another instance of the differential economic location of men and women. Men found cash easier to come by not only because it was easier for them to find paid work outside the local community, but also because they did not have the same day-to-day domestic responsibilities as women. In addition men also had a freedom of movement that was denied to women. A young man who had ceased to be part of his mother's household but was not yet married had few responsibilities and was free to use his time as he pleased. Such "youngsters" (*banyike*) had the added freedom that in their case, unlike that of more senior men (*bakulumpe*), there was no shame attached to their fetching their own water, cooking their own food, and so on. Also, they could often rely on a certain amount of help from their female kin with tasks such as pounding, particularly if they could supply the odd piece of game meat, or some fish, or help out with a male task such as building a shelter. Not only was it perfectly acceptable for such young men to roam about freely—in search of *mapisweki*, to go on hunting or fishing expeditions, or for any other reason that took their fancy—this was the kind of behavior *expected* of young men. It was not so easy for a woman, even one without a husband or children. Any woman, but particularly a young one, who attempted to travel around on her own, was likely to be branded a "loose woman," if not something worse, and would indeed run the risk of being harassed or possibly raped. Should something like that happen a woman could expect little sympathy; such behavior was clearly "asking for trouble." Even men who were married could quite easily fulfill their marital responsibilities and still be free to spend long periods away earning money in one way or another.

An interesting difference as regards the skills of women and men was that while men were perfectly capable of carrying out nearly all the tasks defined as "women's tasks," these were simply demeaning for an adult man; women actually lacked the skills to undertake most specifically male tasks. There was a very practical reason for this. Since a woman's children were a significant source of labor to her, male children in the course of their early socialization were all taught how to do such female tasks as pounding, cooking, or cultivation; and young boys were expected to help their mothers with these tasks, particularly if there were no young girls in the household. At a certain point a boy would manage to detach himself from the world of women and children and would join the adult male world. It was only then, within this adult male world, that boys would learn the specifically male skills, such as building or hunting; since this world was inaccessible to girls, there was no opportunity for them to acquire these skills. Not that local women *wanted* to usurp male tasks—something that some Western feminists have difficulty understanding. As far as the women of Kibala and Bukama were concerned the allotted "female" tasks gave them more than enough work as it was, and they were not about to give up what they saw as their clear and morally inescapable claims to the labor of husbands and other male kin.

With the exception of beer brewing, women's opportunities to earn a little money were usually confined to the worst-paid *mapisweki*. They could earn small amounts of money working on the fields of others, most often being employed by men on *mwafwamu*. Quite often the payment for such work was not cash but small amounts of grain, or maybe some soap or salt. Within rural Chizela wage rates for *mapisweki* were generally low, and the lowest rates of all tended to be paid for the kind of cultivation tasks mainly done by women, such as weeding. Only the most desperate man, maybe one who was disabled or a little weak in the head, would ever consider doing such female, demeaning *mapisweki*.

One of the general characteristics of almost all labor processes in Kibala and Bukama was that they could easily be carried out, and frequently were, by individuals working on their own. I have already described the individual nature of ordinary cultivation (*kujima* that is, rather than "farming"), with men preparing fields on their own and wives being responsible for the growing of the crops. The processing of these crops into food, the pounding of grain, and its processing into flour, for example, were similarly tasks carried out by a woman working on her own with no more help than that provided by her dependent children. It is true that groups of women often worked together, particularly when pounding grain, but each woman would nonetheless have

her own stock of grain that she alone pounded and winnowed to produce her own stock of flour. Sometimes a mother and an adult daughter,
or an adult grandchild helping her grandmother, would work on a common stock of grain, but these were the exceptions rather than the rule.
When women went to collect water or firewood, again, although most
preferred the sociability—and the added security—of going with other
women, as labor processes these were carried out by individuals. Male
tasks, the building of a house or a granary, for instance, also tended to
be undertaken by men working alone, or perhaps with a young boy as
helper. Even hunting seldom seemed to involve more than two or three
men, and again the pattern was often an older man accompanied by a
younger one. Men also frequently hunted alone. The main exception
here was fishing. Fishing, which only some men engaged in, was most
commonly carried out with the use of fish dams which were usually
constructed and owned by a group of men, normally relatives.

In general, however, the process of production in both Kibala and
Bukama was extremely individualized; co-operation at the level of production did not seem to be something people either expected or were
comfortable with. This lack of enthusiasm was not, however, shared
by the state, which has persisted in advocating the formation of co-
operative societies and other forms of co-operative labor as a primary
means of integrating those in the rural areas more fully into the national economy. The final section of this chapter focuses on the notion
of "co-operation," looking both at how this was understood by UNIP's
Ministry of Co operatives and at the place of co-operation in the ordinary economic life of Kibala and Bukama. It also looks at the actual
organizations that had come into being in Kibala and Bukama in the
name of "co-operation."

"Mobilizing the Masses": Co-operation in Theory and Practice

In Zambia as in many other third-world countries, the
co-operative has had a long history as a favored instrument for fos-
tering "development" and enabling the poor and disadvantaged to
share in its benefits. And despite its dismal history, a long legacy of
mismanaged funds, outright corruption, and disappointed hopes,
UNIP never lost faith in the co-operative as a leading player in its

development scenario. Included in the Fourth National Development Plan, published in 1989, for instance, was a Co-operative Development Plan "designed to mobilise the masses for accelerated development in Zambia" (GRZ 1989:423). Rather like Evans-Pritchard's famous Zande witchcraft oracles (Evans-Pritchard 1937), however often actual co-operatives failed, this was always seen as the fault of the particular individuals running them; the idea itself and the assumptions underpinning it were never called into question. The importance of the co-operative in bringing "development" seemed indeed to have a hegemonic authority putting it beyond question. Both Kibala and Bukama had co-operative societies, but to understand the substantive reality these entities had assumed it is helpful to begin with some local forms of "co-operation" and the place of these in rural Chizela's economic life.

The most common form of co-operative labor was *mbile*, the Kaonde term for the work party, common throughout Africa, where people gather to work on someone's fields in return for beer. In Kibala and Bukama *mbile* for meat, dried fish, and soap were also common. In both places many people used *mbile*, particularly at the beginning of the cultivation season for the initial hoeing and planting of fields. At the same time there were plenty of grumbles both on the part of those attending *mbile* and those organizing them. I would frequently come across people returning from *mbile* complaining about how small a piece of meat or soap they were given, or how soon the beer ran out. From the other side I would hear complaints that people had done hardly any work before putting down their hoes. Such implicit struggles over what reward was "fair" for what amount of work can be seen as bringing about something like a local "price"; if people got a reputation for being too stingy then there would be few takers for their *mbile*, while if the amount of work done dropped below a certain level presumably people would not find it worthwhile to have *mbile* at all. In local eyes *mbile* seemed in fact increasingly to be seen as the sale of labor, group "*mapisweki*," as it were, rather than a moment in a more long-term, nonmonetized relation of reciprocity. This shift could indeed be thought of as a concrete example of what the shift from an understanding of human relations based on a notion of reciprocity to one based on the notion of the contract means in practice.

Another work-sharing arrangement also common in other parts of Africa was termed in Kaonde *kilimba*. This is a system whereby a group of people agree to work jointly on each other's fields for one cultivation season, commonly working together for one day in turn on the fields of each member of the group. But although it existed in Kibala and Bukama, it did not seem to be popular. People's experiences of *kilimba* in Bukama illustrate the local distrust of such co-operation. Most people I talked to in 1988 agreed that *kilimba* was a very good system *in principle*, but hardly any were actually practicing this form of co-operation. I was told that a couple of years previously in 1986, when for the first time tractor-ploughing services had not been available on the settlement scheme, many people had tried it, but for most it had not been a particularly happy experience. The problem, as a number of people explained to me, is that those participating can only be relied on to work hard on their own fields. When the time comes for them to cultivate on other people's fields they only work halfheartedly, complaining that the sun is too hot or discovering that they have left their hoe at home and have to go back for it. Then when they do start hoeing they do not exert themselves but just scratch around on the surface of the soil for a bit before stopping altogether; or, a frequent complaint, they suddenly develop some serious illness that prevents them from coming that day at all. This latter excuse was particularly tricky given the local prevalence of malaria and so many other endemic diseases; people *were* often genuinely sick.

The only circumstances it seems in which *kilimba* worked satisfactorily, at least in Bukama, was when those involved were close relatives, preferably who also lived close to one another. There were very few who were planning to use *kilimba* in the 1988/89 season. Among those were, firstly, the three wives of Chief Chizela, and secondly, a man who had been part of a *kilimba* in 1986 made up of his own wife and children, plus his full brother (same father, same mother), and his wife and children. These two brothers lived on neighboring farms, and their joint cultivation was confined to the two men's LIMA fields, their wives' fields being excluded. Thirdly, there was a man who had been involved in a *kilimba* in 1986 that had included several members who were not close relatives. In 1988 he was again planning to use *kilimba*, but this time the group was to be made up entirely from those within his own homestead, because, as he explained, this would make it easier to control people and to tell whether or not they are feigning sickness. In sum, if a system such as *kilimba* is to work, there has to be a high degree of trust between the participants, and it was precisely this trust that seemed to be lacking. It is not that joint productive enterprises were impossible, but in order for them to be successful there needed to be rather special circumstances.

In other words, although co-operation at the level of the labor process could work, it was not, as it were, an organic part of local production, and those involved needed to have overcome the general deep-rooted distrust of others. This distrust, by contrast, very much *was* an organic part of Kibala's and Bukama's daily life.

The distrust of collective productive enterprises, and a certain general suspicion and lack of trust in others, can be linked to a basic character-istic of economic life in rural Chizela. On the one hand, while there was a complex interdependence between husband and wife, individual households had a high degree of autonomy as regards the provision of the bulk of day-to-day consumption needs. In the main, local labor pro-cesses did not compel individuals to come together to produce the basic goods of everyday life. On the other hand, people *were* crucially depen-dent on wider kin networks to meet longer-term security needs. In times of trouble, when there was sickness, when crops had failed, or for some other reason food was short, it was to their kin that people turned— and turned not for charity but for what was simply their moral due. A certain generalized reciprocity was in fact a crucial part of the distribu-tion of the social product. Part of the very definition of kinship was the sharing of surplus; morally it was impossible to deny the appeal of a kinsperson in need. But this was not a reciprocity that involved co-operation at the level of production. Nor did people's unquestioning acceptance that kin *ought* to help one another necessarily translate into the expectation that individual kin could always be relied on to live up to the highest moral standards.

The people of Kibala and Bukama tended to see co-operation beyond the household as inherently problematic, although not impossible. When people did succeed in working together the term that was used to refer to this ability was *lumvwañano*, which Wright translates as "agreement, concord, harmony, (bond of) fellowship" (Wright n.d.). *Lumvwañano* was invoked when people wanted to account for an in-stance of successful working together, or when they wanted to explain to me what was needed if something like a co-operative was to work. Several people explained the problem with *kilimba* in terms of a lack of *lumvwañano* (*lumvwañano kafwako*). Co-operation was clearly something that people did not take for granted and saw as requiring particular circumstances or particular people who were skilled in *lumvwañano*. This distrust, however, was not shared by either the government or foreign aid donors, and in the next section I want to look at the local organi-zations that had come into being as a result of their enthusiasm for "co-operation." The unshakable faith of "the Party and its government" in the co-operative society had resulted in the creation of the Kibala and Bukama Multi-Purpose Co-operative Societies, but just what kind of entities *were* these?

Two Co-operative Societies

The Kibala Multi-Purpose Co-operative Society was formed in early 1987, largely at the prompting of the Village Self Reliance (VSR) team, who had been visiting Kibala regularly since 1986. The VSR scheme was an IRDP initiative that involved a VSR promoter visiting selected wards with the twin aims of promoting "self-reliant development," and establishing a ward secretariat that would serve as an information channel between the ward, the IRDP, and Boma officials generally. Within Kibala itself the driving force behind the attempt to establish a co-operative was the teacher Sansoni, who was both the society's secretary and the secretary of the ward. By July 1988 the total membership was twenty-nine, mostly men, all of whom were supposed to buy three shares at K50 each, giving a potential share capital of K4,350, of which K950 had actually been paid. When I asked Sansoni and the society chairman, the local headmaster, about the projects the co-operative was engaged in, I was told of plans to cultivate two hectares of maize, establish a fish-trading business, open a shop to sell goods brought from town, and buy a hammer mill. As yet, however, none of these projects had been realized. Although there had been a lot of talk about the hammer mill project, and local women in particular were very enthusiastic, the huge gulf between the almost K30,000 that the cheapest hammer mill would cost and the society's actual funds made its realization highly unlikely. As for the other projects nothing so far had been done toward any of them; not one *lima*, for instance, had been cleared for the collective maize plot.

In comparison to the Kibala Society, the Bukama Multi-Purpose Co-operative Society was far more established; it was a member of the provincial-level North-Western Co-operative Union (NWCU), for which it had begun handling input distribution, marketing, and credit within Bukama. At the end of the eighties the provision of such services to the mass of small-scale producers had become the responsibility of the provincial co-operative unions and they tended to see the primary function of ward-level co-operatives as being the delivery of these services. Although the Bukama Society had various plans for a consumer shop and the like, the only activities it was carrying out at the time of my stay in Bukama were those it was undertaking on behalf of NWCU; or rather these were almost the only activities. Two *lima*, one of maize and one of soya beans, were cultivated as Co-operative Society projects in the 1987/88 season, but interestingly I only found out about these accidentally. They were not mentioned to me spontaneously by any of the members when I asked them about the society's activities. The reason they were not seen as relevant is perhaps that they were not undertaken as joint projects by the co-operative as a whole but by small groups within it. The idea behind these collective plots was not to generate funds for the co-operative as a whole but to enable the individual participants to raise money that they could use to help pay their share capital. The story of these collective plots is a further illustration of local attitudes to collective production.

The co-operative's original plan was to divide its forty-four members (twenty-seven men and seventeen women) into four groups and for each group to cultivate a *lima* jointly, but only two of the groups actually carried out the plan. One of these was composed exclusively of men, and included most of the society's board of directors, and the other centered around a rather remarkable group of three elderly widows and was composed only of women. Of the two, only the female group worked successfully together and was planning to repeat the experience. Both they themselves and others attributed their success to their *lum-vwañano* (ability to cooperate). Of the three widows, who were the nucleus of the group, two were siblings and the other was the daughter of their *mwisho* (mother's brother). The three plots on which they lived were adjacent to one another, and the women were unusual in that they often worked co-operatively with one another in all their day-to-day tasks. The experience of the male group was less happy; a little maize had been produced, but by the end of the cultivation season the group had disintegrated amid mutual accusations of failure to work properly on the plot and recriminations about unpaid money owed to individual members. Only in exceptional circumstances, it seems, such as the unusually co-operative living arrangements of the three widows, did such collective undertakings not fall prey to distrust and suspicion.

From the perspective of NWCU, however, the primary function of local co-operatives tended to be seen as the facilitation of the union's delivery of marketing input supply and credit services to the small-scale producer. The 1988 marketing season was the first in which the Bukama

Society handled the buying of crops for the union, and during my stay there it was engaged in handing out, mostly on credit, the inputs for the 1988/89 season. One of the main reasons why people in Bukama had joined the co-operative, it seemed, was that while at that time it was providing these services for members and nonmembers alike, in the future people thought members would be given special privileges. When I asked the chairman, for instance, about the benefits of membership, one of the first things he mentioned was that when the society got its hammer mill there would be a special cheap rate for members, and that, if there were a queue, members would be served before nonmembers. Also, when I asked co-operative members what would happen if inputs, say, were in short supply, almost everybody said that in such a case members would be given preference. The secretary later told me that although the society was currently providing credit for inputs to both members and nonmembers, in the future credit would be restricted to members.

The sense that membership in the society was likely to become important in maintaining access to the support services so crucial for those wanting to participate in "farming" was probably the main reason why those who had joined the co-operative had thought it worthwhile to invest a few kwacha in this way. When I asked members about the advantage of belonging to the co-operative, people were likely to reel off a list of ambitious projects; but when I went on to ask about actual benefits already experienced, the most common answer, sometimes accompanied by a short, was *kufwako* (nothing). The host of potential benefits to be derived from a co-operative, which people produced so readily for me, can be seen as an example of one of the ways hegemony works. It is an example, that is, of how people shape their answers to questions according to what they perceive to be the appropriate and "correct" ones within the particular context in which the questions are being asked. The local skepticism about the practical utility of the co-operative was also reflected in the rather small sums of money most individuals had invested; of the society's fifty-one members more than half had paid less that 50 percent of the K100 share capital demanded, and eighteen had paid only K20 or less.

An important part of the meaning of the co-operative society for the people of Kibala and Bukama was that, like other manifestations of the state at the local level, it appeared to offer a means through which people could link themselves into the powerful world of the Boma. Inevitably it was an entity that came from outside, carrying with it the authentic bureaucratic trappings of the modern world: a board of directors, meetings with agendas, secretaries who keep minutes (in English), and so on, all marks of that which is "modern" and "progressive" as opposed to "backward" and "traditional." The "modern" is literate—consuming vast amounts of stationery, in the 1980s a scarce and difficult-to-obtain resource in rural areas. It is bureaucratic and tends to operate in English. The forms of organization produced by the rural areas themselves were radically different; these were organizations rooted in the hierarchies of kinship and which were primarily oral. For those attempting to forge links with the misty world of power beyond the local, however, it was precisely the alien quality of an institution like the co-operative—an alienness that so clearly stamped it as a thing of the Boma—that gave it much of its legitimacy. This was how things were done in the Boma, and those who wanted to be players in that world would have to abide by its rules.

The co-operative was seen by many as a means, recognized as legitimate by the Boma world, through which it was possible to press claims on that world. What you do if you want the government, NWCU, IRDP, or whoever to provide you with a depot, a hammer mill, or something similar is to form a co-operative. How that co-operative is organized depends on criteria laid down by that external world—for instance, the need to follow certain bureaucratic procedures, at least in theory. The inability of most senior men to operate in English and their lack of basic accounting skills can lead to these procedures undergoing various changes. When I asked the treasurer of the Bukama Society, for instance, how much share capital members had in fact paid, he told me that he had not counted it yet. But a profound dependency on an external and foreign world, and the anxiety to achieve legitimacy in the eyes of that world, is, I would argue, a crucial reality that should never be forgotten if we want to understand the actual entities into which co-operatives have developed in rural Zambia. Nonetheless, the organizational form of the Kibala and Bukama co-operatives was also shaped by local assumptions as to the basic principles underlying *any* organization involving individuals; in particular they were shaped by the deeply ingrained belief in hierarchy and the deep distrust of co-operative productive enterprises. One way such suspicions manifested themselves was in accusations that the local co-operative was full of thieves, which was one of the reasons a number of people in Bukama gave me for not joining the co-operative. At the same time the fact that a co-operative was perceived as an organization run by, and for, the local elite could lead, as in the case of the Women's League discussed earlier, to individuals becoming members primarily to demonstrate that they did indeed belong to that elite.

Reciprocity and Contract

In this chapter I have tried to map out some of the broad contours of the economic landscape inhabited by the people of Kibala and Bukama. These contours, as we have seen, were highly gendered; the economic opportunities and constraints women and men confronted were significantly and systematically different. Monetization and commoditization may have reached deep into virtually every corner of Bukama and Kibala, but the tectonic forces unleashed by them have had different effects on the lives of women than of men. In general, whether it was a question of earning cash by selling goods or by selling labor itself, women had fewer, and less profitable, options than men. Women, that is, faced a number of systematic disadvantages stemming in part from the specific ways in which commoditized and noncommoditized production intertwined with one another. Where men and women were located within those parts of production directly concerned with fulfilling consumption needs also tended to determine how they found themselves situated as regards commoditized production. On the whole, as in the example of "farming," women tended to find themselves in a rather different place to that of men.

This differential location could lead to conflicts of interest between women and men, particularly between wives and husbands. For instance, how should labor be used? Should a husband invest his time in preparing sorghum fields and helping his wife with cultivation, or should he spend his time on his LIMA fields? How much time should a woman spend working on her sorghum fields, growing grain for consumption, and how much working on the LIMA fields (whether these were her own LIMA fields, her husband's, or owned jointly)? The point here is that how access to markets beyond the local community is organized and the way this fits in with production for consumption (which involves such things as state policies on input supply and marketing services) tends to have different implications for men and women. Women, for instance, might have been more interested in expanding the market for sorghum surpluses, enabling them to integrate more easily

production for consumption and for sale, whereas men might have preferred separate cash crop fields, where they were likely to have greater
control over the profits.

Such conflicts of interest were not necessarily fought out in any open,
explicit way, but the fact that such struggles may be implicit and hidden,
present not in what people *say* but underlying what they *do*, does not
make them any the less struggles. There might be a tussle, for instance,
between a woman and her husband or son-in-law as she tried to get him
to clear a field for her when he would rather be working on his LIMA
plot or catching fish to dry and take for sale in town; or husband and
wife might quarrel over whether some of her sorghum harvest should
be sold, and if it were, what the profits should be spent on. Such conflictual relationships between women and men were, however, entangled
with supportive relationships that bound them together in various ways.
A wife, for instance, might be just as keen as her husband that the marketing lorries should come and collect his LIMA crops since although
the proceeds might go to him, this was money to which she had some
claim. A wife had a certain claim to a say in how such money was spent
simply because of the acknowledged obligation of a husband "to clothe
his wife." No man who received a substantial sum of money, from whatever source, could escape pressure from his wife (or wives) to spend
some of it on her, or her children, maybe buying clothes or a blanket,
or paying children's school expenses. Such claims, however, were greatly
strengthened when a wife had worked on her husband's LIMA fields.
This was indeed one explanation I was given for why some husbands
were not particularly anxious for their wives to work on their LIMA
fields.

I began this chapter by drawing attention to the coexistence in rural
Chizela of two different ways of organizing flows of goods and services:
one based on market principles, money, and exchange-value; and one
based on a web of reciprocal obligations between kin. As I have tried to
show, these two mechanisms of distribution can be seen as associated
with two rather different sets of assumptions or indeed cultures; one of
which can be termed a "culture of contract" and the other a "culture of
reciprocity." These can be thought of as "cultures" in that their basic
assumptions have become, to use Bakhtin's terminology, part of "the
fundamental social evaluations which develop directly from the specific
conditions of the economic life of a given group [which] are not usually
uttered" (Bakhtin 1988:13). As we have seen, these two "cultures" co-

existed in rural Chizela in a sometimes uneasy relationship.[12] An example of this was the running battle of wills between fishermen trying to take their bundles of dried fish to sell in the more lucrative urban markets, and local women demanding that they sell to them, their kinswomen, at low prices. The moral pressures on the fishermen could lead to them engaging in all kinds of stratagems to avoid the sharp eyes of their kin, particularly their female kin—from creeping round the outskirts of settlements on their way to town at times when few people were likely to be about to sitting outside their house steadfastly denying that they had any fish despite an unmistakable fishy stench.

Having in the previous two chapters and this chapter mapped out some of the broad economic and political contours of life in Kibala and Bukama, in the next chapter I turn to the question of how the people of these communities themselves saw those contours. How did they themselves imagine their community?

---

12. Even in modern industrial societies, although the "culture of the contract" undoubtedly dominates, "reciprocity" is by no means absent. Some notion of reciprocity is fundamental, for instance, within the family where so many crucial human needs are met through noncommoditized labor. There is a key difference, however, in that in modern industrial societies the "culture of the contract" tends to be *the* hegemonic pattern for social relations in general. The tendency in recent years, seen in various legal developments, to recast marriage and even the relationship between parents and children in terms of a clearly bounded contract is an interesting example of this.

CHAPTER 6

Imagined Locations:
The Dangerous Community

---

*Those that work hard are the ones they point at as balozhi [witches],
those who work very hard and produce enough food. They just say,
"s/he is using bwanga [substance or knowledge associated with
witchcraft]." Even now they are saying that the person who has a lot
of maize is a mulozhi [witch] who is putting children in his maize
sacks [i.e., killing children to increase the yield] so that he can have
a big yield. But me I am not discouraged, because I know that
these people are simply backward.*

Temwa, Kibala, 24.viii.88

*To the extent that ideologies are historically necessary they have a
validity which is "psychological"; they "organise" human masses,
and create the terrain on which men move, acquire consciousness of
their position, struggle etc.*

Antonio Gramsci,
*Selections from
the Prison Notebooks*

Part One: Devouring Kin

---

*The most feared ones [i.e., as balozhi] are the relatives because
they know them very well, they know how they live, they know
how they eat, they have known them from their childhood up to
their growth time. That's how the fear comes in.*

Sansoni, Kibala, 1.xi.88

The first two chapters of this study focused on its theoretical location, my own location within 1980s rural Chizela, and the naming of the people of North-Western Province by colonial administrators and academics. The next three chapters were my attempt to map out some of the broad contours of Kibala's and Bukama's economic and political landscape. In this chapter I want to shift the focus to how those within that landscape themselves imagined their location, and how they themselves named their world. The particular site I have chosen to look at here is witchcraft (*bulozhi*). I chose this site, firstly, because a belief in the reality of witchcraft was an inescapable part of day-to-day life in Kibala and Bukama. The names associated with this dark realm were central to many of the explanations people gave of why certain things, above all any kind of misfortune, had happened to them. A second reason for focusing on witchcraft is that this way of understanding the world was so entangled with the whole discourse of kinship.

As I have tried to show in earlier chapters, while the national state was certainly a very real presence in the lives of the people of Kibala and Bukama and people clearly thought of themselves as Zambian citizens, their primary imagined community remained the community of kinship. The basic assumptions underpinning this community of kin were threaded through the accounts people gave of their lives and their world. But because these assumptions were so taken for granted they were often an implicit rather than an explicit presence; an unspoken substratum informing that which was actually said. There was an elusiveness here stemming from the very indisputability of these "facts" of kinship. These were the kinds of "facts" that Bakhtin was talking about when he stressed how "fundamental social evaluations" are not that which is spoken about. "If an evaluation, is in reality conditioned by the very being of a given collective, then it is accepted dogmatically as something understood and not subject to discussion. Conversely, where the basic evaluation is expressed and demonstrated, it has already in that case become equivocal . . . it has ceased to organize life" (Bakhtin 1988:13). Given this elusiveness, where might such structuring threads have nonetheless revealed themselves (even if only in indirect ways) in the everyday life of Kibala and Bukama? One place where it seemed to me that some of the deepest assumptions about kinship had left their traces was in local beliefs about witchcraft (*bulozhi*).

What I argue in this chapter is that these beliefs can be seen as holding up a mirror, albeit a cloudy one, in which the bonds of kinship were shown in a reversed and distorted form. In the world of *bulozhi* the relations between witches (*balozhi*) and their victims were the relations of kinship, but a kinship that had assumed a fantastic and negative shape. Through an exploration of these beliefs it is possible to glimpse a little of what it meant to live embedded within the hegemony of the community of kin—and what this meant not only intellectually but also emotionally. What kinship meant in 1980s Chizela, however, was very much shaped by the reality that the community of kin was embedded within a wider world of markets, citizenship, and the state.

What this chapter is about is a world of kinship turned upside down: the world of *bulozhi*. I begin with an incident that illustrates both the omnipresence and the essential ordinariness of *bulozhi* for the people of Kibala and Bukama. I then explore the basic contours of the local discourse on *bulozhi*, and some of the images and metaphors at its heart. I go on to look at the relationship between the suspicion of *bulozhi* and certain tensions inherent in the social world of 1980s rural Chizela. Tracing out the links between the suspicion of *bulozhi* and these tensions helps reveal something of the contours of the imagined community of kin and the nature of its entanglement with the market forces already present within it—market forces that were eating away at some of its deepest roots, or rather maybe forcing them to grow in different directions. Through this tracing out it is possible, I hope, to provide some glimpses at least of what it meant to *live* this complicated reality.

Everyday Evil

For the people of Kibala and Bukama the reality of *bulozhi* was a hegemonic fact. *Bulozhi* was an omnipresent reality that cast its threatening shadow over the most basic interactions of daily life. Its everyday, unremarkable nature for local people was brought home to me in an interview I had with the agricultural extension officer in Bukama, Takawali, about the history of the Bukama settlement scheme. He began by giving me a list of all those who had been registered with the scheme since its inception. Among those listed were six men who by 1988 had died. According to Takawali, who had himself come to Bukama only a few months before I arrived, all but one of these deaths had been the result of witchcraft (since we were talking in English, Takawali used the English term). The sole exception was a man who had been beaten to death, and there were rumors that he too had been killed by *bulozhi*. Apart from this man, who may simply have been murdered, it was generally believed that *all* the plot holders who had died had been killed by *bulozhi*. And this fact was recounted by Takawali in exactly the same matter-of-fact tone in which he went on to tell me about the size of the scheme, the amount of land that had been cleared, and so on. That this was not seen by Takawali, or anyone else in Bukama, as in any way unusual illustrates how in both Bukama and Kibala almost all deaths were attributed, at least by some of those involved, to *bulozhi*. In Kibala, for instance, it seemed to have been commonly agreed that a six months' pregnant woman who died after drinking a full three bottles of *lutuku* (the locally distilled, and fiercesomely strong, spirit) had been killed by *bulozhi*. And, as Takawali illustrates, a belief in the reality of *bulozhi* was not limited to unenlightened "villagers," but, in some form or other, was shared by many, if not all, the government employees in both Bukama and Kibala.

Just as kinship relations were seen by the people of rural Chizela as providing the basic ties that wove individuals into a community, so *bulozhi* can be seen as the shadowed underside of that kinship fabric. *Bulozhi* was what happened when individuals substituted their own selfish greed for a proper concern for the well-being of their kin. The local discourse on *bulozhi* can be seen in part as a moral critique that gave people a set of powerful, and morally charged, images and metaphors with which to attribute blame for the various misfortunes and differential success of everyday life. Misfortune and bad luck could always be explained as the result of the personal malevolence of particular individuals and in particular their perversion of the normal obligations of kinship. In other words, a perceived denial of proper respect (*mushingi*) and failure to fulfill the expectations inherent in the *mukulumpe/mwanyike* hierarchy took on a gross and caricatured form in the concrete image of the *mulozhi* (witch). The notion of *bulozhi* provided people, as it were, with a way of naming the failure of kinship.

But while the discourse on *bulozhi* may have had its deepest roots in the community of kinship, it also had its own autonomy. The assumption that malevolent individuals are able to harm others in ways that are undetectable except to those with specialist knowledge of "witches" and their ways has become a basic element of how many people throughout rural Zambia (and much of sub-Saharan Africa) understand causality in general.[1] At the same time the particular stress put on this kind of cau-

---

1. See Comaroff and Comaroff (1993) for a recent collection of articles on witchcraft beliefs in Africa. Karp and Bird (1987) focuses more generally on African systems of

sation and the specifics of the beliefs associated with it vary enormously. For those growing up in a community saturated by such an understanding of causality it provides an immensely persuasive explanation of misfortune and bad luck, as is demonstrated by its hold even over those, such as Takawali and other local government employees, who were normally not part of the local kinship community.

An interesting example of the power of such beliefs and their ability to impose their names on misfortune and sickness at the expense of those of modern "scientific" understandings was the unhappy experiences of the clinical officer in Kibala, Bateya. Bateya was a stranger with no kinship links in Kibala; he was not even Kaonde. Since 1983 he had lived and worked in Kibala, and when I met him at the beginning of my fieldwork he was awaiting his transfer to another clinic. He had completed the full five years of secondary school and a three-year medical training. He very much defined himself as a man of science, and when I first met him he immediately introduced me to his infant son Leon, named for Leon Trotsky. Trotsky's writings, Bateya told me, had transformed his thinking. When I interviewed him about his work in Kibala he assured me that most local people had now come to realize that illnesses are caused by germs not witchcraft, and that they were relying less on traditional healers. I later found out, however, from one of the teachers who was a close friend of Bateya, that the reason why he had asked the Ministry of Health for a transfer was his conviction that local people were attacking him with *bulozhi*. The form these attacks took was insomnia; either he would be simply unable to sleep or, when he did manage to snatch a few minutes' rest, he would be tormented with terrible nightmares. Later I confirmed with Bateya that this was indeed why he wanted to leave Kibala.

One of the difficulties in casting off these kinds of beliefs is that, since they are centered around the problem of misfortune and its causality, they tend to suggest themselves as explanations precisely at those times when individuals are feeling insecure and threatened. A child fails to thrive, someone suddenly falls sick or has an accident, and some kind of emotionally satisfying answer has to be found for the question of "Why *me*, why *my* child?" Then again, it may be, as perhaps with Bateya, that someone living in an alien place far from his own kin simply feels

---

thought and their relationship to particular social contexts, while Arens and Karp (1989) looks at concepts of power.

isolated and vulnerable. It is understandable that someone who has grown up in an environment in which the reality of witchcraft is taken for granted, who lies tossing and turning in the small hours unable to sleep night after night, finds it hard to silence the voices in his head insistently telling him that somewhere, out there in the dark, someone is actively stopping him from sleeping.

Similar beliefs to those that tormented Bateya are undoubtedly common throughout Zambia.[2] My specific focus in this chapter, however, is on the *Kaonde* discourse on evil and how this was linked to the ways in which people in Kibala and Bukama lived the community of kin. As regards its fundamental assumptions, this Kaonde discourse is probably similar to those to be found among a number of neighboring peoples, but what I am interested in here is what this particular Kaonde variant can tell us about the meaning kinship had for those living in Kibala and Bukama in the 1980s.

A good place to begin is with some basic Kaonde terms associated with the domain of witchcraft. However, in attempting to introduce these terms and providing glosses for them we at once run into the problem of finding English equivalents for terms for which there are seldom straightforward synonyms—only words such as *witchcraft* itself, carrying their own baggage of often misleading, but for the English speaker difficult-to-discard, associations.[3] The way I have tried to deal with this problem is, in general, to avoid English language terms such as *witchcraft*, which are so suffused with preexisting European meanings, and, after providing a brief gloss in English, to use the Kaonde terms themselves. The main exception to this rule is when I am quoting from people who were speaking English. It might be objected that since English terms such as *witchcraft* have become a normal part of Zambian English, why not use them? However, the associations conjured up for most English-speaking Zambians by words such as *witchcraft* or *bewitch*, I would argue, remain those of the local discourses on witchcraft rather than those of Europe. I apologize for any difficulty all the unfamiliar words may cause my readers, but it seems to me that this extra effort is

2. Van Binsbergen (1981:135–79) discusses witchcraft beliefs among the neighboring Nkoya. Marwick (1965) and Auslander (1993) analyze witchcraft beliefs in eastern Zambia among the Chewa and the Ngoni, respectively. Turner gives a brief account of Lunda thinking on the causes of disease and misfortune in Turner (1967:300–303).

3. See Larner (1982) for a succinct statement of the essentially peripheral nature of witchcraft beliefs in modern Western society and their radical difference to such beliefs in premodern Europe and Africa.

worthwhile if it enables the non-Kaonde-speaking reader to begin to understand this set of beliefs in its own terms.

My glosses on the Kaonde terms come from definitions of them I was given in my various fieldwork trips to North-Western Province, and from how I have heard them used in different contexts. The terms I am dealing with here are all very basic ones, and there seemed to be general agreement about their definition. These were the ordinary, everyday names that to local people simply identified the "facts" of this aspect of their social world.

The Vocabulary of *Bulozhi*

There is a basic root-*lozhi*, which as an abstract noun *bu-lozhi* is commonly translated as "witchcraft," and as a personal noun *mulozhi* (pl. *balozhi*), as "witch."[4] For people in Kibala and Bukama a *mulozhi* was someone—who might be either male or female (the term is non-gender specific)—who deliberately causes harm, most typically death, to others in ways that do not involve an obvious physical means such as a weapon, but something hidden and impossible to see with the naked eye.[5] *Balozhi* were said to act most commonly at night when it is dark and their victims are asleep. They were believed to kill either for their personal gain (or for that of their fellow *balozhi* since *balozhi*, it was explained to me, often act together with others of their kind) or simply because it is in their nature to kill others. They were described as using various kinds of intermediaries to effect their nefarious ends. There were *tuyebela* (sing. *kayebela*), little creatures that come in a variety of forms, sometimes being described as dolls, sometimes as small animals but always as having the power to transform themselves into a

4. J. L. Wright gives for *bulozhi*, "witchcraft, wizardry, sorcery, enchantment, occult powers, knowledge and practice of the supernatural"; and for *mulozhi*, "wizard, witch, magician, sorcerer, warlock" (Wright n.d.).

5. Kaonde terminology does not seem to contain Evans-Pritchard's celebrated distinction between witchcraft and sorcery (Evans-Pritchard 1937:21). Evans-Pritchard himself, as Turner reminded us thirty years ago (Turner 1964), made it quite clear that what he was describing was a particular distinction of *Zande* terminology. The way this Zande classification was taken up and became a central analytical concept in the subsequent literature on "witchcraft" (particularly, but not exclusively, African "witchcraft") would make an interesting case study in the sociology of knowledge and the history of anthropology.

whole variety of shapes. *Tuyebela* were said to be owned by individual *balozhi*, who were believed to send their *tuyebela* out at night to selected victims; sometimes to steal from them, sometimes to injure or kill them.

As well as *tuyebela*, which could be owned by either men or women, there were also *milomba* (sing. *jilomba*), which normally only men were said to own. A *jilomba* was described as a human-headed snake that enabled its owner to achieve great power and success. The *jilomba's* head was said to have the features of its *mulozhi* owner, and the two were believed to be so closely linked that if a man's *jilomba* were killed, he too would die. As evidence of this I was told about a man from Bukama who had rapidly sickened and died when the dogs belonging to some boys out hunting cane rats by the river found his *jilomba* and killed it. The exact spot where the dogs had found the creature was carefully pointed out to me, the whole story being told to me partly as dramatic proof of the dangers of something so undeniably powerful, but also so evil. Interestingly, this man was one of those deceased plot holders whom Takawali told me had been a *victim* of witchcraft. A *jilomba* (I never heard of any *mulozhi* owning more than one *jilomba*) was said to be far more dangerous than the *tuyebela*, which were always talked about in the plural.

In addition to the ordinary *jilomba* there was also a double-headed variant that some married couples were believed to own, one head resembling the wife and one the husband. There was also the *kimanyi*, which was described as a special type of *jilomba* that helped someone in business amass money. Explaining the *kimanyi*, Mukwetu added the gloss: "People can't have businesses without medicine, they would fail in a year or so" (Mukwetu, Bukama, 15.xi.88, NE). The English term *medicine* here is the usual translation for the term *muchi*, which can be used in a very wide range of contexts. It can be used, for instance, to refer to any kind of curative substance, whether this belongs to western or local medicine, for fertilizer, for yeast—I even heard it used to refer to my deodorant, *muchi wa kwapa* (armpit medicine). In general it seemed to be used for any physical substance used in relatively small quantities to effect some kind of change in or on something larger. On its own the term *muchi* had no necessary connection with *bulozhi* but it was frequently used in a context that in local ears unambiguously gave it that meaning.

There was another term, *bwanga* which had a far more limited field of meaning than *muchi* in that it was only used of things having to do with *bulozhi*, but it was at the same time more inclusive in that it included not only material substances but also knowledge and skills. Both *muchi* and *bwanga* could be used both offensively by *balozhi* and defensively by those trying to protect themselves from such attacks. The more intangible aspects of *bwanga* were possessed not only by *balozhi* but also *bañanga* (sing. *ñanga*), the ritual specialists whose trade is to combat and defeat *balozhi*. Anyone who was ill and suspected *bulozhi*, or who wanted to discover who caused a relative's death or had any problem that seemed to call for the specialist knowledge of someone skilled in this dark realm, could consult a *ñanga* to divine the cause of the problem. Depending on what the *ñanga* found the cause to be, an attack by a *mulozhi* or perhaps some offense to a particular spirit, the *ñanga*'s client would then take the appropriate action, taking the *mulozhi* to court, appeasing the offended spirit, or whatever. Although people relied on *bañanga* to combat *balozhi*, the exact relationship between the *ñanga* and the *mulozhi* tended to be seen as more than a little murky. People tended to wonder: Just how *had* the *ñanga* acquired his or her skills? How could anyone not a *mulozhi* know so much about their ways? This suspicion of *bañanga* skills can also be seen as part of a more general distrust of *any* kind of out-of-the-ordinary knowledge or skill. This distrust was another significant strand in the fabric of rural life.

People in Kibala and Bukama took it for granted that all adult men and women had the skills to carry out all the basic tasks defined as appropriate to their sex. While it was accepted that some people were more skilled than others in certain areas, at fashioning a certain basket, thatching a roof, or brewing beer, for instance; anything that was seen as a genuinely exceptional skill tended to be explained as the result of *muchi*. In other words, such out-of-the-ordinary skills could only have an extraordinary origin. This *muchi* did not necessarily involve *bulozhi*. There were many forms of *muchi* seen as legitimate; in particular there was the whole range of self-defensive *muchi* used solely for protection against attack by *balozhi*. The distinction between legitimate and illegitimate here is, however, a blurred and shifting one. What might be seen by some as clear evidence of *bulozhi* could be defended by the presumed *mulozhi* as no more than sensible precautions *against* attack by others.

One exception to the lack of specialization was the whole area of healing and divination, a realm that certainly was seen as having links with *muchi* and *bulozhi*. Apart from this the only real exception were the skills needed for hunting. Not all men hunted and not all those who did were referred to as "hunters" (pl. *bakibinda*, sing. *kibinda*); the term *kibinda* was reserved for those who were recognized as being successful at killing animals. And this ability was seen by most people, it seemed, as very probably linked with some kind of dealings with dark forces. A central image of the *mulozhi* was in fact that of a perverse and evil hunter who eats not animals but people. Mukwetu provided a vivid image of this perverted hunting:

When *balozhi* are moving about at night in search of victims, they see those they attack as animals. Tall, big people are sable antelopes [the biggest of the antelopes], little short ones are duikers [one of the smallest antelopes] and so on. (Bukama, 20.xii.88, NE)

A number of people assured me that if he were to be successful in killing animals a man needed some kind of medicine. At best, this involved various kinds of legitimate *muchi*; at worst, this meant that a hunter's killing of animals also brought about the death of his relatives. And here again there was something of a slide between legitimate and illegitimate *muchi*. What was apparently clear to everyone was that ordinary human skills, whether acquired through experience or learned from acknowledged *bakibinda*, were not sufficient in themselves: something more was required.

As might be expected, the whole area of *bulozhi* was suffused with a certain secrecy and danger, and people often used euphemisms when talking about it, fearful of being too open and invoking the wrath of those who possess these secret powers. However, it is easy to overemphasize this secrecy, particularly if we are carrying with us the folk models of European witchcraft. Watching how people in Kibala and Bukama used the various concepts within this domain in their daily lives, I was struck both by the omnipresence of this dimension for those around me and at the same time its overwhelming ordinariness, its essential banality—as with the agricultural extension worker who in such a matter-of-fact tone told me that virtually all the Bukama plot holders who had died had been killed by witchcraft. For those living in Kibala and Bukama in 1988 *bulozhi* was simply an unavoidable, but in no way abnormal, hazard of village life. This ordinariness makes this belief in "witchcraft" something quite different from the witchcraft of the folk models of modern Europe or North America. In these modern Western folk models witchcraft is seen as quintessentially strange and bizarre, something that is not part of normal life and that contradicts all the ordinary laws of cause and effect of the natural world. For those living in rural Chizela there was nothing alien about *bulozhi*, it was simply an unavoidable part, albeit a very unpleasant one, of living with other people. Its dangers were as mundane to people as the threat of influenza in the winter is to the inhabitants of London or New York.

Beliefs about *bulozhi*, however, should not be seen simply as some kind of survival of a precolonial past that owe nothing to the colonial or postcolonial world. This is a point that needs stressing. As a number of recent works on witchcraft in Africa have reminded us, such beliefs have apparently not only continued to exert a considerable power over many people in many different African societies, but have often taken on dynamic new forms in colonial and postcolonial contexts. And this is not a phenomenon that has been confined to the rural or "backward" sectors of society; witchcraft, it seems, is often just as much at home in the most modern urban settings. Indeed, it can sometimes be found in the highest echelons of government.[6]

It is important to remember that little of the evidence about African witchcraft beliefs comes from the precolonial period, even if those who recounted such beliefs to the missionary, administrator, or anthropologist claimed to be describing precolonial realities. My information about Kaonde beliefs and practices connected with *bulozhi* comes primarily from conversations I had with people in the 1980s and *bishimi* I recorded then, supplemented by accounts in the colonial archives. The *bulozhi* with which I am concerned is very much a contemporary phenomenon. At the same time, however, I would argue that it draws on an older discourse on evil with deep historical roots. This discourse can be seen as having provided people with a basic grammar of causality and some key vocabulary with which to name a certain area of experience. At the same time, the accounts people gave of specific instances of *bulozhi* were not narrowly determined by this grammar and vocabulary. And as with any living language, not only was vocabulary continually being added, over time even the grammar might change. In the next section, however, I focus on certain key images that ran through all the different accounts of *bulozhi* I heard, and seemed to lie at the heart of the discourse. I also discuss the kind of associations these images seemed to conjure up in the minds of people in rural Chizela.

6. See Richards (1935) and Marwick (1950) for analyses of colonial witch-finding movements in Zambia; and, for the postcolonial period, the recent collection edited by Jean and John Comaroff (1993). The work by Peter Geschiere (1988, 1994, 1995) and Ciprian Fisiy (Fisiy and Geschiere 1991) on sorcery in Cameroon is especially interesting on the links between sorcery and the postcolonial state.

Bulozhi Images

As I have stressed, fear of *bulozhi* was a powerful presence in the daily life of Kibala and Bukama. When illness or misfortune struck, people would invariably speculate as to whether this was *bulozhi*, and on who might be responsible.[7] Such discussions suggest that the possibility of attack was always present as an underlying, inescapable anxiety. When people talked about *bulozhi* there were certain continually recurring images and metaphors that can be seen as constituting a basic core around which a whole discourse on *bulozhi* was elaborated. My account of these key images comes from several different sources. There were the explanations I was given when I asked specific questions. I had normally asked these in a context in which the topic came up spontaneously and I would ask for additional explanations. There were also various disputes I observed, some involving formal court cases brought before Chief Chizela, in which accusations of *bulozhi* were made, or were part of the background to the dispute. Such cases made it possible to see the discourse on *bulozhi* in action; how the ideas and metaphors were deployed in specific contexts by specific individuals.

Another place where ideas about *bulozhi* found expression was in *bishimi* (Kaonde folktales) of which I recorded fifty-seven. After someone told me a story, I would ask them to tell me what they thought the story meant, and what lessons it could teach listening children, for instance. As I stressed in chapter 2, despite the thorny theoretical issues raised by using such explanations, it seems legitimate to me to pick out of such explanations certain very general patterns of association. I make no claims to have done more than to identify some basic ideas and images embedded in the stories that seem to throw light on what *bulozhi* "meant" to people in Kibala and Bukama in the late 1980s. *Bulozhi*, as I shall argue, was a frequent theme in the stories I was told, although it was normally there as an implicit rather than an explicit presence. Characters die or are killed, for instance, and the audience would apparently assume that what the story was talking about was *bulozhi* even though this was not directly mentioned.

When local people described *balozhi* and their habits, perhaps the

---

7. Evans-Pritchard's account of Zande explanations of individual misfortune in *Witchcraft, Oracles, and Magic among the Azande* (1937:63–83, and passim) remains a classic description of this way of thinking about causality.

most dominant image was that of eating. What *balozhi* and their famil-
iars were believed to do to their victims was above all to eat them. The
male *mulozhi*, as I have already mentioned, was commonly linked with
the hunter, but a hunter who hunts not animals but people, maybe with
a special gun made of human bones. One popular story, of which I
recorded four variants, is a good example of the image of the devouring
mulozhi. I have called the story *The Greedy Father*.[8] The essentials of the
story were the same in each variant I was given; the differences had to
do with the length and degree of elaboration.

The Greedy Father

There was once a woman who was married and taken by her husband to
his village. She became pregnant and gave birth to a child, but her husband,
who had been left to look after the child, ate it. Each time the woman had
a child the same thing happened. Finally, when she became pregnant again
and the time came for her delivery, she stole off into the bush and gave birth
alone. She then hid the child in a hollow tree and went back to the village,
telling her husband she had miscarried. Every so often she would then slip
away secretly to the hiding place and feed the baby. Fearing, however, that
the husband would discover the hidden child, she determined to take her
child and return to her own kin. As soon as her husband discovered her
flight, he set off in pursuit. The wife, however, had taken the precaution of
carrying some gourds filled with different grains, and every time the husband
began to get close she would spill one of these on the ground and, unable
to control his greed, he would stop and eat. At last she reached her own
village and told her relatives [i.e., her matrikin] what had happened. They
then dug a pit, which they covered with branches and concealed under a
mat. A rich meal was prepared and when the greedy father arrived he was
lured onto the mat and offered food. As he ate the branches beneath him
gradually began to collapse until at last he fell into the pit and was killed by
his in-laws in just retribution for his murdering ways.

To a local audience it seemed that one of the things this story was
clearly about was *bulozhi*. One of the four people who told me this story
confined her explanation to a simple plot summary, but the other three
glosses on it all mentioned *bulozhi* explicitly.

It means that when a person marries a woman, that is where *bulozhi* can
come from. . . . When her [final] child grew up a little, she thought she

---

8. Storytellers did not usually give their stories titles. I have given the stories titles for
ease of reference.

should run away with the child in fear that her husband would kill it. . . . That is when she went and told her relatives. . . . Her relatives said he is wicked, a *mulozhi* . . . [as they killed him they said] you have finished killing our people, you will now sleep underground. Even now, these things are there, they say a person is a *mulozhi*. (Kibala, 27.viii.88, TK)

There are some men who are very greedy. They like eating . . . [a man can have] a *jilomba* and put it in his house to be eating his children (Kibala, 6.ix.88, TK)

Just like us in this country we do this, you are in a village and a man comes to marry you. You refuse all the good men. Then someone comes who is like a *mulozhi* and you accept him. When he takes you to his village he starts eating your children. When you produce a child he eats it. Now then you go back and tell your parents, "That person was not a proper person but a *mulozhi*." (Kibala, 21.x.88, TK)

These three explanations—by a very old woman, a middle-aged man, and a young woman, respectively—would seem to suggest that whatever else the story might have "meant" to its local audience, the murdering father represented a powerful image of the *mulozhi*. The fact that this was so clear to its listeners even though the story never referred directly to *bulozhi* is, I would argue, a reflection both of the way this naming of the cause of sickness and death as *bulozhi* suffused the whole of rural life and of how certain events and phenomena were automatically seen as synonymous with *bulozhi*. To local eyes, it was *bulozhi* that was the "real" cause of almost all deaths. A story such as *The Greedy Father* can be seen as providing a vivid and compelling image of what it is that *balozhi* do. A child may seem to have died from some illness, but *really* it has been killed by its father's *jilomba*. For someone belonging to this community of belief, the story presents directly the more profound "truth" that the father has eaten his child.

Central to this community of belief were certain general assumptions that run counter to those of the discourse of "scientific" rationalism associated with the development of modern industrial society. For those socialized into this rationalist discourse, it is a taken-for-granted assumption that there is a natural physical world that is governed by fixed and unalterable laws, such as the law of gravity. Such laws are outside the domain of human morality; no breach of human laws, no matter how horrendous, will suspend or alter the law of gravity, any more than any human being can willfully interfere with its operation. By contrast, one of the basic assumptions underpinning the belief in *bulozhi* in Kibala and Bukama was that the human world and the "natural" world are part of one seamless whole; there was no splitting off of an impersonal domain of nature that exists outside, and is indifferent to, the sphere of morality. Within this all-enveloping moral web the essential human community exists as a community of kin bound together in a web of reciprocal moral obligation; but the moral web of expectations reaches out to include the nonhuman. Adultery, for instance, could lead to a woman having a particularly difficult childbirth. Crucially, the notion of causality (A *causes* B, B is *the result* of A) embedded in this general discourse centers on a moral rather than a mechanical relationship; causality tended always to be enfolded in morality and human intentionality. If a nephew (*mwipwa*) shows his uncle (*mwisho*) proper respect (*mushingi*), then the uncle *ought* to reciprocate by helping and supporting his nephew. There is no kind of law-like certainty, however, about his doing so. If a field is properly planted and tended, it *ought* to produce a good harvest, but sometimes it does not. In the space between "ought" and outcome lurks *bulozhi*.

Underpinning the discourse on *bulozhi* was the assumption that the moral conduct of human beings can bring about effects in the nonhuman physical world; what *balozhi* do does not, therefore, violate natural laws, but rather moral expectations. This is why the most sensible and level-headed people, who in other contexts, such as the promises of development planners, could display a conspicuously healthy skepticism, had no problem at all in believing in *balozhi* who can summon thunder, fly about at night in their own magic airplanes, kill people at a distance, and so on. *How balozhi* do what they do was not a question that people found particularly puzzling, the answer was simple: they can do these things because they are *balozhi*. The more pressing question was, How do you cope with *balozhi* and protect yourself against their attacks? A story like *The Greedy Father*, I would suggest, addresses the omnipresent fear of *bulozhi*, providing a satisfying representation of the struggle against, and ultimate defeat of, the evil *mulozhi*.

It is important to stress, however, that the discourse on *bulozhi* is by no means rigid or unchanging. Precisely how *balozhi*, and what they do, are imagined can shift and change, as do the contexts in which such fears can come into play. The belief that some people are able, at a distance and using no obvious means, to kill or bring about all kinds of misfortune provides, as it were, a basic root from which many different narratives of *bulozhi* can grow. *Balozhi* in the 1980s, for instance, were described as traveling about in invisible airplanes and cars. Similarly, as in the case of the clinical officer in Kibala, complaints about attacks by *bulozhi* were very common among the teachers and other government employees throughout Chizela District, even though they were not normally members of the local kinship community. In general *bulozhi*, as might be expected, has a tendency to collect around tensions and contradictions wherever these may occur.

The story of *The Greedy Father*, for instance, can be seen, at least in part, as an expression of an underlying structural tension between the members of a matrilineage and the men marrying into it. This tension was inherent in the combination of matrilineal descent and virilocality whereby the children of a marriage belonged to and reproduced the wife's matrilineage, but were outsiders within the husband's kin group among whom they were likely to live. While it was accepted that there would be strong bonds of affection and obligation between fathers and children, ultimately, despite the undoubted strengthening of patrilineal links over the course of the colonial and postcolonial years, it was still the link between a man and his sisters' children that people described as the most binding. In chapter 3 I quoted a proverb that refers to the contradictory pulls on a man as father and as brother/uncle: "Eat with the chickens, the guinea fowl will fly home." The guinea fowl here are a man's biological children, and the chickens those of his sisters. From the point of view of his wife's kin group a man's commitment to his biological children—particularly as regards providing them with access to any surplus he had produced or acquired—was always suspect. It is not surprising, therefore, that people found the image of the father who sacrifices his children to his own selfish greed so powerful, just as it seemed "right" in the story that it was the wife's matrikin who protected her against the outsider husband.

The suspicion aroused by the stranger-husband with his conflicting loyalties was, so to speak, built into the structure of Kaonde matriliny. But this ambivalence can also be seen as a particular instance of a more general tension around the reciprocal obligations of kinship. Obligations that are at one and the same time vague and diffuse, yet wide-ranging and absolutely binding, cannot but open up a wide space both for resentment of expectations seen as unfulfilled and anxiety that indeed one *has* failed to fulfill one's obligations. The social fabric woven by the threads of moral obligation embedded in kinship is likely to be very different from a social fabric in which the dominant thread is that of the contract. After all, part of the essence of the contract as a social relationship is—at least at the level of ideology—its clearly defined and limited nature. While ambivalence is no doubt inherent in kinship relations in all societies, the emotional charge this carries is likely to be particularly intense when access to basic resources and the distribution of surplus is to a significant extent organized through kinship relations rather than the market, so that individuals' access to basic resources and distribution of surplus actually depends on the honoring of the reciprocal obligations of kinship. It was this kind of highly charged ambivalence, I would argue, that helped to imbue belief in *bulozhi* with such a powerful *emotional* plausibility.

Part Two: Of Mushingi and the Market

Kyo wapana kibwela
  What is given away returns

Kakote wa mukwenu mankumbila
  Your friend's old relative is a rotting mushroom [i.e., no one wants to take care of someone else's aging relative]
  John Ganly, *Kaonde Proverbs*

In the first part of this chapter I explored some of the basic contours of the Kaonde discourse on *bulozhi*. In this second part I want to focus specifically on the links between accusations of *bulozhi* and tensions around the distribution of surplus. Overall the amount of surplus produced in Kibala and Bukama was small; but while this was true in absolute terms, surplus was nonetheless, as in any economy, a crucial part of the system. I am defining *surplus* here as that portion of the social product that is in excess of producers' direct consumption needs. This definition would include, for instance, everything that is necessary to meet the needs of those unable to participate in production, such as the very young, the old, and the sick; as well as everything that is invested in future production.

Individual households in Kibala and Bukama may have been responsible for meeting the bulk of their day-to-day consumption needs through their own production, but this did not mean that households in general were necessarily self-sufficient even as regards basic foodstuffs.

There were always labor-poor households that found it difficult to produce much, and even labor-rich households might face difficulties from time to time. Then again, the labor resources of a single household would vary over the course of its developmental cycle.

A basic reality that was part of the texture of day-to-day life in Kibala and Bukama was the coexistence of, on the one hand, independent households generally reluctant to combine with others in joint productive enterprises; and, on the other, a deep awareness that from time to time any household, even the most prosperous, was likely to find itself needing access to the surpluses of others. Harvests, for instance, were always unpredictable. Crops could fail for a myriad of reasons: drought or rain at the wrong times, disease, animal predators, or because a producer had fallen sick at a crucial moment. Sickness—and people were often sick—was a particularly serious problem because of the individualized nature of cultivation and the difficulty of mobilizing extra labor. But just as crops might fail, so too there could be unexpectedly high yields when everything went right. In short, about all that was predictable was that there would be wide fluctuations in yields, both between households in any year and over time within the same household. As a result there were always some households that had not produced enough to satisfy their own consumption needs and others that had produced a surplus. If they were to meet their needs, those suffering a shortfall needed access to that surplus, and the primary mechanism by which this distribution was effected was the network of kinship claims. Those with surplus were expected to redistribute at least some of it to their kin, whether in the form of "gifts"[9] or loans, or simply by selling it. In an economic environment in which goods, particularly the crops of *kujima* (local sorghum-based cultivation), were not produced in order to be sold, even persuading someone to sell some of their sorghum could depend on the moral pressure of kinship obligation.

Despite increasing monetization and the growing role of the market, a reciprocity based on "gifts" traveling along the paths of kinship from those with surplus to those in need was still a crucial element in the distribution of the social product. For such a system of distribution

9. I use quotation marks here to draw attention to the difference between these gifts enveloped in a tight web of obligation and the gifts of modern industrial society. Central to the modern meaning of the gift is that it is a voluntary transaction that does not demand a return—or at least this is what is stressed in the ideology. Mauss's discussion of the gift (1970) in nonmarket societies remains a classic.

to work it was of course essential that people accepted that they did indeed have an inescapable obligation to make their surplus available to their kin, an obligation that was part of the wide-ranging concept of *mushingi* (respect). One aspect of *mushingi*, for instance, was the general acceptance that, while people tended to work on their own, the products of these individualized labor processes did not belong in any absolute way to the individual producer. In other words, individuals were not seen, and did not see themselves, as having unfettered rights to what they produced. Rather each producer was surrounded by a host of relatives all with some kind of potential claim to a share of his or her surplus, claims described in terms of the obligation to show *mushingi*. Let me go back to the complaint by Banyinyita I have already quoted in chapter 3.

We Kaonde people used to live very differently. In those days elders were given a lot of respect [*mushingi*]. We are not given that respect. It seems the world has changed, they say Zambia now. This is how we lived in those days: we lived in villages with respect. Have you seen people respected nowadays? In those days we used to be given breast meat as gifts [i.e., if a hunter killed an animal]. The young people used to bring us breast meat. (Banyinyita, Kibala, 12.viii.88, TK)

Another elderly headman in Kibala, Mukulu, also stressed the obligation of seniors (*bakulumpe*) to share with juniors (*banyike*). In the past, he told me, those headmen who were hunters did not sell the meat when they killed an animal but gave much of it away to those living in their village.

If you kill an animal, you as an elder [*mukulumpe*] have to give them meat because they are your children [*bana*; figuratively, all those belonging to a village are the headman's *bana*] . . . you have to share with your children in the village. (Kibala, 7.viii.88, TK)

Mushingi ran both ways along the *mukulumpe/mwanyike* relationship. Banyinyita may have stressed the obligation of the young to their elders, but, as is implicit in Mukulu's explanation, *banyike* (juniors) also had legitimate claims on their elders. It was not, however, the weight of moral obligation alone that persuaded people to redistribute their surplus. "Gifts" were also a way of building up concrete relationships of obligation that could be called on in the future when those with surplus might themselves be in need. The distribution of surplus to kin was in part an investment in the creation and maintenance of a network of relations that both constituted the only way of establishing some kind of security for an inherently unpredictable future and beyond bare survival could also be the foundation for the creation of a power network. *Mushingi* can be seen as a way of naming a key mechanism within a "culture" of generalized reciprocity through which certain economic and political relations produced and reproduced themselves. Like any "culture" this culture of reciprocity needed to be continually produced and reproduced through being lived by individuals in their daily lives. Although relatives might have claims on one another simply by virtue of their kinship relation, the transformation of these nominal claims into something more tangible required that these claims be, as it were, continually reactivated through actual material flows and displays of deference.

Given a distribution system that relied so heavily on the diffuse, unbounded, and ever-shifting but always binding obligations of kinship, there were bound to be struggles around access to surplus. Inevitably there was something of a structural tension between those claiming a share of some surplus and those on whom such claims were made. The definition of what constituted a "surplus," could itself be a source of contention; what a producer might see as no more than a bare sufficiency could look like more than enough to a hungry relative. And claims to surplus were not limited to basic consumption needs; money to pay school fees, medical expenses, or even help with some business venture were all potentially legitimate claims. For instance, Desa, an elderly widow in Bukama (one of the group of three widows whom I have already mentioned in connection with the Bukama Multi-Purpose Cooperative Society) had in the past engaged in various business ventures in the course of which she had made use of a car belonging to the son of one of her matrikin. When I asked if Desa had perhaps had to pay something for this, those listening obviously found my question absurd. Very patiently Mukwetu explained to me that since the father of the car owner was Desa's (classificatory) sibling, in a sense the car also belonged to Desa; of course she had access to it. Although over time various socially accepted strategies to limit these kinds of claims by kin have evolved, the form they took tended to be that of concealing the extent of surplus that existed. I have never in any of my trips to North-Western Province heard anyone question the basic moral principle that people have a claim to the surplus produced by their kin.

The ties of kinship that were so crucial, indeed precisely because they were so crucial, contained within them a profound ambivalence. On the one hand, it was to their kin that people in Kibala and Bukama automatically and invariably looked for both material and emotional support; it was kin to whom people turned when they had run short of food or anything else—and in the absence of a state-provided safety net kin were essentially the only recourse people had. On the other hand, precisely because the web of kinship obligation was so diffuse and unbounded and yet so binding, inevitably kin could be seen as *not* having fulfilled their obligations, as having deprived their relatives of what was morally theirs—particularly since individuals were likely to be faced with a number of competing claims by different relatives. The demands of kinship were so all-encompassing that, as people very well knew, it was virtually impossible for any ordinary mortal to fulfill them all to the satisfaction of everyone. Consequently, relatives tended to be profoundly suspicious of one another. Whether or not this suspicion was openly expressed or remained latent, the web of kinship always cast an ambivalent shadow. And one of the explicit forms such suspicion took was accusations of *bulozhi*. As Sansoni put it,

the most feared ones [i.e., as *balozhi*] are the relatives because they know them very well, they know how they live, they know how they eat, they have known them from their childhood up to their growth time. That's how the fear comes in. (Sansoni, Kibala,1.xi.88, TE)

And what people tended to be especially suspicious of was wealth. For instance, when I asked Sansoni what kind of people were likely to be accused of *bulozhi*, he began his answer by saying,

the first ones to be accused [of witchcraft] are those who have achieved something in their lifetime, because most local people think that someone cannot build a ten-roomed house, to them it is impossible, or they cannot believe someone can have a car. Local people do not think anyone can have a very big shop so if they see that you have a shop, then they will say, "No, that one he has used witchcraft to obtain such a thing". If you buy a car they will say, "Ah no", they will accuse you of witchcraft. (Sansoni, Kibala, 1.ix.88, TE)

Just as the people of Kibala and Bukama were distrustful of exceptional skill, so too were they suspicious of exceptional wealth. The feeling that wealth could *only* be acquired through some form of *bulozhi*, or at least required the possession of some kind of *bwanga* or *muchi*, could extend to very minor successes. Nearly everyone kept a few chickens, which were not given any special feeding or care, and apart from being shut away safely at night were left free to forage around the homestead and reproduce themselves as best they could. As might be expected, the mortality rate was high; only the toughest survived. There was one man in Kibala who was noted for his large number of chickens, a success that more than a few in Kibala saw as clearly linked to the possession of some special, and possibly dubious, *muchi*.

There was then a distrust of any accumulation of wealth, and of those who had in any way raised themselves up above their fellows. Any such accumulation, people seemed to feel, *must* have been achieved at the expense of others — a way of thinking that can be linked to the reality that the distribution of the social product did indeed depend to such an important extent on those in need having access to the surplus of those (however temporally) more fortunate. Given the absence of a state-provided safety net, if those with surplus did not make it available to those in need, how were the latter to survive? Those with surplus who did not redistribute it, those who, as it were, denied the culture of reciprocity, were a profound threat to the system as a whole. One way this threat was imagined was in the form of *balozhi*, who in a grotesque reversal of kinship reciprocity kill their kin to create wealth for themselves. There were, for instance, the suspicions that surrounded Temwa, Kibala's richest man, who, as I described in the last chapter, so eagerly embraced the LIMA program. Many people, it seemed, were convinced that Temwa was killing children, whom he then put in his maize sacks to swell them — a wonderfully powerful and vivid image of the entrepreneurial accumulator. I will come back to Temwa and how his attempts to take advantage of new economic opportunities were seen by others in Kibala in the final section of this chapter.

Living with *Mushingi*

If exceptional prosperity was one sign of the *mulozhi*, another was age itself. In local eyes there was a strong association between age and *bulozhi*. After explaining how "the first to be accused are those who have achieved something in their lifetime," Sansoni went on to say,

The other thing [apart from having become prosperous] that causes people to call other people witches is when they develop white hair on their heads.

This is very common. You find someone who maybe grew up in town when he comes to the village with hair white on the head, if anything wrong happens in the village, like a child passing away, then they will say, "That one is the one who is a witch." So the most common characteristic is the age of someone; if he becomes old definitely that name [i.e., witch] is there. Even us who are still growing, that name we are expecting it will be given to us. (Sansoni, Kibala, 1.ix.88, TE)

Similarly, when I was trying to explain to one woman in Kibala how in Britain there were relatively far fewer children than in Zambia, but many more old people, her response was, "Here we would just accuse all those old people of being *balozhi*."

The identification of old people as *balozhi*—apart from throwing an interesting light on the sometimes romanticized picture of attitudes to the old in rural Africa—contained two rather different images of the *mulozhi*. On the one hand, there was the elderly, but powerful, *male* authority figure, the headman, the chief; on the other hand, there was the lonely, old *woman*, often living by herself with no place in any of the formal power hierarchies. Each of these images of the *mulozhi* can be seen as reflecting tensions around the obligation to show *mushingi* (respect) to *bakulumpe* (elders). Both images, I would argue, can be seen in fact as distorted mirror images of the *mukulumpe/mwanyike* hierarchy. Through such mirror images we can perhaps catch a glimpse of what the obligations bound up in *mushingi* could feel like to those living them.

I want to begin with the image of the *mulozhi* as a poverty-stricken old woman (*kakulukazhi*). The figure of the aged crone—this figure seems always to be female—who lives alone, often deep in the bush, poor and neglected, too old to look after her house or herself properly, appears in many *bishimi*. A common narrative has two protagonists, both young (*mwanyike*), who while traveling through the bush come across a pitiful old woman living in squalor. She asks them to help her, to sweep her house clear of its accumulated filth, cook her some food, and so on. One of the protagonists is kind to the old woman, willingly performing the rather demeaning tasks, and in return the old woman provides the dutiful (since the old [*bakulumpe*] *should* be shown such *mushingi*) youngster with some kind of special knowledge, sometimes in the form of an actual object such as a magic feather and sometimes simply instructions. Armed with this knowledge the virtuous protagonist overcomes various obstacles and dangers and acquires an eligible husband or wife, great riches, and generally prospers. This virtuous one is then contrasted with the second protagonist, of the same sex and again young, who takes exactly the same journey, meets the same old woman but scorns her and refuses to help her, and in consequence is not given the crucial knowledge. As a result, in the adventures that follow, which again are precisely those of the first character, this arrogant and foolish person instead of finding riches and happiness meets only trials and tribulations, sometimes even death.

The ambivalent image of the old woman beneath whose repulsive outward appearance lurk potent forces, and who if treated well can re-ward with riches but can also punish if she is denied proper *mushingi*, reflects a general ambivalence toward the old. On the one hand, every-one acknowledged that the old should be shown *mushingi*. While their physical powers might have declined, they were the ones with the great-est knowledge and wisdom—although, as I have stressed, knowledge itself had a certain ambivalence, always tending to carry the taint of having been acquired illegitimately through *bulozhi*. On the other hand, given the continuing significance of distribution mechanisms based on the claims of kinship, those who still had a whole range of claims, but were no longer able to produce much with which to reciprocate could well be seen as something of a burden and simply as a hungry mouth demanding food.

This kind of ambivalence toward the old is present to some extent in all forms of society, especially when there is no welfare state to provide a safety net. It is likely, however, to be particularly extreme when, as here, those who are older (the *bakulumpe*) had such powerful and in-disputable claims to *mushingi* from those who are younger, and given that *mushingi* meant not merely verbal "respect" or a respectful de-meanor, but the giving of goods and services. Contradictory feelings toward the old inevitably create a considerable space for feelings of guilt, feelings that an elderly relative has been wronged. Such guilt is easily projected onto the one wronged to become transformed into a convic-tion that he or she harbors resentment. Add to this the occurrence of some misfortune and, in an environment in which *bulozhi* was always hovering in the air, it was easy to suspect such slighted kin of practicing *bulozhi*.

Despite the general condemnation of *bulozhi*, there was always some moral ambiguity, with the illegitimate use of such powers tending to shade into their legitimate defensive use. Given this and the way belief in *bulozhi* suffused people's day-to-day lives, it is perhaps not so sur-prising that some people would admit to having and using such "knowledge," or at least would make veiled threats. One woman in Bukama, for instance, threatened her ex-husband, a well known local hunter whom she felt should still give her gifts of meat, that he should be careful or he would "see" something when he next went hunting. To local ears this was a clear threat of *bulozhi*, for which she was taken to Chief Chizela's court. The way the elderly and impoverished might use such threats to defend themselves is illustrated by a story Mukwetu told me about Kwanayanga, an elderly woman living in Bukama who had been divorced for many years. Everyone in Bukama, it seemed, agreed that Kwanayanga was a dangerous *mulozhi*. When I went to her home in Bukama to record *bishimi*, one of the women who worked for me remarked how she would never go there for fear of Kwanayanga's *tuyebela*.

Kwanayanga and the Stolen Maize

Late one evening in 1987, the year before I came to Bukama, Kwanayanga was returning home after visiting her daughters in the district center. It was January, the height of the hunger season, when most people have finished last year's grain and this year's is not yet ripe. Kwanayanga was alone and on foot, and carrying a small sack of maize given her by a daughter married to a wage earner. When she was still some way from home, she became too tired to carry the maize any farther and left it by the side of the road, intending to return for it the following day. Before she could do so, however, a local man, Miyenga, happened to pass by and, seeing the apparently abandoned sack, carried it off. When she returned to collect her maize Kwanayanga was furious to discover it gone. On her way back home she announced to everyone within earshot that whoever had stolen her maize would surely die.

Meanwhile Miyenga had also returned home, but in the opposite direction to Kwanayanga so no one had heard her threats. Miyenga gave the stolen maize to his wife who, fortunately as it transpired, did not cook any of it immediately since she too had just collected a sack from the district center. That night there was a terrible storm and Miyenga's house was hit by lightning—a not uncommon occurrence during the rainy season. No one was killed, but everyone in the house was thrown out and Miyenga himself received a burn on the side of his head and down one arm. In the morning Miyenga, who was by now badly frightened (*balozhi* are commonly believed to use lightning to attack their victims) and fearing something worse might happen, went to the Chief, in whose farm village he was living, and told him the whole story, including his "finding" of the bag of maize. Some of those listening realized this must have been Kwanayanga's maize and she was summoned to the chief's presence. Asked by the chief if she was the one who had caused the lightning, Kwanayanga was unrepentant; indeed she had and it was a good thing Miyenga had not actually *eaten* any of the maize since if he had he would now not merely be burnt but dead. She defended her action by saying that she was old now and no longer able to cultivate properly and so depended on the food given her by her children in the district center. The chief gave judgment that as Miyenga was clearly in the wrong for having stolen the maize, Kwanayanga could not be punished in any way and she simply departed with her maize, having presumably provided a powerful lesson to all potential thieves.

If Kwanayanga illustrates the stereotype of the *mulozhi* as a poverty-stricken old woman, the stereotype of the elderly male *mulozhi* seemed to be particularly associated with male authority figures, such as headmen and chiefs. *All* the village headmen in Kibala, for instance, had at one time or another been suspected of using *bulozhi*, and Chief Chizela, as befitted his seniority (he was the ultimate *mukulumpe*), was said to have the most powerful *bwanga* of all. In the context of acknowledged authority figures the line between legitimate and illegitimate use of such powers was particularly blurred, tending to depend on the vantage point of the observer. This ambiguity can be seen as mirroring the generally blurred nature of the limits and legitimacy of the authority of headmen and chiefs. When I asked one headman (who was described to me as one of the most dangerous *mulozhi* in Kibala) about how headmen established a following that would enable them to set up a new village (*muzhi*), he told me, "Love. The people love him. He is humble. He likes people, 'these are my *bankasami* [young siblings], these are my *bak-olojami* [older siblings], let them come and live together' " (Kibala, 7.viii.88, TK). The point here is not that the headman/junior kin relationship, either before or after colonization, was a totally benevolent relationship in which exploitation and oppression of various kinds never existed, but that Kaonde headmen probably always had rather limited powers of coercion. *Compelling* their relatives to live with them was simply not feasible, especially given their lack of control over access to land. Someone who was unhappy living under a particular headman always had the option of leaving him and settling elsewhere. Normally people always had a wide range of relatives from which to choose. Consequently a Kaonde headman's power probably always depended to a great extent on his skills in attaching his kinsmen and women to him; and as far as local people were concerned, these skills were likely to include not merely his ability to inspire love, but *bulozhi*.

It was assumed that an effective headman would almost certainly have special powers. Apart from anything else, how otherwise was he able to withstand the attacks of those under his authority—and inevitably since *bulozhi* was so pervasive, there must be some among them—who were themselves *balozhi*? As Mukwetu put it to me in a slightly different context:

It is like this, if you are boasting, you say bad things to old people . . . now people they will say, "Now, this one must have something [i.e., *bulozhi*]" . . . because you know that if you don't have anything, you don't have anything like *jilomba* and *tuyebela* . . . how can you insult somebody whom you know has got *jilomba, tuyebela* or *nyalumanyi*?[10] Yes, you can fear to say, "No, if I insult this one he may kill me." But if you know that you have also got something, then you can insult your friend. (Bukama, 20.xii.88, TE)

To a local audience any kind of verbal or other expression of power was almost bound to suggest that people daring enough to assert themselves *must* have "something." So too, it seemed to be agreed, must headmen, who by definition claimed authority.

The relative economic autonomy of households meant that individual households, at least in the short term, had no compelling economic need to combine with others in a village. At the same time, an individual's future security depended on their having built up an active network of kinship ties, particularly with those likely to have surpluses to distribute. Putting oneself under the protection of more prosperous senior kin by moving to live with them was one way of doing this. The powerful attraction of prosperity was brought home to me during my Kasempa fieldwork when I was walking one day with a young man, Kiboyi. As we passed one settlement my companion told me how he used to live there and what a wonderful place it was and how much he had enjoyed his time there. With my Western assumptions I asked him if this meant that the people were especially nice. Looking at me with a slightly puzzled air he replied, "No, there was always plenty to eat."

Even if people in Kibala and Bukama did not tend to join together in productive enterprises, they nonetheless took it for granted that the normal way for human beings to live was embedded deep within a community of kin. Those kin need not live in a single settlement, rather they were bound together inextricably in an interlocking mesh of hierarchical *mukulumpe/mwanyike* relationships. That was what, as my elderly neighbor in Kasempa (see above, p. 87) made clear to me, distinguished human beings from brute beasts. As the most senior kinsman within a

---

10. Another kind of familiar.

community, a headman was owed a particular *mushingi*, which of course included goods and labor. The lament of Kyakala, which I have already quoted in the previous chapter, shows us, albeit in a negative form, something of how the obligations associated with *mushingi* gave a headman claims on any surplus produced by all those within his village.

These days you can only expect your own child to give you things or assistance. In those days *every member of a village was a child of the headman*. . . . In the past people were not interested in money; they were only interested in eating [i.e., production for direct consumption] and *helping their elders*. . . . In the olden days *someone who killed an animal first thought of the headman* or his parents for fear of being punished. (Bukama, 21.xii.88, my emphasis, TK)

However, although it might be agreed that a headman should be given *mushingi* (respect), there was plenty of room for debate as to what this meant in any specific context. Also, however hegemonic the obligation to show *mushingi* this did not mean that those in subordinate positions were never resentful of their subordination and never had feelings of hostility toward particular headmen. At the same time, prosperity, which ought of course to be shared with others, exerted its own attraction, as illustrated by Kiboyi's fond memories of plenty. Even this attraction, however, was not incompatible with a certain distrust; there was always the question of quite *how* such wealth had been obtained, just as generosity could always be seen to fall short. In sum, the headman could be both the benevolent provider and the authoritarian senior relative, selfishly withholding his surplus and coercing (possibly in the form of labor or material goods) "respect." This negative aspect could be expressed in the image of the devouring *mulozhi* who kills relatives for personal gain.

Forms of accumulation based on the claims of kinship were still a part of the economic and political landscape of 1980s rural Chizela, but increasingly monetization, commoditization, and the growing importance of market-based relations in general have opened up spaces for other forms of accumulation. These spaces have become new sources of tension in part because of the threat they offer to the old mechanisms of distribution based on *mushingi*. Ensuring security in case of future hardships, for instance, can now to some extent be achieved through savings, possibly stored safely in the post office, and not, as prior to monetization and incorporation into the national economy, solely through the building up of networks of obligation. For the ambitious there are now alternatives to old patterns of "accumulation" whereby surplus through the giving of "gifts" was, as it were, invested in kin so as to create networks of dependents to whose future surpluses the accumulator headman had claims. Monetization means that it is possible to transform surplus into capital; fish, for instance can be bought locally and sold in town, or manufactured goods can be bought in town for resale in the rural areas. Cash can be used to buy the fertilizer and other inputs necessary for "modern farming," and to purchase labor power to be used in "modern farming" enterprises. The chairman of one of the LIMA groups in Kibala referred to this new form of accumulation when I asked him about the differences between the old patterns of cultivation and something like the LIMA scheme.

We used to grow sorghum to feed ourselves, but now we grow maize to sell with the idea that this money can be used the following year to extend one's *lima*. That's the difference. . . . If you have money and many *lima* it's not money that will do the work; you give it to someone to do the work, because if you just put K1 here it will not do any work, you have to give it to someone. (Kibala, 14.viii.88, TK)

While there have always been tensions and contradictions over the distribution of surplus, the new economic opportunities for individual accumulation, however modest in absolute terms, have created a whole range of new, and rather different, conflicts of interest. Although kinship claims and the honoring of them still played a crucial role in the survival strategies of many individuals in Kibala and Bukama, the context in which these claims were made was changing; they were now having to compete with the siren call of capitalist forms of accumulation. Not surprisingly those trying to take advantage of the new economic opportunities tended to be accused of *bulozhi*. In the final section of this chapter I want to illustrate the local association between the newer forms of accumulation and *bulozhi* through the story of Kibala's foremost entrepreneur, Temwa. Temwa, whose keen embrace of the LIMA program I described in the previous chapter, was the most prosperous man in Kibala, but he was also a lonely and isolated figure with a fearsome local reputation as a *mulozhi*.

My biography of Temwa is taken from the narrative of his life as he himself recounted it to me (Kibala, 24.viii.88, TK). When I visited him to record his life history I began by explaining that I was particularly interested in his story because his way of life seemed so different from that of others in Kibala. How had he achieved his obvious prosperity?

The narrative of his life, much of which was given to me in the form of a single uninterrupted monologue, was at one level a response to this question. He began in fact by remarking (before the tape recorder was switched on) how my curiosity about his success demonstrated my superior understanding, and how most people in Kibala would never bother to ask such a question but would just assume that it was all the result of *bulozhi*. These suspicions that attached themselves to Temwa are not only revealing about *bulozhi* beliefs; they also tell us a good deal about the ideology of kinship reciprocity. Part of what *bulozhi* represented in local eyes was precisely a grotesque perversion of this reciprocity.

The Story of an Entrepreneur

Temwa was born in Kibala in 1936. He never went to school, something he now very much regrets.

For me it was not given by God. I did not go to school; I liked where my father was rather than where there was a school. We did not know that there is wealth and goodness in education.

As soon as he was old enough, at the age of fifteen, Temwa went to town to try his luck in the urban labor market, and during the next three years he worked mainly in town. He then returned to Kibala, where he has lived ever since. He used the savings from his second stay in town to buy a bicycle and began trading in fish, buying dried fish from nearby fish camps that he then sold in one of the local urban markets.

Over the next few years his business prospered. He began taking his fish as far as Solwezi, the provincial capital. There he would buy manufactured goods, which he would bring back and resell locally. He also began taking his fish across the border into Zaire where he would buy two-meter lengths of cloth (an indispensable item of dress for all adult women throughout Zambia's rural areas), which he would then smuggle back to Zambia where they were much in demand. In 1966 Temwa began selling the goods he was buying in Solwezi from his house in Kibala. It was at this point that he obtained a trading license. As he became more prosperous he built himself a succession of larger and more substantial houses. First there was a house that still had a grass roof but was of sun-dried bricks; soon, however, the grass roof was replaced by more prestigious iron sheets. Temwa explained to me how he got the idea to "live better." In his travels around North-Western Province selling fish, he saw the way other groups were living and this impressed him very much, especially the Luvale houses.[11]

When we went to Kabompo at the time we used the car for fish trading, I saw that their [i.e., the Luvale] houses are built differently. When I saw that those who were living there were blacks just like us, I said I would also do the same. This thing was in my heart. Whenever I came back from there I carried a chair. Whenever I went to Solwezi I would come back with a chair. I saw that the Luvale people were living well and I said I would also live like them. . . . The difference between me and my friends [i.e., in terms of living standards] is because I work very hard. You cannot just sit and expect God to give things to you. You go and see how others have built their houses. I saw a house with glass windows; they were cleaning them and I said, "I too will have a house with glass." I admired whatever was good and decided I should have them too.

Temwa also bought a sewing machine with which he made women's and children's clothes, and by 1968 he had saved enough to put down a deposit on a car, taking out a loan in the name of a relative in town. The car lasted for five years—about the maximum that can be expected of any vehicle on the rough, untarred roads of North-Western Province. This was the period of Zambia's postindependence prosperity and Temwa's fortunes were at their height.

I started buying many things using the vehicle and bringing them back here. . . . People were just fighting to buy them. I could go to Kitwe, Chingola and buy things from Tops Wholesale.[12]

He also bought more iron roofing sheets with the idea of building more houses and extending his shop. With the car, transport was easy: "I could just pack them into my car with the Coca-Cola." And indeed in 1988 his homestead stood out from others in Kibala by its general air of prosperity. The majority of houses in Kibala were simple pole-and-dagga structures with here and there one built from sun-dried bricks, normally

---

11. In Kaonde areas people have tended not to invest a lot of labor in building substantial houses, something that is probably related to the high mobility of villages in the past, whereas the Luvale (whose staple cassava has enabled villages to be far more permanent) have long been known for their well-built houses.

12. This is one of the private, largely Asian owned businesses that played such an important role in supplying small village shops in the rural areas in the years immediately after Independence.

with a grass roof. Temwa, however, had managed to construct three large cement-reinforced houses, and all with that much-desired marker of true modernity and wealth, the corrugated iron roof.

It was in the early seventies that Temwa began to face difficulties. In 1972, even before the demise of his car, there was a problem with the price control inspectors. At that time the retail prices of almost all goods were, in theory at least, strictly controlled—although the government's power to enforce this was always limited, particularly given the chronic shortages of so many essential commodities. In common with many small village shopkeepers Temwa was marking up his goods considerably more than the tiny amount officially allowed; there were complaints to the district authorities and a visit from the price control inspectors, and Temwa's trading license was revoked. This brush with authority thoroughly unnerved Temwa and he immediately ceased trading. As might be expected, Temwa defended his profit margins and put the blame for his troubles on "jealous relatives." Temwa brought up the subject when I asked him how despite being illiterate he managed to keep a check on the profits and losses of his businesses. In answering this Temwa stressed that his lack of education had not hampered him from running his shop profitably, partly because in this he was helped by his literate children; no, it was only when it came to the bureaucratic regulations that he had run into problems and his enemies had been able to exploit his ignorance.

God gave me business sense and a knowledge of how to keep money. . . . When I bought things I would call one of my children and we would go through and see how much I had spent so that I would know how much profit I had made. The children helped me very much, even when I was packing things I would call my children to put on the price cards [the price regulations stated that all goods offered for sale must have a price shown]. This was from God. I was not making a loss. It was not that people were able to cheat me because I am not educated, no. I would know that I had bought things worth so much and will get so much profit. My children were helping me to check the prices. My problems with selling began when the price controllers came . . . and this was all because of not going to school. . . . I did not fail [in business] because I am not educated, I failed because of the price controllers. I was just selling at reasonable prices, but my relatives here in Kibala were jealous. . . . They saw that I had a lot of things and they did not know how I had managed to achieve this.

In addition to his trading activities, Temwa was also committing to

growing crops for sale. In the last chapter I described how enthusiastically he embraced the coming of the IRDP and "the Germans." As
in the case of his other enterprises, Temwa attributed some of his problems with the LIMA scheme to others who were ill-disposed or lazy.
"The [LIMA] group failed because the others were not working hard
on the land; I was the only one working hard." Temwa, however, insisted he was not discouraged. He even had plans to open his shop
again and had applied for a new trading license, saying, "If God wishes
then I will continue with the business."

Temwa's account of his life did not mention any of his various marriages, and this was clearly a subject Temwa did not want to talk about.
I did discover that he had had at least five marriages that had produced
children, and I was told by others in Kibala that there had been a number
of other marriages, but it was difficult to get a sense of the role played
by his wives in his various business activities. Temwa did in a rather
oblique way seem to refer to his somewhat troubled marital history
when he was explaining some of his mother's *bishimi*, as in the following
general complaint about modern women.

There is a difference in modern living and that of the old days because in
the old days there was respect [*mushingi*]. Women were respectful; when
they got married they married with respect. It's different now; these days
they just meet on the road and get married. Then you just hear they have
divorced. The woman just lives with the man for one day and the following
day she leaves. Because they have not been taught by their mothers to stay
with their husbands . . . women are difficult now, whether you keep her well
or not, it's just the same. (Kibala, 6.ix.88, TK)

From what others told me it was clear that while Temwa's unions were
not very long-lived, he had had many wives, and was usually married—
although never polygamously.

There had been tensions between Temwa and a number of his kin.
Originally Temwa had lived in the village of Mwalu, but he and headman
Mwalu, Temwa's *mwisho* (mother's brother), had quarreled, and Mwalu
and most of the village had shifted to a site some half a kilometer away,
Temwa being left in what was a de facto village, although not recognized
as a "real" one (*muzhi mwine*). Later when I moved from Kibala to
Bukama I came across another piece of Temwa's history. My house in
Bukama turned out to be very close to that of one of Temwa's younger
brothers (a biological sibling), Webster. Until 1982 Webster had lived in
Kibala together with Temwa, but that year he and his wife had fled from

Kibala, accusing Temwa of killing their children with *bulozhi*. Apparently, several of their children had died, another had been sick for a long time, and both husband and wife were convinced that Temwa was murdering their children in order to enrich himself still further. After leaving Kibala, on the advice of Chief Chizela, they and their surviving children had settled at Bukama, where Webster's wife had some relatives. Both husband and wife were quite adamant that if they and their family had not left Kibala, all their children would now be dead.

The two brothers Temwa and Webster were very different in character. Webster seemed to have none of his brother's driving ambition. Webster and his wife, like most of the other Bukama settlers, had continued cultivating in much the same way they did in Kibala: growing sorghum for their own consumption—although, again in common with many others at Bukama, their harvest was never enough to see them through the year—and a little in the way of LIMA crops, maize and some soya beans, for sale to NWCU. The fields of Webster and his wife were anything but extensive. But while they might not have produced much in the way of surplus, they were very generous with what they did have. I experienced this generosity myself during my time in Bukama, receiving a steady stream of gifts from Webster and his wife: one day a basket of mushrooms, another a comb of wild honey or perhaps a piece of dried game meat or some other local delicacy. It seemed to be agreed by everyone I spoke to in Bukama that both husband and wife were a rare example of the kind of unforced generosity all were supposed to practice but few actually managed. Webster and his wife were also very sociable and were regular attenders at neighborhood beer drinks, another contrast with Temwa, who was a strict teetotaler and seemed seldom to leave his homestead. As far as I could discover neither Webster nor his wife had ever been accused of practicing *bulozhi*.

One of those who had remained with Temwa when Mwalu village split was Temwa's widowed mother, Inamwana. Renowned in her youth for her strength in cultivation, Inamwana remained a vigorous and hard-working old lady. She, however, like Temwa also had a certain reputation. As Sansoni explained,

The allegation that [Inamwana] is a witch, it is there. This is generally said by most of the people when they look at the way in which the son is doing the agriculture. Because he is a prominent farmer, producing sometimes 30, 40, 50 bags, so now the hard work that Temwa does has caused the combination of the mother and the son, [it is said] that the mother is assisting the son that they are practicing magic.

After disassociating himself from this kind of reasoning, Sansoni went on to explain the rationale behind the suspicion.

Sansoni: Because of her own hard work she puts in, most of the time she does not run out of food, so now people accuse her saying, "No, she is using some medicines when doing the farming."

Crehan: So this is another suspicious thing, when someone doesn't run out of food in the hungry months?

Sansoni: So that's one suspicion, when you do not go at all for food [i.e., have to buy food] during the hungry periods, because they will say that you used to get your friends' food. That's the food you were feeding on, then the food you had produced was kept safe. In other words, with some magic you were getting some maize from somewhere so the other friends are out of food because of the magic that was being practised.

(Sansoni, Kibala, 1.ix.88, TE)

However much Temwa himself might insist that his prosperity was due to hard work and God having given him "business sense and a knowledge of how to keep money," this was not how others in Kibala interpreted his prosperity. As Temwa himself was only too well aware, to most in Kibala his obvious determination to pull himself up from his local roots and establish himself as a successful farmer and businessman was in itself the clear mark of the *mulozhi*.

Those that work hard are the ones they point at as *balozhi*, those who work very hard and produce enough food. They just say, "s/he is using *bwanga* [substance or knowledge associated with *bulozhi*]". Even now they are saying that the person who has a lot of maize is a *mulozhi* who is putting children in his maize sacks [i.e., killing other people's children to increase the yield]. But me I am not discouraged, because I know that these people are simply backward. (Temwa, Kibala, 24.viii.88, TK)

Temwa has clearly paid a heavy price for his entrepreneurial drive. Despite his material prosperity, he was a lonely and isolated man. Something of his pain came through in his account of his life, as when he told me: "Truly, I know now that it was just lies when some of the elders were told they were *balozhi*. Some died from sorrow. Yes *bulozhi* exists, but some people are not *balozhi*" (24.viii.88, TK). In a community where hospitality and sociability were so highly valued, he remained unvisited, almost shunned by his neighbors. Sansoni, who lived in Temwa's homestead for about a year, confirmed how almost no one visited him. Despite all his brave efforts to legitimate his economic ambitions—not only

to an outsider like myself but also probably to himself—Temwa clearly
suffered from the hostility with which he was regarded. In church once,
I was told, he burst out in an angry denunciation of his fellow Christians
within the Evangelical Church of Zambia (ECZ), who so unjustly ignore him.

A key thread running through Temwa's account of his life, as the
passages I have quoted illustrate, was his identification of himself as a
Christian. His Christian faith was central to his legitimation of himself
and his way of life. It was his sense of living according to the fundamental truths of Christianity that seemed to give him strength to withstand the accusations of his neighbors. He told me, for instance,

God was with me when I was doing business in Solwezi. By taking fish to
Solwezi I had made a good profit. . . . I was the first one to start a business
here. The others who started earlier could not compete with me; God would
not help them because they chased me from their shop.[13] To me God was
generous. (24.viii.88, TK)

Not only did Temwa see his business career as divinely inspired and
God as being on his side, he also saw himself as living in accordance
with the government's gospel of development. For Temwa, it seemed,
the precepts of church and government were virtually synonymous.

The Bible says we should not go and drink beer early in the day. That is
why from my childhood on I wanted to do one job, to believe and to grow
more food. (24.viii.88, TK)

Temwa's church, the ECZ, which originated as the South African General Mission, draws on a fundamentalist Protestant tradition. However,
the significance of Christianity for a would-be entrepreneur like Temwa,
I would argue, lies less in the specifics of this particular brand of Christianity than in the general individualist ethos that was common to *all*
the missionary churches. The point here is that all the different missionary institutions of the colonial and postcolonial period, whether Cath-
olic, Protestant, or Jehovah's Witness, were the products of market-
based societies, and entangled with their explicit religious messages are
a powerful set of assumptions about individuals, individual responsibility, and what individuals can properly expect of society—all assumptions
rooted in the basic structuring relationships of commodity-based soci-

13. Before getting his own trading license, Temwa had briefly sold the goods he was
importing through a shop run by Kabaya, the ward chairman.

eties. A phrase that Temwa used, and which I have heard from many entrepreneurs in rural Zambia, is "God helps those who help themselves." It is easy to understand the attractions of this sturdy individualism for those trying to accumulate and to break free of their relatives' continual claims on their surplus. From the vantage point of those within the community of kin who see such entrepreneurial enterprise as only possible through the unjust hoarding of wealth that should be redistributed, however, such self-help can look more like the *mulozhi* who fills his maize sacks with the bones of dead children.

In this chapter I have taken *bulozhi* beliefs as providing a window through which it is possible to glimpse something of how the people of Kibala and Bukama imagined their social universe. The discourse on *bulozhi* gave people a language with which they could talk about and explain misfortune of any and every kind. It was those actual misfortunes that provided people with what they saw as irrefutable evidence of the reality of *bulozhi*. That people found this evidence so compelling is indicative, I would argue, of the extent to which local realities were viewed through a lens of kinship. Let me be clear here. As I have already stressed, I am *not* saying that the discourse on *bulozhi* was some kind of rigid and unchanging survival. Like any living language, the language of *bulozhi* was dynamic and was continuing to be pushed in various directions by people's need to describe new social realities. What I am saying is that the most fundamental assumptions about the nature of human society on which the whole elaborated discourse on *bulozhi* rest were intimately bound up with certain economic and political relations organized through kinship. At the same time, this powerful discourse also had an autonomy of its own: in 1980s rural Chizela it was part of people's basic mental furniture; it was how misfortune had been named to them from their earliest years. Its hegemonic power to explain why something had gone wrong was such that when misfortune hit, even those like Kibala's clinical officer who claimed to have escaped from such "superstition" (see above, p. 190) seemed to find it almost impossible to think outside it. Nonetheless, it seems to me that ultimately the emotional power of *bulozhi*—why people found it so persuasive as an explanation of misfortune—can be linked to a similarly deep-rooted belief in the inescapable obligations of kinship. For the people of Kibala and Bukama a belief in the fundamental role of kinship in structuring human society was one of those "fundamental social evaluations conditioned by the very being of a given collective" referred to by Bakhtin. What *bulozhi* represented was the shadowed underside of the bonds of kinship. *Bulozhi* was kinship reflected in a dark, distorted mirror. What I have tried to do in this chapter is to look into that mirror to show something of how a life embedded within the hegemony of the community of kin was experienced, and something of how the people of Kibala and Bukama named that experience.

CHAPTER 7

Conclusion:
Of Communities
and Landscapes

*He was, let us not forget, almost incapable of general, platonic
ideas. It was not only difficult for him to understand that the
generic term dog embraced so many unlike specimens of differing
sizes and different forms; he was disturbed by the fact that a dog at
three-fourteen (seen in profile) should have the same name as the
dog at three-fifteen (seen from the front). . . . Without effort he had
learned English, French, Portuguese, Latin. I suspect, nevertheless,
that he was not very capable of thought. To think is to forget a
difference, to generalize, to abstract.*

Jorge Luis Borges, *Funes, the Memorious*

I ended the introduction to this book with a promise to
return to the question of how the mapping of this little corner of Zambia
can help us understand the broader picture of contemporary capitalism.
As a way of trying to answer this question I want to go back to my title,
*The Fractured Community: Landscapes of Power and Gender in Rural Zam-
bia*, and reflect a little on its five key terms: *fractured, community, landscape, power,* and *gender*.

Let me start with that "warmly persuasive" but highly problematic
term *community*. In the introduction I argued that only after tracing out
something of the multistranded and socially differentiated locations inhabited by the people of Kibala and Bukama would it be possible to say
to what "communities" they belong. I hope that having read through
the preceding chapters the reader will have a better understanding of
the difficulty both of defining in some neat and tidy way the nature of

Kibala and Bukama as communities, and of deciding where their boundaries should be drawn. In some *empirical* sense both Kibala and Bukama clearly were communities and identified as such by those living there. But these were not the only "communities" to which the people of Kibala and Bukama belonged. As we have seen, there were many other communities of which they were also a part: some, such as "the Kaonde" or "Zambia," were communities with explicit imagined identities; others, for example, the "communities" created by the global market with its international flows of commodities, while certainly real, lacked such an identity. However, while individuals may not have identified with the latter in the same self-conscious way, those living in Kibala and Bukama were nonetheless tied into these more intangible "communities" in very tangible ways. The traders of the international copper market, for instance, may seem to inhabit a different universe from that of Kibala and Bukama, but the world price of copper has played a crucial role in determining how much the Zambian government has to spend on such things as rural clinics and schools.

A significant global "community" of which those who live in places like Kibala and Bukama are members, albeit shadowy and often silent ones, is the "development" community. It is the members of this community who are responsible for producing the body of knowledge that names "development" and "underdevelopment" in the south, and for prescribing and administering a range of remedies to be applied to the ills attendant on these social "realities." As James Ferguson has put it:

Through Africa—indeed, through the Third World—one seems to find two closely analogous or even identical "development" institutions, and along with them often a common discourse and the same way of defining "problems," a common pool of "experts," and a common stock of expertise. The "development industry" is apparently a global phenomenon. (Ferguson 1990a:8)

It is important to note here that the "development industry" includes a number of Africans and other individuals from the countries of the south; this is not a simple north-south divide.

Those who live in areas like rural Chizela, who are sometimes referred to in the militarily accented language of development-speak as the *target population*, may seem at first sight hardly to be present in the jet-setting world of "development experts." The voices that dominate in the development industry's decision-making arenas are those of the international "experts." It is they who *name* the world within which rural Zambians live. In fact, however, those rural lives themselves do play at least some part in the process by which those names are produced. Even if, as I have tried to show, it is difficult for those living somewhere like rural Chizela to articulate their own accounts of reality, let alone effectively challenge the prevailing hegemonic accounts, these hegemonic accounts are, to however small a degree, shaped by the concrete conditions that they attempt to explain. The discourse on development is after all an attempt to provide an account of certain realities capable of producing real answers to real problems. Of course, the strength of any hegemonic discourse can in part be measured by its ability to impose its names on the world and its facility in explaining away apparent contradictions, but nonetheless it has always to engage with various refractory experiences that stubbornly refuse to be contained within its smooth skin. The "target population" may seem to exist outside the self-referential community of the "development" industry but in reality it is present at its very heart. Its speech may not be easy to hear but it is not dumb, just as the Chizela women sitting in polite silence on the margins of a meeting to discuss "development" may "speak" in powerful ways in the heads of their menfolk, who know all too well what they can and cannot demand of their wives and sisters. "Development experts" may have little real understanding of their "target populations," but, over time, they cannot but take *some* account of what people do and do not do.

As I explained in my introduction, I have deliberately used a very broad definition of *community* as a way of calling into question this deceptively straightforward term, and focusing attention on the problem of exactly what is it that makes a community a community. Or, to put it another way: what kind of links between people create communities? These, it seems to me, are questions that are most usefully asked and answered in the context of *specific* communities, whether these are empirically existing collectivities or analytically defined sets of relationships. And it is in the specific context of rural Chizela in the 1980s that this book has tried to explore these questions. Understanding the complicated ways in which individuals in Kibala and Bukama were located vis-a-vis the many different kinds of communities that impinged on their lives necessarily involves tracing the various ways in which these communities were *fractured*, which brings us to the second term in my title.

Part of the baggage carried by the term *community* is a sense of homogeneity and an assumption that those who belong to a "community" are bound together by a set of common interests. There is a sense then that a "community" can be treated as a single entity with a single set of interests. The problem here is similar to the problem of "household" as a category, which I discussed in chapter 3. Like households, communities, or at least those with an explicit imagined identity, are sites where conflictual and supportive relationships are inextricably entwined. As in the case of the household, it is important neither to romanticize "the community" as an invariable source of all that is warm and authentic, and which by definition always has a single set of interests, nor, in reaction to such romanticization, to go to the extreme in the other direction, to see it as so fractured as to make any collective identity impossible. What we need to do is to analyze the particular lines of fracture of particular communities—whether these are cleavages of gender, of economic inequality, ethnicity, or whatever—and then trace out the implications of these in specific contexts. In this study I have concentrated on some of the broad fractures, such as the way in which women and men tend to be differentially located both politically and economically, the cleavage between the Boma and rural Zambians, and so on. Inevitably this has meant neglecting other fractures that exist within these broad patterns. I hope, however, that my approach to mapping out the general contours suggests how such an analysis could be taken further to explore in more detail, for instance, the different locations of different women, and different men, or of the politicians and bureaucrats, who in the eyes of the people of Kibala and Bukama constituted the undifferentiated category of the Boma.

Moving on to the third term in my title, *landscapes*, there are several reasons why I used this particular metaphor to think about the social environment within which people live. Firstly, physical landscapes are the product both of underlying geological formations with their associated tectonic forces, and of human activity. Landscapes always have, as it were, two levels of history: the extremely *longue durée* of geological time and the relatively far shorter one of human history (within which again there are of course many different levels of historical time). Landscape as a metaphor, therefore, provides an image of history as the complicated intertwining of conscious human activity and underlying larger structural forces. Secondly, although we can draw boundaries demarcating particular landscapes, landscape is always also continuous; there are always other boundaries that could be drawn. Finally, landscapes have a certain hard reality that cannot be ignored, and yet at the same time the ways in which any particular landscape is inhabited (both practically and in people's imaginations) is not determined by this reality, and indeed how people use a landscape is part of what shapes its fundamental character.

I would like to consider the final two terms in my title in reverse order. Before reflecting on that hugely complicated subject *power*, I will look first at *gender*, whose significance in the social landscape of rural Chizela is one of the central themes of this study. Maureen Mackintosh, in her superb study of gender and class in rural Senegal, suggests a very useful way of thinking about their relationship. She writes,

One of the most general results of feminist-inspired research in the last ten years has been the understanding that class experience — and class change — is gender specific . . . not only do men's and women's experience of class differ, but changes in the relations between men and women, including the sexual division of labour, is one of the ways in which new class structures become established. (Mackintosh 1989:35)

At first sight my story of Kibala and Bukama, while saying a good deal about gender, may not seem to have much to say about class or class formation. Let me, therefore, first explain why I think class is in fact present in this story, before going on to think about the relevance of Mackintosh's formulation linking class and gender for an understanding of rural Chizela. It is certainly true that *within* Kibala and Bukama there was no real class differentiation. Everyone was poor, although some were a little less poor than others. Neither was there any clear pattern of differentiation with respect to people's relationship to the structures of production, except for that based on gender and to a lesser extent on age. Nonetheless, I would argue, the story of rural Chizela does have something interesting to say about the processes of class formation in Zambia that may well be relevant to other areas of Africa.

The first point to make is that once we begin to think about how people in Kibala and Bukama were located, not merely within North-Western Province but within the larger economic and political world of the nation and beyond, then clearly they *were* located within more general patterns of inequality, even if it is difficult to pin down the exact nature of these patterns. Mapping out the historical development of particular patterns of stratification and determining the most useful ways of theorizing these remains is, to my mind, one of the most crucial tasks for those attempting to understand the contemporary world. And here I am not yet ready to give up "class" as a way of naming this inequality, even if the class analysis of substantive historical realities is clearly a lot more complicated than certain crude versions of Marxism would have it. My account of monetization and commoditization in one little corner of rural Zambia is of course only concerned with a tiny fragment of the grand map of capitalism, but understanding such fragments is perhaps a necessary first step to producing the larger maps. It seems to me, for instance, that we need these kinds of carefully located fragments if we are to have any hope of coming up with broader maps of capitalism that accurately describe *African* historical trajectories and contemporary realities, rather than simply forcing these to conform to theoretical templates carved from Western history.

Secondly, precisely because economic differentiation within Kibala and Bukama was so embryonic, it was possible to see the detailed patterning of the roots of the emerging differentiation in a rather clear way—how, for instance, economic relations based on exchange-value and the logic of the market were gradually, unevenly, and sometimes painfully, increasingly tending to displace economic relations based on the production of use-values and nonmarket distribution mechanisms. Even if there were as yet no clear class differences within Kibala and Bukama, various processes of differentiation were undoubtedly taking place; and these were processes that, as I have attempted to show, were strongly gendered.

A central element of my analysis of gender in rural Chizela has been the exploration of, on the one hand, the gendered nature of processes of differentiation; and, on the other, how existing gender relations, such as a specific sexual division of labor, themselves tended to create certain forms of differentiation. My concern has been to trace out the thread of gender, teasing out the complex ways in which it wove itself through the entire social landscape. Mackintosh's way of approaching the question of the significance of gender and the relationship between gender and class suggests how it is possible to focus on both gender and class in a way that pays proper attention to each and avoids setting up a sterile opposition between them. An illustration of the relevance for this study of Mackintosh's approach is the LIMA project. What the coming of the LIMA project meant for the women of Chizela was in part determined by the existing sexual division of labor and local definitions of the "proper" roles of women and men, but it was also determined by the particular location within the national market, and within the state, of Chizela's rural producers as a whole. A key task for feminist analysts, it seems to me, is exploring the particular ways in which gender operates in particular contexts, and just how the thread of gender interacts with other social threads.

Finally, now, I would like to consider *power*. Despite the fact that the question of power is at the heart of my study of Kibala and Bukama, I deliberately chose not to begin with some tidy definition of the term. What I set out to do was rather to map out the particular contours of some of the actual power relations in which the people of Kibala and Bukama were embedded. As a way of organizing this mapping, I have made some separation of the different dimensions of power, focusing on political and economic relations in different chapters, for instance. I did this, however, simply because this seemed the most clear and straightforward way of describing the landscape of power, not because these dimensions actually were separate; ultimately all these contours combined together to constitute a single landscape.

As I explained in the introduction, my mapping of power was shaped by Gramsci's problematic of hegemony. What I have tried to do is to provide a map, albeit a very incomplete one, of the particular tangle of different hegemonic relations that existed in Kibala and Bukama in the 1980s. My starting point was the inescapable reality of power. As Gramsci put it in a formulation I have already quoted, "It really must be stressed that it is precisely the first elements, the most elementary things, which are the first to be forgotten. . . . The first element is that there really do exist rulers and ruled, leaders and led" (Gramsci 1971:144). However enterprising and creative the people of Kibala and Bukama might have been in their responses to the world in which they found themselves, the fact remains that most of the basic realities of that world were not controlled by them. But if power is inescapable it is also complex and multifaceted, manifesting itself in innumerable different ways.

Part of the usefulness of hegemony is that it poses the problem of power in a way that acknowledges both the hard reality of certain over-arching power relations and that however impregnable such structures of power may seem they always contain within themselves their own fractures and contradictions. Hegemony is always a *process* involving struggle, whether or not this struggle is explicit or remains implicit and hidden. There is always a potential counterhegemony, whether or not this has achieved an articulated, coherent form. However much hegemonic power may approach a totality of control, there is always some space for contestation, or at the very least passive resistance. Hegemony provides us with a way of thinking about power as a terrain of contending forces that can never achieve a genuine stability—a terrain of ever-shifting *relationships*. The value of this approach to power, it seems to me, is that it focuses our attention both on the question of just *how* particular power relations are maintained and reproduced and on the points of potential fracture where these structures of domination are, or might be, challenged. It also allows us to ask questions about the effectiveness of various kinds of challenge without denying the reality of that challenge. What kind of threat to male authority, for instance, does the ridicule of an old woman working in her fields pose (see above, p. 135)?

Throughout my explorations of the day-to-day realities of life in Kibala and Bukama I have tried never to lose sight of the broader contours of power. I hope, however, that the reader has not taken me to be saying that individual lives are no more than the mechanical reflection of these. Rather my intention has been to map out the contours of the landscape within which individual lives were lived. In certain respects this landscape necessarily shaped those lives, but it was itself also shaped *by* those lives—just as any physical landscape with a history of human habitation is always the joint product of its particular physical properties and human activity. At the same time, however, as always trying to keep in sight the broader contours of power, my concern has been with the ways in which the people of Kibala and Bukama lived these power relations in their day-to-day lives. What did they mean in terms of material realities, and how were they imagined?

In mapping out the landscape of power I have tried to explore both what I persist unfashionably in calling material relations and the ways in which people understood, imagined, and named these relations. Starting with the case study of the colonial uses of the term *tribe*, a key theme of this study has been the power of naming. In my telling of the story of Kibala and Bukama, I too, of course, have been engaged in the exercise of naming. It seems to me that however much we may try to reinvent the project of anthropology, inevitably we are bound, in some form or another, to end up imposing *our* categories and *our* names. That is what intellectuals do. The key question, it seems to me, is the constitution of that "*our*." In other words, who participates in the process of naming?

As with the RLI anthropologists, whose use of the concept "tribe" I discussed at the beginning of my story, those in society who are given the role of producing knowledge, the "intellectuals," do not simply spin their accounts of reality out of their own heads. Rather, starting from the understandings and categories already present in their social milieu, they attempt to answer questions that seem important. And ultimately it is the historical and political context rather than the predilections of individual intellectuals that determines what questions seem important, just as it shapes the terms in which those questions are formulated. In the context of colonial Zambia, for instance, it is not surprising that the problem of order and disorder in the colonial state loomed so large. Intellectuals necessarily view the world from a particular historical location, and whether they are conscious of it or not, the knowledge that they produce cannot but be linked to this location, albeit in complex and subtle ways. The production of knowledge is always a profoundly *social* enterprise, even if it is difficult for the individual producer within this enterprise to see all the links clearly.[1] What such an individual *can* do, however, is to acknowledge the existence of such links and continually endeavor to understand them better, while at the same time trying to be as explicit as possible about just where he or she is writing *from*. It is this *from* that ultimately defines who it is who participates in the process of naming—who makes up, that is, the *we* who imposes *our* categories and *our* names. I tried to explain something of my particular location in the introduction and the first part of chapter 2.

As I see it, the names I have used in my telling of the story of Kibala and Bukama in part reflect my particular theoretical location and my working through of a particular intellectual legacy, but that is not all they reflect. What I observed in rural Chizela and what people told me about their lives, even if inevitably refracted through my own preconceptions, also fed into my naming; ultimately my account of Kibala and Bukama was the product of a *dialogue* between this experience and my theoretical (and other) preconceptions. This is the kind of dialogue that the classical anthropological approach, with its close examination of particular lives in particular contexts, seems especially well suited both to produce and to explore. Let me then, appropriately enough for an anthropologist, end both this conclusion and this book with a brief defense of the anthropological case study approach.

I believe that through its careful mapping of small corners of contemporary capitalism, such an approach *can* help us understand the broader picture. In the first place it can do this because its concern with the small

---

1. Gramsci's discussion of what it is that defines the activities of "intellectuals" is relevant here.

The most widespread error of method seems to me that of having looked for this criterion of distinction [i.e., that defines intellectual activities] in the intrinsic nature of intellectual activities, rather than in the ensemble of the system of relations in which these activities (and therefore the intellectual groups who personify them) have their place within the general complex of social relations. (Gramsci 1971:8)

details of people's day-to-day lives in particular times and places allows us to trace out something of what the large abstractions of monetization, commoditization, the state, and so on actually mean at the level of individual lives—and to trace out what these translate into both as regards the material realities they produce at the local level and in terms of how these realities are understood and imagined. This focus on the lived realities of particular places at particular historical moments can also pose the hoary old question of structure and agency in a potentially more fruitful way. Precisely because of its narrow focus, the carefully located case study enables us to explore both the creativity of individuals and the structuring of the spaces within which that creativity is exercised— and explore this not in some vague and generalized way but through particular empirical realities. Thinking about this complex and multidimensional structuring as a range of different *locations* is one way of separating out the different strands, and of examining the different ways particular strands are entwined in particular lives. Such an approach allows us at the same time as teasing out all these different strands, also to see how the various, different locations come together in various configurations to constitute a single landscape.

Secondly, for those of us who still believe that the Marxist problematic gives us an extremely useful set of questions with which to begin the mapping of contemporary capitalism, the anthropological case study can offer a way of bringing the broad narratives of commoditization, accumulation, and so on into dialogue with the complicated and messy stories of particular places. It is through such dialogue, I would suggest, that, on the one hand, we can begin to understand something of the role of overarching global relationships in creating local heterogeneity; and, on the other, also begin to rethink some of those broad narratives. In other words, this approach can help us find a way of naming the particularity of places like Kibala and Bukama that is sensitive to the violence we do to that particularity by our abstractions and our systems of classification—the violence which so disturbed Funes in Borges's story—but yet still allows us to think about such places in ways that enable *their* reality, *their* history to speak in the debates about the nature of contemporary capitalism.

APPENDIX

Kaonde Kinship Classification

ENGLISH LANGUAGE DEFINITIONS OF KAONDE KINSHIP CATEGORIES

Inanji (pl. *bainanji*) — Ego's genitrix plus all her female siblings and her female matrilateral parallel cousins from the first to the *n*th degree.

Mwisho (pl. *bamwisho*) — All the male siblings and all the male matrilateral parallel cousins of all ego's *bainanji*.

Kolojanji (pl. *bakolojanji*) — All ego's older siblings who share the same genitrix and all ego's matrilateral parallel cousins whose genitrix is *kolojanji* to ego's *inanji*.[1]

Nkasanji (pl. *bankasanji*) — All ego's younger siblings who share the same genitrix and all ego's matrilateral parallel cousins whose genitrix is *nkasanji* to ego's *inanji*.

Mwana (pl. *bana*) — All ego's biological children and all the children of a female ego's *bakolojanji* and *bankasanji* plus the biological children of a man's *bakolojanji* and *bankasanji*. Only in the case of a female ego are her *bana* her matrikin.

1. Whether or not ego's matrilateral parallel cousins will be classified as *kolojanji* depends on which of the original pair of ancestor siblings with the same biological mother—that is, ego's ancestor or the ancestor of the cousin—was the elder. In other words, the relationship of relative seniority created by an original group of siblings sharing the same biological mother is perpetuated in succeeding generations. The principle involved is the same as that in English kinship classification, which designates certain groups of kin as senior branches of a family and other groups as junior branches.

Mwipwa (pl. *bamwipwa*)   All the *bana* of ego's *bakolojanji* and *bankasanji*. Only when ego is male are ego's *bepwa* his matrikin.

Nkambo (pl. *bankambo*)   All those who are *inanji* or *mwisho* to any of ego's *bainanji* or *bamwisho*. *Nkambo* is also used for affinal relatives in the second ascending generation.

Munkana (pl. *bankana*)   All children of both ego's *bana* and *bepwa*.

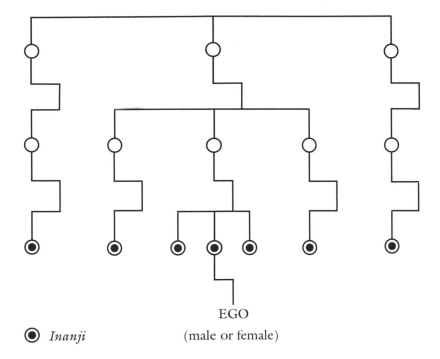

EGO

⊙ *Inanji*   (male or female)

Figure A1. *Inanji*

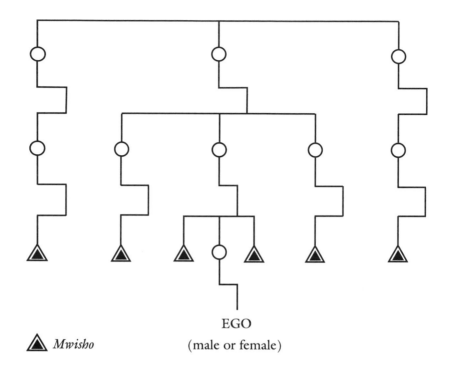

EGO
(male or female)

▲ *Mwisho*

Figure A2. *Mwisho*

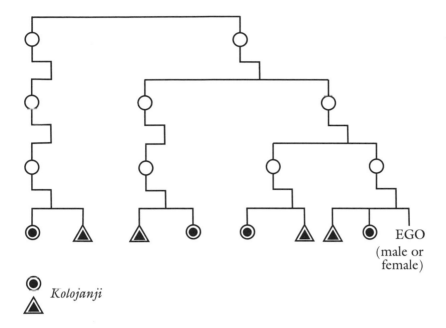

⊙ *Kolojanji*
▲

Figure A3. *Kolojanji*

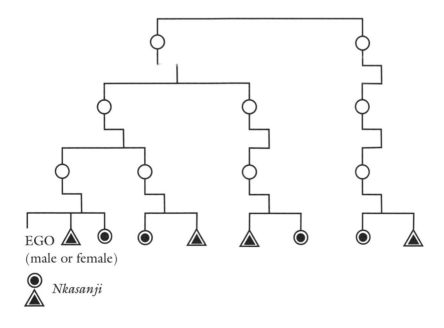

⊙ *Nkasanji*
▲

Figure A4. *Nkasanji*

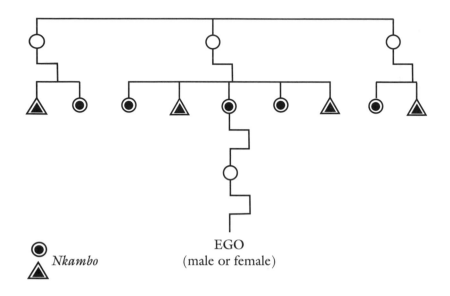

Nkambo

EGO
(male or female)

Figure A5. *Nkambo*

Bibliography

Allan, William. 1965. *The African Husbandman*. Edinburgh: Oliver and Boyd.

Allen, Christopher. 1977. "Radical Themes in African Social Studies: A Bibliographical Guide". In *African Social Studies: A Radical Reader*, edited by Peter C. W. Gutkind and Peter Waterman. London: Heinemann.

Anderson, Benedict. 1991. *Imagined Communities*. 2nd ed. London: Verso.

Anderson, Perry. 1976–77. "The Antinomies of Antonio Gramsci". *New Left Review* 100 (November 1976–January 1977).

Arens, W., and Ivan Karp, eds. 1989. *Creativity of Power: Cosmology and Action in African Societies*. Washington: Smithsonian Institution Press.

Asad, Talal. 1973a. "Political Inequality in the Kababish Tribe". In *Essays in Sudan Ethnography*, edited by Ian Cunnison and Wendy James. New York: Humanities Press.

———, ed. 1973b. *Anthropology and the Colonial Encounter*. London: Ithaca Press.

Auslander, Mark. 1993. " 'Open the Wombs!': The Symbolic Politics of Modern Ngoni Witchfinding". In *Modernity and Its Malcontents: Ritual and Power in Postcolonial Africa*, edited by Jean and John Comaroff. Chicago: University of Chicago Press.

Bakhtin, M. M. 1981. *The Dialogic Imagination*. Austin: University of Texas Press.

———. 1984. *Rabelais and His World*. Bloomington: Indiana University Press.

———. 1986a. *Speech Genres and Other Late Essays*. Austin: University of Texas Press.

——— [V. N. Volosinov, pseud.]. 1986b. *Marxism and the Philosophy of Language*. Cambridge, Mass.: Harvard University Press.

———. 1988. *Bakhtin School Papers*, edited by Ann Shukman. Oxford: Russian Poetics in Translation Publications.

Barnes, J. A., J. C. Mitchell, and M. Gluckman. 1949. "The Village Headman in British Central Africa". *Africa* 19.

Bayart, Jean-Francois. 1993. *The State in Africa: The Politics of the Belly*. London: Longman.

Beckett, Samuel. 1983. *Worstward Ho*. London: John Calder.

Bernal, M. 1987. *Black Athena: The Afroasiatic Roots of Classical Civilization*. Vol. 1, *Fabrication of Ancient Greece, 1785–1985*. London: Free Association Books.

Bernstein, Henry. 1978. "Notes on Capital and Peasantry". *Review of African Political Economy*, no. 10.

———. 1979. "African Peasantries Towards a Theoretical Framework". *Journal of Peasant Studies* 8, no. 4.

Berry, Sara. 1993. *No Condition Is Permanent: The Social Dynamics of Agrarian Change in Sub-Saharan Africa*. Madison: University of Wisconsin Press.

Bird, Jon, Barry Curtis, Tim Putnam, George Robertson, and Lisa Tickner, eds. 1993. *Mapping the Futures: Local Cultures, Global Change*. London and New York: Routledge.

Borges, Jorge Luis. 1962. *Ficciones*. New York: Grove Weidenfeld.

Bozzoli, Belinda. 1981. *The Political Nature of a Ruling Class: Capital and Ideology in South Africa, 1890–1933*. London: Routledge and Kegan Paul.

———. 1991. *Women of Phokeng: Consciousness, Life Strategy, and Migrancy in South Africa, 1900–1983*. Portsmouth, N.H.: Heinemann.

Brown, Richard. 1973. "Anthropology and Colonial Rule: The Case of Godfrey Wilson and the Rhodes-Livingstone Institute, Northern Rhodesia". In *Anthropology and the Colonial Encounter*, edited by Talal Asad. London: Ithaca Press.

Buci-Glucksmann, Christine. 1980. *Gramsci and the State*, translated by David Fernbach. London: Lawrence and Wishart.

Bundy, Colin. 1979. *The Rise and Fall of the South African Peasantry*. London: Heinemann Educational Books.

Burdette, Marcia M. 1988. *Zambia: Between Two Worlds*. Boulder: Westview Press.

Buttigieg, Joseph A. 1995. "Gramsci on Civil Society". *Boundary* 2.

Channock, Martin. 1985. *Law, Custom, and Social Order: The Colonial Experience in Malawi and Zambia*. Cambridge: Cambridge University Press.

———. 1991. "Paradigms, Policies, and Property: A Review of the Customary Law of Land Tenure". In *Law in Colonial Africa*, edited by Kristin Mann and Richard Roberts. London: James Currey.

Chipungu, Samuel N., ed. 1992. *Guardians in Their Time: Experiences of Zambians under Colonial Rule, 1980–1964*. London: Macmillan.

Clark, Katerina, and Michael Holquist. 1984. *Mikhail Bakhtin*. Cambridge, MA: Harvard University Press.

Clifford, James. 1988. *The Predicament of Culture: Twentieth Century Ethnography, Literature, and Art*. Cambridge, MA: Harvard University Press.

Clifford, James, and George E. Marcus, eds. 1986. *Writing Culture: The Poetics and Politics of Ethnography*. Berkeley: University of California Press.

Colson, E. 1958. *Marriage and Family among the Plateau Tonga of Northern Rhodesia*. Manchester: Manchester University Press.

————. 1960. *The Social Organisation of the Gwembe Tonga*. Manchester: Manchester University Press.

Colson, E., and Max Gluckman, eds. 1951. *Seven Tribes of British Central Africa*. Oxford: Oxford University Press for Rhodes-Livingstone Institute.

Comaroff, Jean, and John Comaroff. 1991. *Of Revelation and Revolution: Christianity, Colonialism, and Consciousness in South Africa*. Vol. 1. Chicago: University of Chicago Press.

————, eds. 1993. *Modernity and Its Malcontents: Ritual and Power in Postcolonial Africa*. Chicago: Chicago University Press.

Cooper, Frederick. 1993. "Africa and the World Economy" [revised version]. In *Confronting Historical Paradigms: Peasants, Labor, and the Capitalist World System in Africa and Latin America*, by Frederick Cooper, Florencia E. Mallon, Steve J. Stern, Allen F. Isaacman, and William Roseberry. Madison: University of Wisconsin Press. Original article published in *African Studies Review* 24, nos. 2/3 (June/September 1981).

Coquery-Vidrovitch, Catherine. 1969. "Recherches sur un mode de production africain". In *La Pensée*, 144. Paris: Editions Sociales. Translated in *Perspectives on the African Past*, edited by M. A. Klein and G. W. Johnson. 1972. New York: Little, Brown and Company.

Crawford, Peter Ian, and David Turton, eds. 1992. *Film as Ethnography*. Manchester: Manchester University Press.

Crehan, Kate. 1987. "Production, Reproduction, and Gender in North-Western Zambia: A Case Study". Unpublished Ph.D. thesis. University of Manchester.

Crehan, Kate, and Achim von Oppen. 1988. "Understandings of 'Development': An Arena of Struggle. The Story of a Development Project in Zambia". *Sociologia Ruralis* 28, nos. 2/3.

————, eds. 1994. *Planners and History: Negotiating "Development" in Rural Zambia*. Lusaka: Multi-Media Press.

Davies, D. H. 1971. *Zambia in Maps*. London: Hodder and Stoughton.

Edholm, Felicity, Olivia Harris, and Kate Young. 1977. "Conceptualising Women". *Critique of Anthropology* 3, nos. 9–10.

Epstein, A. L. 1981. *Urbanization and Kinship: The Domestic Domain on the Copperbelt of Zambia 1950–1956*. London: Academic Press.

Evans-Pritchard, E. E. 1937. *Witchcraft, Oracles, and Magic among the Azande*. Oxford: Oxford University Press.

Fabian, Johannes. 1983. *Time and the Other: How Anthropology Makes Its Object*. New York: Columbia University Press.

Fagan, Brian M., ed. 1966. *A Short History of Zambia: From the Earliest Times until A.D. 1900*. Nairobi: Oxford University Press.

Feierman, Stephen. 1990. *Peasant Intellectuals: Anthropology and History in Tanzania*. Madison: University of Wisconsin Press.

Femia, Joseph V. 1981. *Gramsci's Political Thought: Hegemony, Consciousness, and the Revolutionary Process*. Oxford: Clarendon Press.

Ferguson, J. 1990a. *The Anti-Politics Machine: "Development", Depoliticization, and Bureaucratic Power in Lesotho*. Cambridge: Cambridge University Press.

————. 1990b. "Mobile Workers, Modernist Narratives: A Critique of the

Historiography of Transition on the Zambian Copperbelt" [pts. I and II]. *Journal of Southern African Studies* 16, nos. 3–4.

Fisiy, Cyprian S., and Peter Geschiere. 1991. "Judges and Witches, or How Is the State to Deal with Witchcraft? Examples from Southeastern Cameroon". *Cahiers d'Etudes Africaines* 31.

Fontana, Benedetto. 1993. *Hegemony and Power: On the Relation Between Gramsci and Machiavelli*. Minneapolis and London: University of Minnesota Press.

Forgacs, David. 1988. *An Antonio Gramsci Reader: Selected Writings, 1916–1935*. New York: Schocken Books.

Ganly, John C. 1987. *Kaonde Proverbs*. Ndola: Mission Press.

Gann, Lewis H. 1964. *A History of Northern Rhodesia: Early Days to 1953*. New York: Humanities Press.

Geschiere, Peter. 1988. "Sorcery and the State: Popular Modes of Action among the Maka of Southeast Cameroon". *Critique of Anthropology* 8.

———. 1994. "Domesticating Personal Violence: Witchcraft Courts and Confessions in Cameroon". *Africa* 64, no. 3.

———. 1995. *Sorcellerie et politique en Afrique: La Viande des Autres*. Paris: Karthala.

Gibbon, M., and M. Neocosmos. 1985. "Some Problems in the Political Economy of 'African Socialism' ". In *Contradictions in Accumulation in Africa*, edited by H. Bernstein and B. Campbell. Beverly Hills, CA: Sage.

Gluckman, Max. 1945. "Seven-Year Research Plan of the Rhodes-Livingstone Institute of Social Studies in British Central Africa". *Journal of the Rhodes-Livingstone Institute* (December).

———. 1955. *The Judicial Process among the Barotse of Northern Rhodesia*. Manchester: Manchester University Press.

———. 1961. "Anthropological Problems Arising from the African Industrial Revolution". In *Social Change in Modern Africa*, edited by A. Southall. Oxford: Oxford University Press.

———. 1965. *Politics, Law, and Ritual in Tribal Society*. Oxford: Basil Blackwell.

Godelier, M. 1972. *Rationality and Irrationality in Economics*. London: New Left Books.

Government of the Republic of Zambia [GRZ]. 1988a. *UNIP Constitution*. Lusaka.

———. 1988b. *Statistical Handbook no. II: North-Western Province*. Solwezi: Provincial Planning Unit.

———. 1989. *Fourth National Development Plan, 1988–1993*. Lusaka.

Gramsci, Antonio. 1971. *Selections from the Prison Notebooks*, edited by Q. Hoare and G. N. Smith, London: Lawrence and Wishart.

———. 1978. *Selections from Political Writings (1921–1926)*, edited by Q. Hoare. London: Lawrence and Wishart.

———. 1992. *Antonio Gramsci: Prison Notebooks*. Vol. 1, edited by Joseph Buttigieg. New York: Columbia University Press.

———. 1995. *Antonio Gramsci: Further Selections from the Prison Notebooks*, edited by Derek Boothman. London: Lawrence and Wishart.

Guyer, Jane. 1981. "Household and Community in African Studies". *African Studies Review* 24, nos. 2–3.

———, ed. 1994. *Money Matters: Instability, Values, and Social Payments in the Modern History of West African Communities*. Portsmouth, NH: Heinemann, and London: James Currey.

Hall, Stuart. 1987. "Gramsci and Us". *Marxism Today* (June). Reprinted 1988, in *The Hard Road to Renewal*, by Stuart Hall. London: Verso.

Hamalengwa, Munyonzwe. 1992. *Class Struggles in Zambia, 1889–1989, and the Fall of Kenneth Kaunda*. Lanham, Md.: University Press of America.

Hansen, Karen Tranberg. 1989. *Distant Companions: Servants and Employers in Zambia, 1900–1985*. Ithaca: Cornell University Press.

———. 1994. "Dealing with Used Clothing: *Salaula* and the Construction of Identity in Zambia's Third Republic". *Public Culture* 6, no. 3.

Harries, Patrick. 1989. "Exclusion, Classification, and Internal Colonialism: The Emergence of Ethnicity among the Tsonga-Speakers of South Africa". In *The Creation of Tribalism in Southern Africa*, edited by Leroy Vail. London: James Currey, and Berkeley: University of California Press.

Harvey, David. 1982. *The Limits to Capital*. Oxford: Basil Blackwell.

———. 1985. *The Urbanisation of Capital*. Oxford: Basil Blackwell.

———. 1989. *The Condition of Postmodernity: An Enquiry into the Origins of Cultural Change*. Oxford: Basil Blackwell.

———. 1990. "Between Space and Time: Reflection on the Geographic Imagination". *Annals, Association of American Geographers* 80.

———. 1993. "From Space to Place and Back Again: Reflections on the Condition of Postmodernity". In *Mapping the Futures: Local Cultures, Global Change*, edited by J. Bird et al.. London and New York: Routledge.

Hindess, B., and P. Hirst. 1975. *Pre-Capitalist Modes of Production*. London: Routledge and Kegan Paul.

Hobsbawm, Eric. 1982. "Gramsci and Marxist Political Theory". In *Approaches to Gramsci*, edited by Anne Showstack Sassoon. London: Writers and Readers.

Hobsbawm, Eric, and Terence Ranger, eds. 1983. *The Invention of Tradition*. Cambridge: Cambridge University Press.

International Labour Office [ILO]. 1981. *Basic Needs in an Economy under Pressure*. Findings and Recommendations of an ILO/JASPA Basic Needs Mission to Zambia, Addis Ababa.

Jaeger, Dirk. 1981. "Settlement Patterns and Rural Development: A Human Geographical Study of the Kaonde". Ph.D thesis. Amsterdam: Royal Tropical Institute.

Joyce, James. 1937. *Ulysses*. London: John Lane The Bodley Head.

Kahn, Joel S., and Josep R. Llobera. 1981. "Towards a New Marxism or a New Anthropology?" In *The Anthropology of Pre-Capitalist Societies*, edited by Joel S. Kahn and Josep R. Llobera. London: Macmillan.

Karp, Ivan, and Charles S. Bird, eds. 1987. *Explorations in African Systems of Thought*. Washington, D.C.: Smithsonian Institution Press.

Kaunda, K. D. 1967. *Humanism in Zambia*. Pt. I. Lusaka: Government Printer.

————. 1974. *Humanism in Zambia*. Part II. Lusaka: Government Printer.

Larner, Christina. 1982. "Is All Witchcraft Really Witchcraft?" In *Witchcraft and Sorcery*, edited by Max Marwick. 2nd ed. Original published in 1970. Harmondsworth: Penguin.

Leach, E. R. 1954. *Political Systems of Highland Burma*. London: Bell.

Leys, Colin. 1994. "Confronting the African Tragedy". *New Left Review* 204.

Mackintosh, M. 1977. "Reproduction and Patriarchy: A Critique of Meillassoux, *Femmes, Greniers, et Capitaux*". *Capital and Class* 2.

————. 1989. *Gender, Class, and Rural Transition: Agribusiness and the Food Crisis in Senegal*. London: Zed Press.

Mamdani, Mahmood. 1996. *Citizen and Subject: Contemporary Africa and the Legacy of Late Colonialism*. Princeton: Princeton University Press.

Mann, Kristin, and Richard Roberts, eds. 1991. *Law in Colonial Africa*. London: James Currey.

Marwick, Max. 1950. "Another Modern Anti-Witchcraft Movement in East Central Africa". *Africa* 20.

————. 1965. *Sorcery in Its Social Setting: A Study of the Northern Rhodesia Cewa*. Manchester: Manchester University Press.

————, ed. 1982. *Witchcraft and Sorcery*. 2nd ed. Original published in 1970. Harmsworth: Penguin.

Marx, Karl. 1963. *The Eighteenth Brumaire of Louis Bonaparte*. New York: International Publishers.

————. 1964a. *Pre-Capitalist Economic Formations*, edited by E. J. Hobsbawm. London: Lawrence and Wishart.

————. 1964b. "Letter from Marx to Engels, March 25, 1868". In *Pre-Capitalist Economic Formations*, edited by E. J. Hobsbawm. London: Lawrence and Wishart.

————. 1970. *A Contribution to the Critique of Political Economy*. London: Lawrence and Wishart.

————. 1973a. *Surveys from Exile*. London: Allen Lane.

————. 1973b. *Grundrisse*. London: Allen Lane.

————. 1976. *Capital*. Vol. 1. Harmondsworth: Penguin.

Massey, Doreen. 1984. *Spatial Divisions of Labour: Social Structures and the Geography of Production*. Basingstoke: Macmillan.

————. 1991a. "The Political Place of Locality Studies". *Environment and Planning A*, no. 23.

————. 1991b. "Flexible Sexism". *Environment and Planning D: Society and Space* 9, no. 1.

————. 1993. "Power-Geometry and a Progressive Sense of Place". In *Mapping the Futures: Local Cultures, Global Change*, edited by Bird et al. London and New York: Routledge.

————. 1994. *Space, Place, and Gender*. Cambridge: Polity Press.

Mauss, Marcel. 1970. *The Gift: Forms and Function of Exchange in Archaic Societies*. London: Cohen and West. Originally published in 1925 as *Essai sur le don*.

Mbembe, Achille. 1992. "Provisional Notes on the Postcolony". *Africa* 62, no. 1.

Meillassoux, C. 1964a. *Anthropologie économique des Gouro de Côte d'Ivoire*. Paris: Mouton.

———. 1964b. "Projet de recherche sur les systèmes économiques Africaines". *Journal de la Société des Africanistes* 34.

———. 1972. "From Reproduction to Production". *Economy and Society* 1, no. 1.

———. 1973. "The Social Organisation of the Peasantry: The Economic Basis of Kinship". *Journal of Peasant Studies* 1, no. 1.

———. 1981. *Maidens, Meal, and Money*. Cambridge and New York: Cambridge University Press.

Melland, F. H. 1923. *In Witch-Bound Africa: An Account of the Primitive Kaonde Tribe and Their Beliefs*. London: Seeley, Service and Co.

Mitchell, J. C. 1956. *The Yao Village*. Manchester: Manchester University Press.

Moore, Henrietta L. 1988. *Feminism and Anthropology*. Cambridge: Polity Press.

Moore, Henrietta L., and Megan Vaughan. 1994. *Cutting Down Trees: Gender, Nutrition, and Agricultural Change in the Northern Province of Zambia, 1890–1990*. Portsmouth, NH: Heinemann.

Mouffe, Chantal. 1979. "Hegemony and Ideology in Gramsci". In *Gramsci and Marxist Theory*, edited by Chantal Mouffe. London: Routledge and Kegan Paul.

Mwanza, Jacob. 1979. "Rural-Urban Migration and Urban Employment in Zambia". In *Development in Zambia*, edited by Ben Turok. London: Zed Press.

O'Laughlin, Bridget. 1977. "Production and Reproduction: Meillassoux's *Femmes, Greniers et Capitaux*". *Critique of Anthropology* 2, no. 8.

Papstein, Robert. 1989. "From Ethnic Identity to Tribalism: The Upper Zambezi Region of Zambia, 1830–1981". In *The Creation of Tribalism in Southern Africa*, edited by Leroy Vail. London: James Currey.

Pateman, Carole. 1970. *Participation and Democratic Theory*. Cambridge: Cambridge University Press.

———. 1989. *The Disorder of Women*. Cambridge: Polity Press.

Phillips, Anne. 1991. *Engendering Democracy*. Cambridge: Polity Press.

———. 1993. *Equality and Difference*. Cambridge: Polity Press.

Poewe, Karla. 1981. *Matrilineal Ideology: Male-Female Dynamics in Luapula, Zambia*. London: Academic Press.

Pred, Allan, and Michael John Watts. 1992. *Reworking Modernity: Capitalisms and Symbolic Discontent*. New Brunswick, N.J.: Rutgers University Press.

Rey, Pierre Philippe. 1969. "Articulation des modes de dépendence et des modes de reproduction dans deux sociétés lignageres (Punuet Kunyi du Congo-Brazzaville)". *Cahiers d'Etudes Africaines* 9.

———. 1971. *Colonialisme, neo-colonialisme, et transition au capitalisme*. Paris: Maspero.

———. 1973. *Les Alliances des classes*. Paris: Maspero.

———. 1975. "The Lineage Mode of Production". *Critique of Anthropology* 3.

Richards, Audrey. 1935. "A Modern Movement of Witch-Finders". *Africa* 8, no. 4:448–61.

———. 1940. *Bemba Marriage and Present Economic Conditions*. Livingstone: Rhodes-Livingstone Institute Paper, no. 4.

———. 1950. "Some Types of Family Structure Amongst the Central Bantu". In *African Systems of Kinship and Marriage*, edited by A. R. Radcliffe-Brown and C. D. Forde. London: Oxford University Press.

Roberts, Andrew. 1966. "The Age of Tradition (A.D. 1500 to 1850)". In *A Short History of Zambia: From the Earliest Times until A.D. 1900*, edited by Brain M. Fagan. Nairobi: Oxford University Press.

———. 1976. *A History of Zambia*. London: Heinemann.

Sassoon, Anne Showstack. 1982. *Approaches to Gramsci*. London: Writers and Readers Publishing Cooperative Society.

———. 1987a. *Gramsci's Politics*. Rev. ed. London: Hutchinson.

———, ed. 1987b. *Women and the State: The Shifting Boundaries of Public and Private*. London: Unwin Hyman.

———. 1990. "Gramsci's Subversion of the Language of Politics". *Rethinking Marxism* 3, no. 1.

Saul, John, and Roger Woods. 1987. "African Peasantries". In *Peasants and Peasant Societies*, edited by T. Shanin. [Rev. ed. Original published in 1971.] London: Penguin.

Scott, J. C. 1976. *The Moral Economy of the Peasant: Subsistence and Rebellion in Southeast Asia*. New Haven: Yale University Press.

———. 1985. *Weapons of the Weak: Everyday Forms of Peasant Resistance*. New Haven: Yale University Press.

———. 1990. *Domination and the Arts of Resistance: The Hidden Transcript*. New Haven: Yale University Press.

Shanin, Teodor, ed. 1987. *Peasants and Peasant Societies*. London: Penguin. [Rev. ed. Original published in 1971].

Short, R. 1973. *African Sunset*. London: Johnson.

Smith, W., and A. P. Wood. 1984. "Patterns of Agricultural Development and Foreign Aid to Zambia". In *Development and Change* 15.

Soja, Edward. 1989. *Postmodern Geographies: The Reassertion of Space in Critical Social Theory*. London: Verso.

Terray, Emmanuel. 1972. *Marxism and Primitive Society*. New York: Monthly Review Press.

———. 1974. "Long-Distance Exchange and the Formation of the State: The Case of the Abron Kingdom of Gyaman". *Economy and Society* 3.

———. 1977. "Autocritique". *Dialectiques* 21.

Thompson, E. P. 1978. *The Poverty of Theory and Other Essays*. London: Merlin.

Turner, Victor. 1957. *Schism and Continuity in an African Society: A Study of Ndembu Village Life*. Manchester: Manchester University Press.

———. 1964. "Witchcraft and Sorcery: Taxonomy Versus Dynamics". *Africa* 37.

———. 1967. *The Forest of Symbols: Aspect of Ndembu Ritual*. Ithaca: Cornell University Press.

Turok, Ben, ed. 1979. *Development in Zambia*. London: Zed Press.

Vail, Leroy, ed. 1989. *The Creation of Tribalism in Southern Africa*. London: James Currey.

van Binsbergen, Wim M. J. 1981. *Religious Change in Zambia: Exploratory Studies*. London: Kegan Paul International.

———. 1985. "From Tribe to Ethnicity in Western Zambia: The Unit of Study as an Ideological Problem". In *Old Modes of Production and Capitalist Encroachment: Anthropological Explorations in Africa*, edited by Wim van Binsbergen and Peter Geschiere. London: Routledge and Kegan Paul.

———. 1987. "Chiefs and the State in Independent Zambia: Exploring the Zambian National Press". *Journal of Legal Pluralism and Unofficial Law*.

van Binsbergen, Wim, and Peter Geschiere, eds. 1985. *Old Modes of Production and Capitalist Encroachment: Anthropological Explorations in Africa*. London: Routledge and Kegan Paul.

Vincent, Joan. 1990. *Anthropology and Politics: Visions, Traditions, and Trends*. Tucson: The University of Arizona Press.

Watson, William. 1954. "The Kaonde Village". *Rhodes-Livingstone Journal* 15.

———. 1958. *Tribal Cohesion in a Money Economy*. Manchester: Manchester University Press.

Watts, Michael John. 1989. "The Agrarian Question in Africa". *Progress in Human Geography* 13, no. 1.

———. 1990. "Visions of Excess: African Development in an Age of Market Idolatry". *Transition*, no. 151.

Werbner, Richard P. 1984. "The Manchester School in South-Central Africa". *Annual Review of Anthropology* 13.

White, C. M. N. 1948. *Material Culture of the Lunda-Lovale People*. Occasional Papers of the Rhodes-Livingstone Museum, no. 3. Livingstone.

———. 1953. "Notes on the Circumcision Rites of the Balovale Tribes". *African Studies* 12, no. 2.

———. 1960. *An Outline of Luvale Social and Political Organisation*. Rhodes-Livingstone Paper no. 3. Manchester: Manchester University Press.

Williams, Raymond. 1977. *Marxism and Literature*. Oxford: Oxford University Press.

———. 1983. *Keywords*. 2nd ed. London: Fontana.

Wright, J. L. 1977. "Kaonde Grammar". In *Language in Zambia: Grammatical Sketches*. Vol. 1, *Bemba and Kaonde*. Edited by Michael Mann et al. Lusaka: Institute for African Studies.

———. 1985. *English-Kaonde Vocabulary*. Ndola: Christian Publishers.

———. N.d. "Kaonde-English word list". Unpublished.

Wright, J. L., and N. Kamukwamba. 1958. *A Kaonde Notebook*. London: Longmans.

Young, Iris Marion. 1989. "Polity and Group Difference: A Critique of the Idea of Universal Citizenship". *Ethics* 99.

Index

Abraham (polygynist), 151, 152
accumulation. *See* commodities and commoditization; surplus, distribution of; wealth, suspicion of
adultery, 200
Africa: creation of tribalism in, 53; crisis of the postcolonial state in, 12–13, 19. *See also* British Central Africa
African Socialism, 80
age: association with witchcraft (*bulozhi*), 207–12; (relative) distinctions in Kaonde kinship, 35, 98–103, 108, 155
agriculture: commercial (by white settlers), 79; government attitude toward, 52; preparation of fields for (*kutema*), 156; by "progressive farmers," 4–5, 122, 167–71; shifting cultivation (*citimene*) in Bukama, 6, 48; shifting cultivation (*citimene*) in Kibala, 3–4; women's role in, 135, 155–60, 167–68. *See also* cultivation (*kujima*); development; "farming" (*mwafwamu*); Integrated Rural Development Project (IRDP); maize, growing of; sorghum, cultivation of
alcohol: brewing of, 116, 162, 168–69, 174; state regulation of sales, 126–27
Anderson, Benedict, 12
anthropological methodology: case studies, 232–33; interviewing, 40, 44, 51; participant observation, 38–46
anti-Semitism, 68–69n21

BaKaonde. *See* Kaonde "ethnic group"
Bakhtin, Mikhail (V. N. Volosinov, pseud.), 1, 13; on collecting information, 39; on "fundamental social evaluations," 88, 99, 184, 187, 222; on naming of reality, 30, 31, 32; on nonverbal assumptions, 40
bulongo (kin), 92
balozhi (sing. *mulozhi*) (witches), 113, 192, 198. *See also* witchcraft (*bulozhi*)
bamfumu (chiefs), 97–98. *See also* chiefs and headmen
ba munzubo ("those belonging to the house"; household), 94
bañanga (sing. *ñanga*), 194
Banyinyita, 145, 204
Bateya (Kibala clinical officer), 190
Bayart, Jean-Francois, 14
Beckett, Samuel, 37, 51
beer. *See* alcohol; brewing; sorghum beer
birth mothers (*inanji wasema X*) ("mother who bore X"), 90
bishimi. See folktales (*kishimi*, pl. *bishimi*)
Boma: definition of, 119–20; view of "villagers" by, 121–23, 165. *See also* state
Borges, Jorge Luis, 224, 233
brewing: state regulation of, 126–27; by women, 168–69
British Central Africa, Indirect Rule in, 56–57, 63, 65, 73, 110
British South Africa Company (BSAC), 3, 78–79

Index:	Barbara Cohen
Map:	Bill Nelson
Composition:	Impressions Book and Journal Services, Inc.
Text:	10/13 Galliard
Display:	Galliard
Printing and binding:	The Maple-Vail Manufacturing Group